True Wealth
How to Enjoy the Most of Your Beautiful Life, Especially in Finance

By Andy Lee

ISBN:
978-1483936246

i

True Wealth
How to Enjoy the Most of Your Beautiful Life, Especially in Finance

Words of Recommendation:

"I am very proud to know Andy Marlinata and his family as their Financial Advisor. Over the years that we have known and shared with each other, I am always reminded of his gracious spirit and positive outlook towards life.

His passion for providing for his family and being used by God as a vessel in this world to help and assist others has always impressed me and I am the better because of it. Andy has grown much over the years and has applied what he has learned toward his finances and I personally can attest that what he has done financially is just short of remarkable compared to any standard here in America.

With the normal resources that any average American would possess, Andy and his family have not only become debt free, but have also paid off their home mortgage in just a very short period of time. Also, they have been consistently saving and building wealth utilizing mutual funds (as well as investing for their children) that any average American would be envious of.

Learn from someone who has applied financial principles and continuously lives by disciplines that we all should apply in our own lives."

- Jeff Rimer, President of Rimer Financial Group

"After scanning his manuscript I can say that, not only can he put pen to paper but he does it rather brilliantly. He has applied his engineering background to the world of personal finances. Like all good engineers they see things as "systems". Personal finance and life are such systems. In the end you "get from it what you put into it." Andy not only preaches this, he actually lives it. He has proven that his family can achieve great things by taking the small and right steps in their lives. Their sacrifices have a purpose; their hard work has a goal in mind and in doing that; they keep their children and their faith foremost in their hearts and minds. It is an honor to know Andy and his family.

I hope that as you read this book you will feel the warmth and sincerity that Andy exemplifies and exudes. His cup isn't half full; it overflows, and he shares that with his customers every day that he walks through our door. His is an infectious attitude and as Andy would say 'Have a blessed day.' Read his book and you will have a 'Blessed Life."'

- Carl S. Milam, President of Western Concepts Restaurant
  Group

"Having known Andy and his family for about eleven years, I know that they have accomplished their amazing achievements by prayer, good will, planning, determination, commitment, and hard work. Andy's book will open your mind to what is possible for you to accomplish sooner than you thought possible."

- L.G. Parkhurst Jr., retired reverend, author and Daily
  Oklahoman weekly Bible columnist

"This book is a great tool in today's times. Not many people have money/debt/life planning figured out as well as Andy does. If everyone could start out life with these basic principles Andy speaks of in this book then we would not have a nation in a debt crisis like we do now."

- Scott Sabolich C.P. L.P., owner and Clinical Director of
Scott Sabolich Prosthetics & Research

"Who is Andy Lee? Andy is a personal friend and inspiration to us all. No matter what trials and tribulations he may be facing, Andy will always tell you "I am blessed!" They say that smiling and laughter is very healthy for you. With Andy, he should be the healthiest person in the world. :) Andy wrote this book for those who are struggling with being persistent in their life skill goals. Knowledge from this book will help you stay focused and have a winning attitude for anything happening in your life. He has put a lot of sweat and tears into this book (his own experiences) and will always be my friend and my mentor. God Bless You, Andy!"

- Jimmy Parker, IT Project Manager of Seagate Technology LLC

"Andy's book is the manifestation of his remarkable attitude along with good, simple living and practical advice. I hope it leads all readers to a new positive outlook on life and a financial freedom!"

- Kristian Kos, President and Chief Executive Officer of New Source Energy Partners

"I have studied a lot about life and financial success under his extraordinary care and diligence. I did more in 2 years than I have been able to do in the previous 10 years. And I really am thankful for him and what he does. I have never met any person in my life with the same level of personality and ability that Andy has. I believe that his book can help anyone else like he helped me."

- Midori Carrisoza, Sushi Neko General Manager, Andy's supervisor at work and Andy's student at life and finance

Gratuitous words from people who have known Andy or have experienced Andy's teaching/leadership in their life:

"I first met Andy ten years ago as my martial arts instructor. Over the past ten years he not only has taught me martial arts, but has taught me many life lessons which have helped me grow into the strong disciplined individual I am today. Andy's faith and positive outlook on life is truly inspirational."

- Kevin R. Buttross (Business and Management graduate, a good friend and martial arts student)

"I am very privileged to have met someone like Andy. He is the exact definition of a good hearted person. His work ethics are phenomenal and he genuinely cares about his surroundings, coworkers and friends. His knowledge about life, business, and world events are extravagant. He knows just the way to bring people up when they are feeling down and always seems to know the right things to say. He has made so much of himself at such a young age due to his magnificent leadership skills. I can honestly say that I have never met anyone like Andy and for that I am blessed and extremely grateful."

- Melissa Hatcher (Office/HR Manager of Western Concept LLC)

"I've known and worked with Andy for about 5 years now and I have learned a lot from him. He is such a good person who has great passion in everything he does. Thus, his accomplishment is way beyond what others only dare to dream. This man is the true definition of living the 'American Dream.'"

- Danny Tran (Sushi Neko staff trainer, Andy's former trainee who has become a trainer himself at a great workplace)

"Thank you so much for directing our small group. You are so professional and have worked hard to develop our simple talents. It is apparent that you love the Lord and want to serve Him and we love you for it. Thank you for your patience, understanding, and sharing your talents with us."

- Mel and Shirley Baker (engineer and retired IRS staff)

"I just want you to know how much I appreciate your time and effort you give to us. We just love working with you and are learning so much. Don't give up on us, Ha! Thanks again for what you do for us."

- Sarah Willis (Christian singer)

"You are a very talented and kind person, loving husband, nourishing father, and most of all, a great steward of Christ. The Lord has so richly blessed us with your live and your talents. Thank you for sharing yourself with us."

- L.G. and Pat Parkhurst Jr. (former pastor family)

"Andy makes a lasting impression - you are immediately struck by his genuine enthusiasm and positive attitude. What strikes me as unique is that his optimism has never wavered. Andy sees things in a way that always emphasizes the positive aspects of his life, and selflessly always offers an honest smile. The one thing I most appreciate in a character is integrity - that a man lives according to his own moral code and builds his life accordingly. What Andy presents to the world and who he is at home are one and the same thing and because of this he has created a circle of virtue where what he does positively influences those around him. I am grateful for knowing him and the conversations that we have together. If you stay focused on what you hold most dear everything else will follow, and staying positive means good things happen!"

- Kristian Kos (President and Chief Executive Officer of New Source Energy Partners)

A few words from Wienke, Andy's wife of 12 years, 18 years partner in life:

"I am really thankful to God for sending Andy into my life. He is very kind, caring, loyal, diligent, detailed, and intelligent. I couldn't ask for a better husband or a better father for my children. He can explain everything in a very detailed but fun way. It really shows in how he supports and helps me in my daily life and how he raises and educates our children.

He always believes that if anything is worth doing, it's worth doing well. And he really applies that in all aspects of his life, including this book. Sometimes I worry that he will get stressed or drained too much since he always wants to do his best in everything, from preparing a Bible Study to teaching Mixed Martial Arts, and trust me, he has a lot more on his plate. The amazing thing is that he always has the necessary heart and energy to do them all. 'If we do everything in our life for God's glory, then we will have the willingness to always do our best and God will always provide the ability to do so' he explains that with a warm smile and I love him for that (and thanking God for sending him my way)."

I believe that this book will open our eyes to how Andy sees life so that all of us can achieve what he has achieved in his beautiful and meaningful life. Go ahead read it, I promise you won't be disappointed."

This book is dedicated to all who want to have a warmer heart and cooler head in facing anything in their life, especially in finance.

Special Thanks to:

- God, He who has created, protected, blessed, guided (and forgiven) me and everyone else in our life.
- My wife, Wienke, and my two young children, Joshua and James, who are the sunshine in my life and always give me strength and good conscience when I need it.
- Cora Yamada, who helped with editing this book, is very good at what she does and she does it with her genuine kindness and great effort. What a treat to have the chance to work with her caliber of professionalism and compassion. Seriously, without her, this book might never be in your hands right now.
- Jimmy and Kartika Parker, an awesome couple who welcomed us to America with their warm hearts and pure kindness. They are always helpful and supportive to everyone in their life and we are blessed to experience it ourselves, including the making of this book.
- My parents, who raised and educated me the best they could so that I became who I am right now.
- L.G. and Pat Parkhurst Jr., a great couple who treats us like their own children with their parent-like love and concerns.
- My sister, Evelyn (and her husband, Daddy), who keep raising the bar for me to catch in their own way. Fortunately, that keeps me properly motivated with whatever I do.
- Kevin Butross, a good friend and student, who always amazes me with how far he's come to grow as an individual and a martial artist. His eagerness to improve and his positive attitude really make a better me.

Preface

Who is the writer? Why should we buy this financial book while there are so many of them already? Andy Marlinata was just a permanent resident (green card) holder when he arrived in Oklahoma, USA, with his sweet wife, Wienke, in May 2002 with an Engineering degree from Indonesia. In Indonesia, he has worked in different fields and companies but most of his earnings came from his work as a private tutor for Math, Physics and English, a hired instructor for Martial Arts, Vocal Technique and Choir Director for multiple individuals, churches, and private schools in Indonesia. He generated a better income and schedule by doing all of the above compared to working as an industrial engineer.

After he arrived on American soil in May 2002, Andy could not use his degree and experiences from Indonesia in America, so he was determined to try his best to accomplish something and be financially secure without going to school again. He has worked at fast food restaurants, a women's shoe department in a retail store, a golf club, a vending machine company, martial arts schools and a popular Japanese restaurant in Oklahoma during his life in America. In less than three years, in February 2005, he and his wife bought a three bedroom, two full bathroom home. In about three and a half years, in September 2008, he and his wife paid off their home and currently have no debt at all of any kind, so his family only needs to pay for their daily living costs. In addition, he has also created and contributed routinely to their retirement accounts, to their children's college fund and some other investments. Andy was 31 years old at that time, and started writing this book when he was 32 years old (2009).

The interesting part is that Andy and his family are just like the majority of us, the hard working middle class American citizens, perhaps closer to the lower class, some may say. He is currently still working at the same nice Japanese restaurant and his wife is currently working at a retail store and a child development center where their children go while writing this. So if he could be debt free, have even paid off his mortgage, and also enjoy his life while doing so in his first six and a half years he lived in this great and proud country, why can't others do that, too? All of us want to be debt free and able to pay off our mortgage as soon as possible, so we don't have to worry about making payments except for our current living costs! If Andy can do it joyfully with his income level, most Americans can do it, too. The question is whether other Americans (or people anywhere else, too, actually) want it badly enough to gain the same financial security and freedom.

This book will not just tell you what to do, because most of us might know already. He'll talk about how we could live our lives fully, work our best happily, enjoy the little things, not worry about how others judge us, have our own standings, love others genuinely, and dream about our future and how to accomplish it. While doing so, he also will present all the facts, his real life data (not exaggerated ones) and experience, and of course, what and how to do everything, too, will be in the later part of the book. He will first speak about the emotional part in order to be ready for doing the real steps, just like priming before painting, pep talk before a big game, previews before actual movies, stretching and warming up before going into an MMA fight, etc. After we understand (and agree) about the ideas, then he will guide us step-by-step in simple, practical and inspiring ways. We will smile, get amazed, get awaken back to reality, get inspired and fired up and also get tutored (like private tutoring by Andy himself) so we can be ready to face this recession with our own Re-Ce-S-sion (Re think and Check our vi Sion and mi Ssion). Basically we will have a warmer heart and cooler head in order to face any situation in our life, especially in finance. Now enjoy his LoVEly (Lee on Vital Evolution ☺) ways.

Table of Contents

Chapter I: Introduction

Chapter II: The LoVE-ly Way To Prepare or Fix Our Financial Path

Chapter III: The Simply Great Strategy

About the Author

In 2001, our family was financially middle class in our former country, Indonesia. Now we are still in middle class family but have no debts of any kind and have managed to pay off our home mortgage in 2008. In the previous year, 2007, we were so blessed and proud that we could become American citizens. I graduated in Industrial Engineering and my wife graduated in Manufacturing Engineering. Even though we were pretty good at our jobs, we didn't really love or feel especially talented in those fields. We just got those degrees because our parents wished us to get them (that is one of the problems we will discuss later in this book). We tried to work using our degrees, for a bank, a giant house wares factory and also a big food supply company. None of them really captured our heart. First, because we did not really love to do those jobs. Second, we were not really excelling in them. In addition, the income was not worth our energy, time and effort. Then, we decided to focus on what we love to do, which fortunately we already started doing as part time jobs since we were in college. We really enjoyed doing and teaching what we were good at, logic and numbers, music and sports.

My wife played in Surabaya Symphony Orchestra and gave private lessons on violin, piano and guitar, from which she made a living. I taught vocal technique and choirs privately, at churches and schools. I also gave private lessons on Mathematics, Physics, English and Martial Arts (I am a second degree black belt in Porbikawa Jiu Jitsu, which mixes traditional Japanese Jiu Jitsu for real life self defense, Qun Tao kung fu for speed and agility, and karate for posture, breathing and power). I also joined Surabaya Oratorio Society (the choir team that performs with the Surabaya Symphony Orchestra) and was honored to be one of the soloists in 2002. I did not get paid for being a choir member there, unlike my wife who was a musician, since vocalists usually don't spend a lot of money to buy or maintain a musical instrument. Our main and only musical instrument is our health and vocal cords.

We made a good living and had great schedules. At the same time, we kept our mind, soul and body sharp, since we had to be good enough to be able to teach some particular subjects. We also learned while we taught since we had to completely understand the subjects and know how to break down the subjects in detail and in an attractive way so that our students could always be connected, understand it and have fun while applying the lessons themselves. The noble ultimate goal in our profession was that our students excel and do their best in the subject(s) they wanted or needed to learn.

Then suddenly, we got another wonderful yet challenging situation at the same time. In May 2001, my wife received a notification letter mentioning that she (and spouse, if married) won a green card lottery through USCIS, United States Citizenship and Immigration Services (it used to be INS, Immigration and Naturalization Services)'s Diversity Visa (DV) program. First, we thought it was just a scam, since they asked us to pay a $400 fee per person. Just for your information, the US $1.00 is worth Rp.10,000.00 in Indonesian currency (most people could live a middle class lifestyle at that time with about Rp.3,000,000.00 per month, which is only $300 per month in US currency!). So the $400 fee per person was worth about 40 days living cost for a middle class person in our former country! Trust me, there are a lot of really good scammers back in Indonesia... I mean a lot.... and I mean really good.... so we did not want to be their next victim by risking our hard earned income for the "American Dream" used to lure us, so I threw it away. Fortunately, God is great, He gave us a second chance (actually, He might just keep finding ways to make us realize what a beautiful plan He has for us). About two weeks later, we got another package from USCIS with all the seals and symbols. It was pretty thick and weighed about 2.5 lbs. Then we started to wonder whether that was for real or just a scam, so we made an appointment and went to the US Embassy in our city, Surabaya (the second largest city in Indonesia) which fortunately was pretty close from where we lived. Then, we tried to get some confirmation. They said," Yes, it's a real package from the USCIS. Congratulations, you just won a green card lottery, but there are still a lot more steps you need to take to finalize whether you get the green card or not. Just follow all the instructions in this package; such as, reconfirm your application with all the requirements needed, required pictures, background check, police report, educations qualifications, work experiences, bank account, health test and interview."

We were so excited, grateful, and worried at the same time. We are the fifth generation of a Chinese family who were born and had been living in Indonesia; so we are islanders, even though we are Chinese descendants. Officially, we were Indonesian citizens, but there were some racism in social, political, economic, educational and religious areas. In almost all aspects of our life, to a certain degree, we were treated differently (sometimes a little and sometimes a lot). So we really had to work hard to be able to live there in balance and also learn how to blend and understand other people's perspectives. I am not complaining, just sharing. Actually, we were blessed that we could live in a pretty hard environment (not the hardest, there are many worse environments we could have lived in, so we're still thankful). So someday, if we lived in a better and fairer environment, it would be much easier for us. We believe that whatever happens in our life, none of these things are accidents. Everything happens for a reason. Actually, we believe that everything happens for the best reasons for all of us, though sometimes it is hard to know what the good part is if something bad happens to us. But trust me, the most important thing is what we do with what we have or with what happened to us, not what we have or what happened to us itself. So we were already excited and grateful to be Indonesian citizens and islanders. We were even more excited and grateful we won a US green card lottery (just like anyone who ever won a lottery). We were pretty sure that, if God allowed, we would be able to fulfill all the next requirements and we would go and live in one of the best countries in the world! Much fairer and better, just like what we all dream about! However, we were also worried since we would have to leave all of our 25 years of life in Indonesia behind. We would leave most of our family, most of our friends, teachers, students, colleagues, church, our jobs, lifestyle, hobbies, etc. Basically, we would leave all of the things to which we were already attached for 25 years; things we love, people we love and who love us, things we are already good at, our lifestyle and comfort zone! Our savings would drastically shrink in value because of the extreme currency rate (after all the US $1.00 is worth Rp.10,000.00 in Indonesian currency)! Furthermore, one more reason to worry was that we had never even lived in other towns or states in Indonesia, let alone lived in another country (just like the movie "The Truman Show" starring Jim Carrey)!! So we had to totally go out of our comfort zone in our former country (actually, our former city!) if we wanted to immigrate to America. Just like a fish out of the water. Actually that's too harsh of an analogy because the fish would surely die if it's out of the water, while we wouldn't surely die. We might just be miserable, homesick, have weather and cultural shock, get really embarrassed if we could not find a job or do a job which might not be as cool or have a potential based on what our families and friends think. Anyway, you get the point.

We finally decided to immigrate to America after a long, serious thought and decision-making process. We reasoned," We are still young. We are healthy and not dumb enough to do anything reckless that might ruin both of our lives for good. If we fail, we can always go back to our former country. Though we might feel embarrassment, since we went to the greatest country in the world, but failed to make the best out of it." We arrived in Edmond, Oklahoma, USA in May 2002. Why Oklahoma? Because I have a sister (and her husband and one baby boy, at that time) who lives in Oklahoma. She has been in the USA since 1998. She went to college and got a work sponsorship from her company. So, I felt not as uncomfortable anymore coming here, even if it was my first time going out of our former country to the biggest country in the world, America. Since I knew someone that I could trust, at least, could help us avoid all kinds of mistakes that we might make. It was not as bad as we thought, it was worse! Especially for me, I'm a normal guy so I had normal post power syndrome (feeling like we are not needed or appreciated like we used to be). Why? We applied for jobs about 4 days after we arrived in the USA. No one called us back. We were homesick. Weather was a shock. We suffered a little bit of culture shock, too. Anyway, we realized that employers would not just call us back since that is not how it works here. We, the applicants, were the ones who needed to be active in calling and checking to show how much we really desired the jobs! In our former country, Indonesia, companies really do not like to take calls from applicants. If they are interested, they will call us. We just wait in Indonesia. That is not the case here. So, even after difficult attempts to follow up and still no desirable job openings, after about ten days of living here, we decided just to go to work at any place we could. The job did not need to be what we were really good at or what we really desired to do.

We started working about 11 days after our arrival in the US (May 17, 2002). Our first jobs were at McDonald's, the well-known fast food chain restaurant. After about two weeks of working there, we started a second job at Arby's Beef Corporation, which is another great fast food chain (our first employer's competitor). After about 60 days (in late July, 2002), we started to try other fields, not just fast food restaurants. We tried to apply in the retail field. We both got hired! My wife got hired as a men's department sales associate at JC Penney, a nationwide department store and I got hired as a women's shoes sales associate at Dillard's, another nationwide department store. Both were located in Quail Springs Mall, Oklahoma City, a very nice little mall near where we lived at that time in Edmond. Those department store jobs were our main income sources. We got our extra money from working at the fast food restaurants. Soon, we both resigned from the second fast food jobs we had, properly and respectfully (we gave two weeks notice and we still did our jobs with our best efforts until the last second we worked there, loving everything we did and all the people we met, as much as possible).

In August, 2004, we were willing to try another field besides fast food and retail. Since those two fields have the tendency to please customers during most national holidays, we had to work on holidays, and that was not desirable for either of us. We both applied and started working at Japanese restaurants and worked at our other jobs (McDonald's) part time. My wife and I worked at two different Japanese restaurants across from each other. They are two different types of Japanese restaurants. My wife worked at Musashi's, an exquisite teppanyaki and/or hibachi style (they have great food and most of all, it is very entertaining with the chefs doing some tricks in front of customers). I worked, and still do, at Sushi Neko, a lovely little traditional style restaurant (a regular dining floor and kitchen format). We also have a nice sushi bar at the center, displaying all the fresh fish. We have a cozy liquor bar, with a wide range of liquors, from wine, sake, beer and mixed drinks. At that point of time, we both worked hard at multiple jobs and saved as much as possible; not much relaxing time for things such as vacation! Our church, family, friends and work were our vacation since we genuinely love all those things!! We really did enjoy that lifestyle! Even when I started to write this book (September 2009), we were both still amazed at how crazy we worked at that time, almost like workaholics: yes almost, I said, still not falling into that workaholic category!

I left my retail job (same way, properly and respectfully) and began working full time for my Japanese restaurant employer, and started teaching martial arts part time at two different martial arts schools. My wife maintained her two main jobs (JC Penney and Musashi's) during 2004!

In February 2005, my wife only kept her retail job and left the Japanese restaurant job, because she was too tired from working two full time (about 70 hours) jobs for about

6 months. I kept working two jobs until around May 2006. Then, we both focused on our main jobs; by doing so, we were more focused and we climbed the career ladder pretty well, thanks be to God only. And thanks to whoever He uses in our life in the past, present, and also future, since we believe and know that God will always be good and life is always beautiful even if it's not easy or pleasant, sometimes, it is still beautiful overall in Him.

After doing that, I started writing this book in August, 2009; we are so blessed and guided by God. Today, we are considered an average income family. Since 2006, we still work at the same places. I work in the restaurant business (no.. I'm not the owner, just work there) and my wife works in retail (in this case, I believe you all have figured it out that she's not the owner either, we would be way well off if my wife owned her own decent size department store). So, we are an average income American family with two children born in the USA. The only thing different is just how we think about life and how we act toward our life (not react). We try to commit. I really mean commit. No turning back or even to the right or to the left. We use all of our focus and energy to make our commitment work, which takes discipline. We are similar to other ordinary people, with an ordinary life, who are willing to commit and discipline themselves to get their extraordinary dream. In our case, our dream is much simpler than being a UFC (Ultimate Fighting Championship) world champion, a movie star, one of the richest guys in the world, an American Idol, or something like that. We just have a simple dream which every family or person in our society is supposed to have, a dream in which we are able to live our life with security. In this book, of course, I will write about how you can achieve financial security.

Remember when we arrived in the US the first time? On May 18th, 2002, with all the fun, joy, struggles, activities, stresses, etc. We were able to save money and buy a standard house (three bedrooms and two full bathrooms, a 2 car garage, one living room and one dining room) in

February, 2005, for $125,000. I will show you how to get a good bargain, too, later in this book! We bought a home in less than three years after we came for the first time to America in May, 2002!! We put $43,000 down, and we had a $5,000 emergency fund in our banks. We also helped our family back home in Indonesia, sending about $8,500. Then in September 2008 (about three and a half years after we bought our house) we were able to pay off our home mortgage!! We have no debts at all and have already started saving for our retirement and our children's future on a monthly basis (deducted automatically from our bank accounts). We have always liked to work hard and save so we can secure our (and our children's) future, while also having balance and enjoying our present life in the most effective and efficient way we can. Our retirement and children's future investment options and planning were also inspired by Dave Ramsey with his FPU (Financial Peace University) class, which was held at our loving little church in 2007. We combined our Christian values, our Asian culture, our dreams and the knowledge we gained from that class to prepare the best we could for our and our children's future. What a great feeling knowing for sure that we were able to pay all of our present bills easily (with no debts at all) at that time and have already started to secure our family's future (only if God allows us to live until that future ☺) while enjoying our lifestyles in the process. It's only with God's blessing that we heard, learned, understood, agreed and really applied all those things to our life. And the main thing is that everyone can do it, too, as far as they really want it!! Regardless of the genders, genes, backgrounds, current conditions, etc. Some people say that their current condition is too dire; that they do not know where to start. To start, we definitely have to dream it, make a plan to reach our dream (with prayers and struggles) and just do it!! Do it with all your focus and energy! Never give up on your discipline, then you will be there!

There's a great one liner from Walt Disney's PIXAR "The Incredibles" movie, one character is the superhero outfit designer, named Edna Mode, she said,"

Pull-yourself-together! "What will you do?" Is this a question? You will show him you remember that he is Mr. Incredible, and you will remind him who "you" are. Well, you know where he is. Go, confront the problem. Fight! Win!" then she reached her petite arms up high and smiled with one pure enthusiasm! That made me laugh hard .... and think hard, too... There is also another great line in the movie "The Matrix", the Lawrence Fishburne character told Keanu Reeves character (Neo)," Stop trying to hit me and hit me!" That one line made me really think and got deeply inspired, too, just like the one from "the Incredibles" movie.

Stop only trying to do something, and just do it! Just like when we are about to do a bungee jump, the more we are trying to do it, the more fear will get in the way. The right way is this: when we already put a good amount of thought and time into something, what's left is to really just do it! Again, this only applies after we have already put a good amount of thought and time into deciding something, it doesn't apply to compulsive (spontaneous) decisions.

By the way, we are not problem-free either. During those years after we came to the United States, we also experienced some unexpected conditions/events which forced us to spend our money. Fortunately, we have great discipline so we never really touched our real emergency fund. We kept saving more and more so that we would be secure enough not to hurt our financial security. We faced and paid for medical problems just like other Americans. My lovely wife got two surgeries to remove tumors in a couple of different places at different times (2005 and 2009) and I broke my left foot in an MMA sparring session in May 2010 (boys will always be boys). We brought my wife's parents to the United States 3 times (every two years since 2004) with all expenses paid for, airfares, living costs, vacation with us, souvenirs, etc. They lived with us for at least a month per visit (most friends and colleagues were shocked when they knew that we had our parents live with us for a whole month, especially for a pretty long period one time, 5.5 months in 2006). At that time, a roundtrip ticket (US to Indonesia then back to US) was about $1,300 for economy class for one person. We also sent them a small contribution monthly to help with their living costs in Indonesia. They have already paid off their house, too.

How about my parents? My parents are pretty well off in Indonesia, so we just help out a little as a good gesture and they perfectly understand. In 2007, we became U.S. citizens. Since God always protects, blesses, and leads us (and forgives us, too), we were (and still are) sure that we will stay here in the United States for the rest of our lives. We enjoy and contribute our best to our new homeland. In 2009, we successfully sponsored my parents to come to America as permanent residents, since it had been their dream to come and retire in the United States with their two kids (my older sister and me). My oldest brother wants to live in Indonesia. Trying to be good and grateful children, we did our best to make their dream become a reality while they were still pretty healthy for their age. My father was 72 and my mother was 68, when we sponsored them. We never know when God will call any of us back home to heaven, so we wanted to do it while we could. Even though 2008-2012 were the years when the recession hit us pretty hard, We were able to start upgrading our lifestyle progressively closer to our dream since 2010. I believe in the wise saying "No pain no gain", at least most of the time except if we win a big lottery (ticket) (which I personally never do nor suggest anyone to do it) or having such luck. God is good and life is beautiful, even though it's not always easy, pleasant, or smooth, it's still beautiful overall. The most important thing is to keep moving forward using all of our focus and energy, which makes it a committed discipline. Remember, when any not too great (bad) things happen, or any problems arise, just confront the problem, fight and win! ☺

Chapter 1: Introduction

1) The Nowadays Lifestyle

Our lifestyle has been changing a lot since the beginning of time as we all know. But not just that, it changes at a very fast pace, too. We can see that from our parents' generation to our generation, lifestyle has changed a lot. Even only in my lifetime, lifestyle has changed a lot! Now, everybody has a cell phone, even the younger generations (including younger kids!!). Most of them have all the extra features, such as a camera, a video camera, GPS, TV broadcast, internet, with many more features in the years to come. It's as though all of our communication or even lives depend on cell phones a lot. The after-sleep-alike (bed head) messy hairstyle is a big fashion. Having a tattoo (tattoos) is a very common thing for almost everyone in the younger generation. Phrases; such as, "life is hard," "life s***s," "that's not fair!" "I deserve ...," "I hate this ...," "I can't stand him/her" are being thrown around like never before. Getting in debt is a normal thing, or even worse, it is a culture! They say, "Everybody has to have debt at one point in their life. It's normal here! If you go to school or college, you will already be in debt." True, but sad! Competing with others, being cool or having the biggest property is a big thing. Making celebrities (from pop stars, athletes to politicians) into idols is huge everywhere. Darker themed movies are big hits, raunchier comedies are booming, product marketing is too good to be passed and the lists go on. With all of the lifestyles around us, it is really hard not to join in them and fall into the "everybody does that!" excuse. Be careful, when everybody does it, it doesn't always mean that they are right, right? If we fall in with the wrong group of people or environment and everybody is doing the wrong things, deep in our hearts we know that it still does not make it right. Just because everybody else is doing it does not make it right. Why even bother joining them?

The really important questions that I kept asking myself before we made our life changing decisions were actually basic, fundamental questions. Do we really want to always join or follow these fashions? Do we really want to be led all the time? (Just like what Loki states in Marvel's "The Avengers" movie, the most epic superhero movie yet) Do we really need those things? Do we really want just to be as good as everybody else? Do we really think that we can never change this situation or culture? If "Yes", why? If any of you who are reading this book answer "Yes" to all of the above questions, then this book might be able to help you find a different point of view of life. If you can give clear reasons for each "yes" answer that you strongly believe, then you might not agree with this book at all. It is still worth a try to see what a few debtless people have to say (just kidding, it's all up to you). If any of you answer "No" to all of the above questions, congratulations, you are one step ahead, a huge step actually, because changing people's beliefs that are already set is almost impossible. We always believe what we want to believe. If you have good reasons for your belief, that is even better! You are that much closer to being financially peaceful. I would love to help you figure out and do the "how".

What about the "what," "who," "where," and "when?" The "what" we are trying to change is our way of life so we can have a joyful, healthy, and peaceful financial situation and life. I call it "Happy, healthy and wealthy in God." That is the easy way to remember it, and that is in the right order, too. The "who" is anyone who really wants to change their way of life or wants to add some unique way of thinking to their arsenal for facing life and finances. The "where" is basically everywhere. Some programs provided by the states might have different details, but overall they are all based on the same principle. The "when" is actually up to us, but I strongly suggest that you begin as soon as possible, since time is one of the biggest factors of these winning techniques (you will find out why soon).

There are two major groups of lifestyle followers. The first group is the "competing with your neighbors". Or, we also might say, "The neighbor's grass always seems greener than ours." The first group always does what others do or what most people do. They feel comfortable if they can blend in with other people's standards or habits, whether they can afford them or not. Even if they are able to afford them, the question is, "Are others' standards or habits really the right ones for them?"

The second group is the "idol follower". This second group always wants to copy or be their idol. They have a particular someone (could be a superstar athlete, a movie star, a religious leader, a news anchor, a politician, or even their father or mother who they want to copy). Again, sometimes we are just not equipped as they are, so actually we have to find our own strengths and weaknesses and work on both of them. Even if we are as equipped as our idol, the real question is, again, "Do we really have the right idol to learn from and copy?" Like I said earlier, it is almost impossible to change someone's belief unless they themselves are willing to open up to a new angle of thinking; then, they are able to change their belief. So when we are already willing to open up to the new angle of thinking of our idol, hopefully our idol can improve most aspects of our life, including financial. I said "hopefully," because not every change is good. We might change in a better or worse way, but for someone to improve, one has to change. If he or she does not change, it is impossible to say that they are improving. Here is an analogy: not every animal is a horse but a horse is for sure an animal. In this case, the horse symbolizes better and the animal symbolizes the change. So: Not every change is for the better, but better is for sure a change.

Those are the two major groups of lifestyle followers. How about the others? The minor ones? There are a couple of different kinds of groups, but the one that interests me and my family is the one that I call the lifestyle promoter group. Some lifestyle promoters become lifestyle leaders. The rest become unique lifestylers (doesn't necessarily mean good or bad, it depends on what perspective we use). Those in this group do not really care about any fashions or trends in the world. They know what they need and how to get what they want. People might say different things about them, good or bad; such as, simple, down to earth, old school, out of fashion, old fashioned, weirdo, ancient, stingy, smart, efficient, tight, etc. It depends on who gives the opinion; but again the lifestyle promoter group does not really care what others think or say because they are all set with what they believe, which is different than what the fashions or trends have to offer.

2) Idols Influence

Most of us have our own idol. It might be a superhero, a movie star, an athlete, a celebrity, a politician, an author, a religious leader, a friend, our parents, someone we know, a character in history or Bible or holy book in any religion or belief (legal ones, hopefully) or even our own glory days! We can pick our own idol from many choices (by idol, I mean someone to look up to and set as our example by ourselves, not in any other meaning like idols to replace God or some kind of black magic. If you are hoping to find ideas like black magic in this book, you will be totally disappointed ☺). Only few people that I know do not have someone they admire and look up to. I feel kind of sorry for them, since there are so many incredibly great people that God has provided for us to look up to in this life. This is important; since nobody has really
appealed to them in their life as worthy of being set as an example, it is hard for them to know what they want to do, or more importantly, what or who they want to be in their life. So I personally suggest that we have our own idol to look up to as a good example. But, I strongly suggest that we really use our heart and mind to seriously pray (if you do pray, if you don't, you might want to start praying), feel and think, before we decide who is the best idol (or idols, as long they compliment one another) for us. Once again, idols are important in order to inspire us to follow their spirit, characters, principles and their journey to their success; not for us to be them, but for us to be as good as them, or hopefully, even better!

Since an idol(s) is important to be set as our example, so we want to make sure we choose the right idol. There are three important filters/signs of the right idol(s) that I can not emphasize enough.

First, choose an idol(s) we admire and want to follow as an example because of their overall life. Consider their background, their progress or journey toward their greatness or success, and how they end their journey up to their most current condition. If we choose an idol(s) based only when they are already great and well known without knowing all the information I mentioned, then we will only see that side of their life when they are in the spotlight. We need to know a lot more than that if we want to set somebody as our example in the long run.

Second, the idol must have a good influence on our life. If by idolizing that particular character makes us and our life worse from a third party point of view (I strongly suggest a third party since they will be more objective than us. And they must be someone who truly cares and loves us enough to tell the truth if we ask them), then we have chosen the wrong idol. What is the point of idolizing someone who only will make us and our life worse? We need to find some good influence in our life. That is why we have to filter our idol(s) by making sure when we are setting them as our example so that we can be better people and have a better life. We need a happy, healthy and wealthy life, in that exact order. We want to be happy first of all, so even if we are sick or not rich, we can still be grateful, happy, and enthusiastic. Being happy leads to contentment. If we are wealthy, healthy, and strong, but we are always worried, mad, and not happy, what's the point of being wealthy and healthy? So always go with the right order, happy, healthy, then wealthy. People might ask about wise. Wise is included in the "healthy" category since I think healthy can be physically, mentally and spiritually healthy.

Actually, this technique for filtering our idol(s) is also

applicable for everything else in our life: choosing friends, people around us, movies, hobbies, our life partner, and most other things. If we have a great life partner, very kind-hearted, patient, great looking and in shape, pretty decent in financial wisdom, smart, diligent and humble, that sounds perfect, doesn't it? But if all of their good qualities make us, as their life partner, become lazy, arrogant, and sloppy, so we do not care about their or our welfare, I personally prefer to have a regular life partner who can stimulate my motivation to be my best! Of course, it is the best if we both are already in great shape and both have a healthy morale so that we both keep trying our best to get better all the time, to be the best we can. This is just one example, it applies to our choices of movies, hobbies and everything else, too. If any of those things is a bad influence, we really should stay away from it as much as possible! Always stay close to the things or people who can make us a better person. If I watch too many movies or read too many books with many curse words, I immediately pick them up in my language which is very bad for me, my family and whoever/whatever I represent! Nowadays, many lifestyles are totally different. As I mentioned earlier, there are so many people throwing curse words, bad language and bad attitudes that we do not need to add more! So, we really should try to stay away from any bad influence, trust me! Don't play with fire if you don't want to get burned, sooner or later.

Some people might say that they are strong enough not to get influenced by bad behavior, even if they are around people who act badly all the time. For example: smoking weed, drinking, smoking, cursing, being in debt, etc. Really? I think they are already weak just by wanting to be around that kind of environment and people, if they know it is not what they want to do on a regular basis, just as our parents or teachers taught. If we do not want to do those things, why do we bother exposing ourselves to that kind of people or environment? Doing so already shows our weakness. We can get a bad influence, and we might begin to copy our environment or people around us. To not admit that is denial. So it is a combination of weakness and being in denial. I am sorry if I offend anyone here, but it is true. If I did the same thing, I would fall in the same category of being weak and in denial. We are vulnerable to becoming the people around us (family, friends, etc.) and what the environment around us is like, sooner or later, in a big or small way. If we have a very strong way of life and sound morale principles, then we might have one strong and great "filter" already. We might share our lifestyle with them, and not the other way around. But if you are not at that stage yet, please do not try playing with fire. Trust me, you will get burned sooner or later.

Third, the right idol(s) is the one(s) that will always be admired and we can keep as our example as time passes. So, even if we have another idol(s), we still always admire and get inspired by our previous idol(s). If we have more than one idol, all of them are supposed to compliment one another and not conflict with one another. If our idols' principles are conflicting with each other, this means we are not consistent in choosing our idol(s); or even worse, we do not choose them right. We might not pray or think about it enough. We might just follow fashions or trends, or we keep changing our values in life, etc. Then we have to come back to square one. So, make sure you do your best to plan how you will choose your idols so you do not have to waste your energy, time (and perhaps money) just to come back to square one. There is a great old teaching: "If you fail to make a plan, you are planning to fail".

3) Nowadays Economy

When I began writing this book in 2009, our country's economy was in bad shape. The downturn started around the end of 2007, and then the whole of 2008 got worse! 2009 got even tougher! Even now, our economy is still struggling. Since the world is so interactive, the whole world's economy is (at time I finished this writing) in trouble. How come? Well... there are a lot of reasons: unpredictable markets and resources and all other normal causes that we can not predict nor control at the level where most of us desire. Our economy and life is always up and down, that's life as it is, not a fairy tale. There are also some reasons that make matters worse which actually we can control but we don't! So everything is all messed up now! I really mean now because it will be better later, sooner or later, if God allows us to live that long. We never know the days God will let us live, and we do not know the day our economy will get better. Anyway, I said "we" not "them", because we are all part of it, too, especially if we do not live within our means. How come? It all comes back to our nowadays lifestyle again, to our living beyond our means which is definitely bad! Well, even living below our means, it is sometimes not good either because that is still not our means.

For example, most people say they do or get stuff because they can... really?

The first possibility (and the worst!) is that they get stuff because they have a magic plastic card called a credit card. Then, they don't even care, or let alone check, if their expenses are more than their income. So, actually they are weak because they can not control themselves. They buy what they can not afford, and they are in denial when they say they can afford whatever they want by using a credit card!

The second possibility (this one is better, but there is still something to think about with this, too) is, they really can afford what they want, which is great, but do they really need everything they want? What if they do not get what they want? Will something massive happen to their life? It's all up to them. They earn and really have the income in their hands as excess money, so why not? We should live to the fullest, too, as far as we are responsible and not violating other people's rights. But sometimes, our excess money is the result of some "skipped" or "forgotten" needs for later on. If we are not careful with our excess money at hand, we might honestly forget later need or we do not care about that later need. The "don't care" possibility can be dangerous. It is similar to the beginning of the end when you watch a UFC match or any other sport match.

The third possibility (this is the best; I do not mind this one, I am just trying to present the facts) is, they really have the money after they do their real budgeting (I'll explain in more detail later).

If we really want our economy and the rest of the world's economy to get better, we really should avoid the first two lifestyles noted above. Always buying what we can not really afford is not a wise move at all, and it does not represent an adult characteristic. The Bible and many old teachings say "we should not eat if we do not work", and by work I mean real and honest work. We should never have a dishonorable profession or line of work. Remember that we should always do to others what we would want them do to us. I believe in that simple teaching and that it is still applicable now and forever more, in every aspect in our life. We also can say this in a more universal way, "If you don't do your part, you don't get your part." It could mean, "If you don't work hard enough to get something you want, you don't get it," or "If you don't workout and prepare hard enough for the UFC championship belt, you won't get the belt," or even "If you don't do your part to love, care and protect your girlfriend, you don't deserve to be her boyfriend." This can go on, of course, for school, tests, work, bonus money, etc. It seems that this simple, yet great, teaching is being forgotten nowadays.

The kind of thinking like "Life's too short, so better enjoy as much as possible now," "Later needs can be taken care of later," is changing our actions. When an action has been done repeatedly, it will become a habit, then from a habit it turns into our lifestyle before we know it. A lifestyle of always getting what we can't really afford is horrible and that kind of lifestyle opens up the opportunity for loan sharks. A loan shark is someone who will lend us money for a certain period of time; then we must return the money we have borrowed, plus pay the interest or their "kindness" fee. Since they are charging a fee or interest, I personally do not think that they are kind, it's just business. If they were truly kind, they would not charge interest or even a fee. Even when they charge interest, it should not be a much higher interest rate compared with the interest we might be charged from a bank. In addition, if our credit rating is good, our loan interest rate should not be much higher than our saving/checking interest rate anyway.

So, loan sharks are very smart! They can see opportunities and exploit them. That's how it works in most aspects of our life; in sports, in politics, at work, and especially in business. I think loan sharks are smart in capturing the opportunities that's working to their advantage, but are they really nice (working for our advantage)? Let's break it down. They seem nice (I'm pretty sure they want it that way) because they are helping people (in this case is the borrower) to get something that they really want or need while they don't have the money at that time. Why does the borrower not have the money at that time when they really need or want something?

a) Something really bad happened. In this case, I feel sorry for them, but that still does not mean that they are right. If the borrower lives a healthy and right life (working to make money, saving, budgeting, taking some preventative steps like buying insurance, etc., loving other people, honest, always genuinely kind, etc.), they usually have enough savings or prevention like insurance, etc. Even if they do not, some of their family or friends, seeing their loving and kind family or friend in unexpected deep trouble, will most likely offer or give them some help. And just in case, in the worst possible scenario, if the people who need money do not really have family and friends (even though they are so kind and loving, but still have no family or friends who are able or want to help) at least the one giving the service (the hospital or some other agency), will understand and believe that they are genuinely kind and honest people who are really in an unexpected deep trouble; so they will most likely help with the financing with no interest, even with some fee or interest, it would still be much better than going to loan sharks.

b) Nothing really bad happened, but something happened as a result of their own unwise or self-centered action. In this case, I don't feel sorry at all, I just hope that they can learn from this hard way they have chosen. For example, consider gambling (wanting to be rich easily and quickly is very unwise), wanting to get things they can not really afford (which is unwise and self-centered).

With those two possibilities about people who need (or want) money while they don't have it, it's clear that they will be better off not getting involved with any loan sharks so that they will not be in deeper trouble! It's a double trouble if they keep thinking they can afford anything they need or want which they (actually) can't, and they still have to pay much higher interest on top of that!! So, the loan shark business is misleading and it benefits from weak people, weak emotionally since they can not control themselves from getting something they can not afford at that time, or weak financially because they just simply do not have the money, or both. We must always remember that we are supposed to have control over our own life. If loan sharks exploit someone, it is partly the fault of the person being exploited.

Sometime in the '70s, we were introduced to a magic plastic card called the credit card. Just like everything in our life, it is not always about what kind of thing or system that matters, just the one who uses them and what the usage is for that matters. If we use credit cards in a proper manner, they will be of good use and to our advantage. If we use them wrongly, then their use will put us in deeper trouble. The 2008 recession happened mostly because of too many people or businesses at all levels (smallest to biggest) getting into debt that they could not afford to pay back, or giving too much of a loan to someone (or some business) who could not afford to pay the loan. One factor was too many banks giving pre certified loans that amounted to more than the borrower could afford to repay. The basic rule of thumb is never get loans totaling more than 25% of your monthly income. But too many banks or financial institutions misled people to believe that they would be fine if they had loan obligations more than 40% of their monthly income (which was greedy because they just wanted to close a bigger loan). But again, it was not just the banks' fault. The borrowers were also at fault. They should be able to think for themselves enough not to do such unwise or greedy things such as borrowing beyond their ability to repay. The result was too many foreclosures, too many borrowers unable to repay their loan. When the banks took over all the assets of the borrowers who could not repay their loans, they could not resell their homes since too many people were affected by the foreclosures. The consumers' buying power was adversely affected, which led to low demand then low employment. Before we knew it, it was like a contagious disease. We had a recession (yes, I said "had" not "have" unless it is still not over when you read this book. I really believe that all will be fine and that we are, at least getting out of the recession gradually).

So basically, being in debt is really bad. Having debt is something else, as long as we have the money to pay off our debts anytime we want. So there is a big difference between "having debt" and "being in debt". Having debt means we do have the money to pay the debt, but for whatever reason we do not pay the creditor yet (because the loan is not due, so we are not in default). Being in debt means we really do not have the money to pay our debt, meaning we have spent what we do not have yet. So, if it is up to us, I strongly suggest not being in any debt. By any means, don't spend what we do not have yet. We do not deserve to get what we want if we do not have anything to trade for it, at the time. It means we are not ready to have it yet.

4) Multiple Choices

There are a lot of perspectives about life. The most important thing is which perspective we would like to use. Perspective is like our "glasses" to see all the things around us. In some sense, it usually can be divided into two perspectives. The first perspective is the positive one, and the second one is the negative one. Remember the parable or story about the half full (or half empty) bottle in the desert? Let me remind all of us again about the wisdom in that story. Just imagine we are already in the middle of desert (no matter how we got there; similar to most of our financial problems, suddenly we are in the middle of a hardship or debt). After a long journey under the blazing heat of the sun, we are almost hopeless. We see nothing but sand everywhere. We suddenly find a half-filled bottle of water. We think, "Is it real? This isn't Fata Morgana (seeing an illusion of something we really want or need but it's not real, after a long dragging heat attack that has dehydrated our body), is it? Oooh..yay!!... This is real water!! Thank God!!" Then, we become so grateful. We enjoy every drop of that water, and it keeps us going. Our hopes rise. But, in the same scenario, another person might think like this," Whoa..whoa.. Is this a bottle of water? Hmm.. and it's real, too.. Yup, it's about time! But what kind of a cheap person would leave a half empty bottle! Why didn't they just take the whole bottle with them?!! Are they too lazy to clean up after themselves? Do they think we are not tired enough after being tortured in this ridiculously stupid sand and sun, they want us to clean up after them??!!" The scenario is the same, but two different people can think and act in two totally different ways. One person is so grateful that they find a half full bottle of water to fuel their hopes. The other is so angry to find a half empty bottle that it fuels their anger. This second perspective (the negative one) sounds like a bitter person on steroids; but trust me, there are many people who fall into this category when a little hardship comes into their life.

The perspective we choose to use, the positive or negative,

can apply to most aspects in our life. I personally choose to use the positive perspective. Why? Because choosing the negative one will not change anything; it actually will make everything worse in every case. The positive perspective will usually make everything better, at least mentally. For example, I got into debt because of unexpectedly high doctor and hospital bills. I received their services, and then the bills came one-by-one. The bills totaled a decent amount of money that I did not have at that time.

There are two ways to react to a situation such as this.

1) On the one hand, a person could get shocked, then mad, and then freak out: "What? How come these bills are so high?! Are the doctors and hospitals trying to give me an extra problem? Do they want me to have a heart attack?!! Do they want me to go bankrupt?!!" A shocked person could become depressed and keep asking themselves, "Ouch... How can I pay all these bills? I'm already in bad shape physically! Now I'm gonna be in bad shape financially, too. I'll be bankrupt and sick! Who will take care of me? I really don't like this kind of life (my life)." These reaction examples are negative ones. One person explodes with anger and emotion. The other person responds with a sad, depressed emotion. If we have either of these two reactions, our life will become full of anger and complaining, or we will be full of timid and weak emotions. With these reactions, we cannot do our best relating to other people at work, or in trying to pay our debts, and a lot more aspects in our life. Will the debts and bills be gone by reacting in these negative ways? No! If we become mad or sad, our energy and time are being spent (or actually wasted) by focusing on being mad and sad all the time, and it will not change the fact that we still owe that debt. If we keep being stubborn in our perspective, then other people around us will get annoyed by our complaining and negative attitude. Even worse, all of our nerves, cells, blood flow, muscles, etc. will follow what our brain is saying

and what our heart trying to show, which is depression and timidness. Our anger will make us tense which will make us to get tired quickly. Our timidness will also make us get tired quickly. Both of them will also take over our good judgment. With the physical and emotional decline caused by our anger or timidness, we may get depressed, and become slow and weak, then we will have no enthusiasm. With all these negative emotions and their consequences, we cannot enjoy every moment of our life and we will not pay off any debt as effectively as possible.

With our weakened mind, body, and soul (since all of our focus and energy are being wasted by us being mad and sad), we will not perform our best in relating to other people which might prevent them from having the willingness to help us. Some people think that if they complain all the time then God or their family or friends will notice their problems and offer help. No! Trust me, too much complaining, sadness, and anger will not help us get their help. It will surely get their attention! But a different kind of attention, and not a sympathetic one, believe me. With that dark condition, we just cannot relate to others healthily. We also cannot perform our best at what we do or at our work, which is worse! So, if we cannot get a grip on ourselves and try to solve the problem ourselves, we also close all possibilities from others to help us, too. Then we will suffer more stress. We may become more sad or angry. The cycle will keep going on and on and on, a dark/negative cycle.

2) On the other hand, a person could get shocked and learn they have a big problem at hand. So, they need to step it up!! They need to be ready to face whatever happens as a consequence in their life, and the most crucial thing to remember is that everything happens for the best reason in our lives. I believe everything happens in our life for the best reasons. How about this case? Same application. If we go to the hospital because of a foolish accident, then we learn the hard

way not to do the same kind of foolish thing again, especially after this very expensive lesson! If we go to the hospital because of an accident not our fault, then we learn that many things happen that we can not control in this life. Someone or something with a greater power has more control (or even total control). In my case, I believe that Someone far greater than we can imagine has the total control over our lives in long run. In the present short run, we cannot really feel that, since we have free will to change our minds, or so we think. You need to watch Jim Carrey's Bruce Almighty movie about testing God's total control, especially the part when Jim Carrey's character was trying to cheat on God to prove his own free will with his finger counting, it's hilarious! It is a comedy with a good message. So, if the accident was not caused by us at all, we will learn to depend and rely on God more. Accident means we never expect it to happen. If we expect it to happen, then we should be prepared for it. If we do not prepare ourselves, then it will not be an accident anymore, but more like being ignorant, and that's foolish and should be considered our own fault. For example, say I want to show off to a girl I like in high school or I want to show that I still have athleticism in me, even though people might think the opposite. All of the examples above may be considered foolish. Except in any accident (let's say auto for example), even if I do/treat (drive) in a proper manner but someone else is the one who's being reckless, then it is purely an accident, and not our own fault at all. Those are the great truths we can learn from the accident itself. The great truth is that we actually can prevent some accidents in our lives by not being ignorant, or at least from accident that is caused by our own ignorance.

How about the financial problem presented by the hospital bills after the accident? Well, if we successfully have ourselves accept the fact that we are responsible for all the bills, then it will be in our best interest to impose our will fully to do anything we can to pay off our debt as soon as possible. The most logical and right ways are: first, trying to get any good deeds available for us from the hospital (a discount, no interest payment, etc.) or good deeds given to us from our state/federal government (some sort of aid, grant, etc.). Second, just enjoy every moment so we can perform our best to generate income as much as possible and as fast as possible, as long as we are not violating other people's rights. From those two steps above, I can learn two things or skills to better myself: The communication skill (yes, it takes skills and a humble heart to admit that we need help and can communicate that to others so that others feel that they would like to help us) and the uplifted spirit/mentality to generate income as much and as quickly as possible, which we can call a focused discipline (and yes, these two skills will carry us a lot further in our life).

So, there is always more than one way to look at anything, anybody, or any condition. The two basic ways to see them are the positive (or bright) cycle or the negative (or dark) cycle. The choice is ours to make! These repetitive ways of thinking and acting become our lifestyle; they will really shape our lives. Whatever our financial level, we can learn very important basic logic and apply the real life techniques and tips in this book. Even an average income family, one open to God's guidance, can choose to live according to their own trend until they enjoy a debt free lifestyle (including the elimination of a home mortgage and every other kind of debt). They can also have retirement savings, a kids' future and college savings account, and extra funds in about 7 years (we did those in about 6 years and we are an average income family with earnings come from working in restaurant and retail). If you are already successful and debt free or already wealthy, then this book may not be of much use to you, but it might be a little friendly reminder of your reasons for success. I am really joyful and grateful if those already successful or wealthy still read this book, and I wish you all the best in life!! If you fall in the average financial level or below, I welcome you to excel, because my wife and I were in exactly the same place when we first began to build from scratch in May of 2002. So, this book usually fits ordinary people with an average income or lower. It might not fit people with more advantages or those who have been in the "dream" position, and that is what we're shooting for in this book. But, by no means, don't stop your learning after reading this book. There are a lot more potential possibilities for this beautiful life of ours. God is incredibly good and life is awesomely beautiful. We are the ones who make the world as it is right now, so let's keep doing our best (or better, our excellence!). Let's do our best in whatever is under our control! Whatever is beyond our control, we should give it to God. My strong motto for my life is, "Let's keep praying and doing our best and He'll take care of the rest!"

Chapter II : The LoVE-ly Way To Prepare Or Fix Our Financial Path

1) Preparing or Fixing Our Way of Thinking

To prepare or fix our lifestyle, we really should start from the way we think. An inspiring Christian writer, Rick Warren, wrote in his book, the "Purpose Driven Life", that we have to change our way of thinking first before we can change the way we act. Then if we keep acting or behaving based on our new way of thinking repetitively, it will become our new habit. After a long enough time doing our new habit, it will become our new lifestyle. So this chapter is the most crucial part of the book since we will discuss how to prepare or fix our way of thinking which is the root of all actions, habits and ultimately, lifestyles.

I can never emphasize too much how important it is to always learn the basics well. Our way of thinking is our basics. Just like when we build a building, we need a strong and good foundation. If not, everything built on top of them will easily fall apart. It's the same with martial arts, too. All the fancy moves won't work for real life or a real fight, they are only great for showmanship such as demonstrations or movies. But the well mastered basic moves are the ones that work in real life or a fight. For example, in the UFC, there are no fancy back flip front kicks (Bruce Lee in Enter the Dragon, Jet Li in Fist of Legend, Tony Jaa in The Protector, etc.) 580 degree kicks (Xtreme Martial Arts, Capoeira, Scott Adkins in Undisputed 3 etc.), cart wheeling kicks (Tom Cruise in Mission Impossible 2, Mark Dacascoss in Only the Strong, etc.), flying reversed crescent kicks (Tony Jaa in Ong Bak, Scott Adkins in Undisputed 3, Van Damme in Knock Off, Jackie Chan in many of his movies, etc.) ever used, let alone ever succeeded. The small chance that all those fancy moves would work only exists when the opponent is way too tired or too unprepared to react. Only basic strikes and submissions work in a real fight with real athletes or martial artists. It applies the same way for the way we think. Well mastered basics always work, not the fancy ones, the fancy ones only have a very little percentage called luck and luck won't have a steady result as often as good perseverance in hard work! I guarantee that! And also, it is statistically proven.

By the way, by no means have I tried to offend anyone with my examples above. I personally really admire and love all those martial artists/actors and the movies above, but they themselves and we all know that they are only movies. I guarantee none of the people I mentioned above will use those fancy moves if they are in a real fight.

a) Have a Different Attitude, Don't Get Caught by Trends

Trends or fashions are usually made by human beings, in a few cases are made or influenced by nature, cultures, or even traditions, but again, most cases are influenced or made by humans themselves. They usually are either powerful, brilliant, cool, idolized or influenced by a popular person (or group). The similarity of all the reasons and why they can influence others is that they are different. Whoever starts or gives a big influence to a trend/ fashion is usually different than others, because if they're not different than others, then they won't give any influence, let alone start a new trend/fashion since they are the same way as others who just follow the flow.

Just like I mentioned in the introduction, not everybody can afford to keep up with the trends all the time since there will always be new popular people/icons, new fashions, new trends, new culture, new atmosphere, new cool stuff, etc. So do not try to keep up if you really can't keep up with the trends even though you have tried your best. Just like anything else in life, if we can't keep up with what others demand from us then don't demand from them to begin with.

Here's an example, let's say a guy has been practicing tai

chi for a long time and he is getting really good at it. That is great for him since he has mastered that particular style. Since MMA is very famous right now, he wants to be dominant in MMA (Mixed Martial Arts) competition, too. I'm pretty sure that any true martial arts master will not do that to prove anything, but this is just an example. I am sure (and I believe most of you will agree me) that a pure tai chi master will be less likely to win in MMA competition, let alone dominate MMA. He will get a wakeup call physically and emotionally. How so? Because it's not what he does, he never practices any MMA, he is like a baby in the MMA world while on the other hand he is a master in tai chi. This applies the exact same way if any MMA champ wants to compete in any tai chi competition, they would look like fish out of the water. They just never train tai chi, they are using different breathing technique, different movement and muscle, even a different way of thinking! They all have their own strengths and weaknesses. If one side tries to keep up with the other which have a different daily practice, experience, etc., it would be almost impossible to keep up or achieve something close to the other one.

So if we really can't keep up with the requirements or demands for trading in with what we want to accomplish, then don't try to accomplish it! Do we have what it takes to accomplish what we want? We have to be honest with ourselves! If we can, sure! Why not? But if we know we can't and are still saying that we can, we are in double trouble. If we don't have enough money to keep up with all the super cool stuff, newest trends/ fashion, don't have enough diligence to keep track of the newest trend, don't have enough time to do all the renewing or being reintroduced to the next level of technology that's way beyond our means, or most important of all, if we don't have enough focus and energy left for something more important in our life since we are using them way too much for all the trends around us, then stop following the trends! If we have enough money, time, energy, curiosity and are not abandoning other important things in our life while we always try to keep up with the fashion/trend, then go ahead. But again, important things in our lives depend on our priority. I won't talk about priority in this book, since it's all up to us. But if you're still holding and reading this book now, I know at least you have a similar matter in mind, financial.

Most people are afraid to be different, they are afraid that others might think of them as, or even worse, call them, weird. Let's see it this way: if we're different, we're not weird, we're unique! Unique is different in a good way but weird is different in a bad way. What is good and what is bad? Again, it is relative to our way of thinking. If my way of thinking is totally the opposite of your way of thinking, my perception of good is gonna be your perception of bad and vice versa. But wherever you are, most people in your area or even country, usually have a major similarity in the way they live and what they use as far as they are in the same financial level (of course, the rich people's lifestyle won't be the same as the medium class or lower group's lifestyle). If we are already in the financially medium class or higher (a real one, I mean debt free, not the higher class lifestyle but mostly supported by debts!) and we are content with our lives, then it's great. Stay with what our lifestyle is now whether it's in the same direction as the trends around us or not. But if we are still in debt (yes, any debt, school loan, mortgage, car payments, credit cards, loan from friends or family, anything we enjoy now but we still have to pay sooner or later, those are all debts!), either having a cool or simple lifestyle or if we are not content with our lives (including unhappy with our lives, feel that life is not fair, feeling jealous of others' successes) and the trend around us is like that, then we really have to get a grip on our life and use all our focus and energy to get out of those trends as blazing fast as possible, and flee from it! The longer we dwell in that environment the more we feel justified since everybody else is also thinking or doing things the same way. We will feel more comfortable or justified since everybody is doing/experiencing them, too. This kind of thinking is totally not healthy: why?

The real problem hasn't been fixed yet, it just feels right or more comfortable. Just like if we take pain killers (aspirin, ibuprofen, etc.), they don't heal us, just make us feel good. We don't feel our pain anymore, but the real problem which caused the pain is still there, we just try to "ignore" it. Other worse examples are some people try to get drunk when they are having pain or facing a problem in their life, some people keep doing their darkest desire without any control at all, and some are doing drugs, etc. All that won't fix the problem, those are just an easy instant way to forget or ignore the real problem and they cost money, too! And even worse, there will be more problems to fix. Remember the negative/dark cycle? The same exact thing will happen to us if we get comfort from "everyone else is doing it, too" or "it's a common problem" or "it's just the way it is". How so? First, we have a problem to fix and second we are in denial. I know it's harsh, but that's true. We complain about this and that but instead of trying hard to get out of it and be a winner, we feel comfortable by flowing with the current trends and say that we are fine. That's double trouble!

At the same time, that way of thinking also makes us happy or content to be a blend in the mix or of an average quality. Being content emotionally is good but if we feel content logically but never content emotionally, that'll make us lazy and lack of enthusiasm and hurt inside. Try to think and be better than average, just like another favorite writer of mine named David J. Schwartz, in his greatly inspiring book, "The Magic of Thinking Big": "Average is the best of the worst and the worst of the best!" Do we really want to be average? It's all up to us...actually, if you say "yes", then just put down this book and don't waste your time reading it. My purpose is at least to make people want to get out of the incorrect trends and make a change for their own winning way of life. Just kidding, since you already have the spirit and made some effort to buy, borrow or may be are even standing up reading it in the bookstore aisle, I admire all that willingness and effort. So as a nice guy as I am, I let you slip this time and go ahead and read the rest of this book (if you still want to ☺). And I truly wish that this book can help you prepare or renew your way of thinking so that you can act on it, then keep repeating them as habits, then before you know it, you are already there, the first step is always the hardest step! But once you roll then you'll keep going, just like pushing a minivan that won't start. Just use all your focus and energy to do it! First, you might feel "It's impossible" then "It's difficult" then "It's done".

So never let your unique personality get caught in the wrong trends. Don't be average, be better than average, be your own best and have your own trend! Who knows? You might be a trend setter? Don't get hypnotized by all the trends that surround us, they usually cost you more than the benefits you can gain from them. Is the juice really worth the squeeze?

b) Love Means Joyful Sacrifices (Then Prioritizing Them)

Love means joyful sacrifices. It's as simple as it sounds. If we love something or someone, we will joyfully sacrifice our time, energy and finances (treasures) for that particular something or someone. If we don't sacrifice anything or if we sacrifice but don't enjoy doing our sacrifices, that means we don't really love that particular something/someone. For example, if I really do love my family, I will make time for being with them, give and support them with all my might (my time, heart, energy, skills, talents and finances) to make them joyful and happy, healthy and wealthy as much as I can. And on top of that, I enjoy every moment of doing all those things.

I also love martial arts so I put a pretty decent amount of time, energy, and finances into it since martial arts is my healthy hobby (which is my 4th priority) so I have to be committed to my priority order. My personal priority order is 1) God, 2) Family, 3) Responsibilities (work, help others in need, etc.), 4) Healthy Hobbies: that make me a better person directly since I use serious effort and energy (martial arts, singing, finances) then 5) Personal Hobbies: purely for my leisure (watch movies, eat, read books). That order works the best for me, personally. Each of you might have a different priority order. Usually, the more we love something/someone, the more we will put them as our priority. So our priorities usually reflect what we love/care about most in our lives. If someone put a lot of time and energy in their work then we know that he/she loves to work, meaning that work is his/her priority. If someone always put a whole lot of time and energy into a sport, he/she must love the sport so that's going to be their priority. After deciding our priorities (it may be a whole long list of them) then we need to rank our priorities.

In my case, I love God (by frequently reading, listening and watching/experiencing Him to learn, understand and apply more and more from His lessons), love my family (by always being thoughtful about them and intentionally giving my best time, energy, skills and financially for them), love my work (actually I try to love whatever I do so that I can excel in all of them, whatever it is, I will explain more about this later), love my hobbies (that's why it's called hobby, right? Duh?! Hahahaha....my hobbies are all kind of sports especially martial arts, and some other arts, especially singing and dancing), and love my personal hobbies (by enjoying things for purely myself, don't care whether it's productive or not, will better myself or not, or helps others or not). All of them are priorities in my life because I love them all so I need to rank them from their necessities in my life and I myself have ranked them just like I mentioned above.

c) Learn to Love Working Hard, Whatever We Do

After we all learn not to get caught easily by trends or fashions around us and learn to enjoy our sacrifices for someone (some people ☺) or something we love, now we are ready to aim all our focus, energy, time, skills, talents and financial (the last aspect only if available and required ☺) for the main strength of our financial builder, our income. Without any income, we won't be able to do anything as we really wish. Surely money is not everything in our life but everything still needs money. So it doesn't matter how wise and smart we are in spending and organizing our money if we never have any! Income is like the bullet in our gun, the oil in our fryer, cattle in our farm, camera in a photographer's hand and so on.

There are a lot of ways to make money but only a small percentage of all of us who really enjoy what we do for a living. It doesn't matter what we do to earn our income as long as we have the right mind and attitude toward what we do, we usually excel. It should be in our best interest to have something that we love or are good at as a living. But most of the time, that doesn't happen, at least for some period of time in our life. When that doesn't happen, it's fine, just seize the opportunity to be successful at whatever we do. Some people keep waiting for the right opportunities to come that fit their desire and talents. This choice has two possibilities, first, they might really get their opportunities and their patience and perseverance will pay off, or second, they'll never get their opportunities and their stubbornness wastes their time, energy and their other talents. I won't judge whatever others decide but I personally prefer to go ahead do whatever lies ahead of me while still looking for (or even better, making it ourselves) the opportunity to find a job I really desire! So, at least, I got some income while I'm looking for (or in the making of) my ideal.

In these stepping stone or time filling careers, we might be way out of our field specialties. An engineer from another country, future anesthetists, future engineers, future doctors, work in restaurant business, a young pastor works as a paper or pizza delivery, non-A-list movie stars work as bartenders, etc. Most of the examples above are happening around me! Actually, I'm one of them, too. My wife and I are both engineers (refer to "about the author" first passage) and we both work in restaurants and retail, consecutively. Many people are so surprised to know that fact but few people understand how it happens in life.

We both chose to work with what we had at that time, starting both at a chain fast food restaurant, trying our best to learn and do them so we can take pride in what we did and most importantly how we did them. With all our heart and mind, we focused all our talents and energy at our workplace at that time, the fast food restaurant. We used our best skills to communicate with coworkers, supervisors and customers (tactful, compassionate, enthusiastic, honest), used our best logic to do the most ergonomic (the most comfortable way with the least injury risk for our body) way to lift and move all the heavy stuff and share all those with other coworkers. We always do more than what we are expected, always help without being asked first, and always have a great attitude toward other people and our work. All those made us perform our best at our workplace. And the benefit of it is, at least God is always watching our true intention and value, at most God is watching and so are the owners, supervisors, coworkers and customers, too. So sure enough, we got promoted while we were still looking all the time for better opportunities which we got about two months after working at those fast food restaurants.

Our supervisors at work are not blind or stupid (at least they're not supposed to be). Even if they are, just approach them politely. If they're still the same way, or even worse, if they disrespect our polite approach, then approach the higher level supervisor above them. If the higher levels are all still blind or stupid, just put in your two week notice! We don't want to work for companies whose management level all the way up are either blind or stupid. That's like we don't want to jump out of a ship to a life raft even though we knew that the ship will sink sooner or later. But again, I don't mean that we should be rebellious to our supervisor or company, I said they're not supposed to be blind (doesn't see anything, good or bad things happening under their watch) or stupid (doesn't care about anything, good or bad things under their watch). If they are, there are chances that the good employees won't get what they deserve and the bad employees will get what they don't deserve, and that's frustrating! So just leave them! But always in a good way, never burn a bridge behind us. Always put in a two week notice, never leave our workplace just like that. We never know what will happen later. Always be respectful and honorable (both are signs of our maturity).

And the important thing is that every job is important as long as it is legal! Do not let anyone look down on us just because we work in fields that most people think are dead end jobs! Here is the best defense against people who are judgmental: It's much better for a person to work (make a living) in fields that are looked down on by others yet they are able to pay all necessities and bills in their life properly than for a person to work (make a living) in fields which are well respected by others but still aren't able to pay all necessities and bills in their life properly. Examples: It's much better for someone to work at a fast food restaurant yet able to buy property (and pay it off) than for someone to work at a property business but are not able to dine at a fast food restaurant without their credit cards. It's much better to work in retail and still be able to pay all the medical expenses properly than to work in a medical field for a living but aren't able to pay all their retail expenses without using their credit cards (in debt). It's better for someone to work in a public school and be happy and have no debt than for someone to work as a successful businessman but can't be happy or have all kinds of debt caused by their fancy lifestyle.

Just as I refer to in the multiple choice section of the introduction, we can be positive or negative in our way of thinking. Personally I choose the positive one since it will make me better, at least at the mental stage, and at most at other aspects, too. The positive thinking in my mind and heart can fuel my spirit, enthusiasm, focus and energy to do whatever I do and wherever I am so that my performance will be better and others will notice the results, too. Then the greater rewards will come which will make me more passionate about what I do and the positive cycle will keep going like that.

Learn to love your job whatever it is! Why? Here's why: There are only two choices if we don't like our job, change our job to the one we love or change ourselves to love our job! It's that simple! Just as simple as take it or leave it. In this recent economy, I believe the first choice is way harder to achieve than the second one. If we can find another job that we love (permanently, not just love it since it's new!) without jeopardizing our life, financially at least, then go ahead! Great for you! But if we cannot find other job that we love for whatever reason, then we are stuck at our current job since we need income. If we know we are stuck anyway, might as well love our job! We know we have to work on a regular basis! So, instead of regularly having a mentality that we are about to do something we hate with people who we hate, let's just have a positive mentality regularly as if we are about to do something we really love with the people we love. I know it's almost impossible for most people to have a real world like that, but we might as well have the happy and positive mentality and attitude since it's not going to change the fact that we have to go to that particular work anyway! Loving our work/job will make us excel in the work field. We have to try to find the good things/points about that particular work that we do and the people around us at work. If we are open minded and honest enough, we all will be surprised at how many good things we can find at our job!!

The biggest reason why we can't find any good things about our job or people at our job is this: our jealousy of other people at work. We are jealous that they get the better position, why they get the higher salary, why we are the one who have to do this, why we do all the work but they're the one who got the rewards, etc. If we focus on those things, we will never be happy! I guarantee that! The most important thing is whether or not we are happy with what we do and what we get for what we do. If not, try to find another one that makes us happy with what we do and what we get for it. If we can't find any other like that, then, might as well, enjoy what we must do and enjoy what we get for what we do, too, right? "KISS: Keep It Simple, Stupid!" That's what my former youth choir director advised me long time ago while preparing me to fill his spot when I was 20 year old.

We really shouldn't be jealous of others who earn higher than us in our work. Why? Here's how it goes:

First fact: the higher earnings we make, usually the higher energy and time it takes from our lives so that we have less energy and time for other things in our life. Other things could be good or bad, it all depends in how we want to live our life. But basically, the high earner usually has less energy and time for other things in their lives. That's a fact even though some people might not agree with it.

The high earner might deny that fact since they are so passionate about their work which makes it seem like a hobby, too, for them. So, they might be content with that. But if we honestly compare the high earner with the middle/low earner, we will see that the middle and low earner have a lot more energy and time on their hands for other things.

The middle or low earner who says that the high earner has more time than them, are usually just people who are jealous of the high earner. Trust me; if someone has climbed their way to the high earner level and can keep it that way, they sacrifice a lot for that. For example, a McDonald's fast food restaurant owner will have much less time and energy to watch movies, play video games, hang out, chatting at the computer, vacationing, relaxing, etc, in their overall life, compared to any of their crew members, regardless of their demographic background (gender, age, ethnicity, etc.) That's a guarantee. A doctor spends about 11 years after graduating high school in order to be a real doctor (4 years pre med school, 4 years med school, 3 years residency), that doesn't include a specialist. And it costs a lot of money, too!!! The average doctor without any grants/scholarships involved, will have a $240,000 - $300,000 debt at their graduation, depending which school they attend. It's really hard and expensive to be a doctor here in the US. So we cannot (and should not) be jealous of them.

Second fact: the higher earners usually have higher positions. The higher the position we have, the higher responsibilities and stresses we have also. This is very true, if we are the manager of a restaurant. Everything and everyone under our watch is our responsibility. So let's say if all our crew members have great working mentalities and qualities but since they all are human, they still have a small possibility to make mistakes/failures. So, we, as the manager, will accumulate all our crew members' possibilities to make a mistake, which makes the possibility for a mistake to happen bigger, plus we also have to deal with our own possibility of making a mistake. On top of that, we have to do all our responsibilities and make sure everyone under our watch does their responsibilities, too. That's a lot of responsibilities! And if anything is wrong, we have to stand up and fix the wrong the best we can. If not, the customers might get really upset and never come back. Or even worse, the upset customers might tell their bad experience which happened under our watch to many other people/customers which might make them not to come to our restaurant also. And there's a chance that the upset customers might know our direct supervisor, CEO or owner who might penalize us or even terminate us for that incident. That's a lot of responsibilities and stresses!

I'm not trying to say that it's better to be a regular position employee all the time. No! I personally suggest that everyone should try their best to set and then reach their dreams! I'm just saying that it's not easy to be in a higher position or the one who has higher pay, that's why there are some wise sayings, like "no pain no gain" or "is the juice worth the squeeze?" It's all our decision! My point is that we really need to love what we do, whatever it is, be content and not to be jealous of other who we might think have better positions, income or luck. We have to focus on finding the best for us and do it the best we can. We should not be too picky except we still can survive by doing so. For example: many people complain that they couldn't find any job for months (or even years?!!) already, saying that the economy is bad right now, etc. but they always think that they're too good or too smart/classy or whatever else they might think, so that they never want to work in many vacancies available in work fields other than what they want! But yet, they complain that they don't have any money?? What an immature attitude! If we don't like something and start whining about it, then do something about it! Don't complain until we really try to do something about it; don't be like a little whining child or a childish person.

If we really love what we do, whatever it is, whichever phase we are in now (surviving phase, stepping stone phase, reaching the dream phase, etc.), we will excel in it because we really love our work so we will love to work hard on it, just like our hobbies. That's good for whatever plans we have. If we plan to move up the ladder (which I chose personally and strongly suggest for you, too), that attitude will make us shine in our productivity and other work results so that we will get promoted and be ready for the bigger rewards, appreciation and also the challenges and stresses, too. It's a whole package deal :) If we decide to do the other plan, just stay where we are (not my personal choice and I don't suggest that, but it's all up to us, of course), at least we will enjoy our work and we will be good at it so we will be content and people will really love to see us, know us and work with us.

d) Ever Improving Contentment

We have learned how to be independent in our own trend or fashion, choosing and making our own lifestyle. We have learned about loving someone or something that goes along with our decided lifestyle and learned about the meaning of true love which is joyful sacrifices and making what we love a priority. Then in the last lesson we learned about the main weapon for our financial battle which is our income generating source, our work, how to choose and love what we do so that we love to work hard on it and be content.

Being content is being grateful. Satisfied with what we have or do. The key to being content is to know (or at least believe) that what we have or do is the best fit for us even though others might say the opposite. Others might say the opposite since they might have their own perspective that fits the best for them. Feeling content is one of the best feelings we ever have. If we never feel content, it would be so sad and hard for us since we never like our jobs, never love our life, are always jealous of our neighbor's property or our friend's belongings, always envious of other people's successes, always feel that we get less than what we deserve, constantly think that others always have better luck than us, continuously being resentful of our relationship, etc. Basically, not being content is similar to being negative (as I mentioned in the introduction chapter, part d) multiple choices). On the other hand, being content is not exactly the same as being positive because being positive has more coverage (anything toward us and toward others) than being content (only for things toward or around us). So being content is very important since everything starts from us. It is impossible to be positive if we ourselves aren't content. For example, there's no way to say that I am a positive person but yet I am not content like: I always hate my job, always am resentful to my wife and sons, etc.

But it is possible for someone to be content but yet they have negative point of view or attitude toward other people or the world. For example, I am so content with my life, family and career but I always think that the system in our government or world is crooked, the world we live in is full of really bad things and people, etc. So we need to be content first then we can be positive!

There is also a danger in this matter though, since sometimes people get mixed up between being content and being dreamless. If we are truly content, then we will be thankfully satisfied with what we have and do, then we will feel secure enough to try to improve our contentment to a higher level. A strong sign of our contentment is that even when we fail in achieving our higher level of contentment, we are still content with our earlier level of contentment. That's why I called it an ever improving contentment because it is pretty self explanatory. So whichever contentment level we are in, we are content! We are thankfully satisfied with what we have and do, so even if we can't achieve our higher contentment level, we will still be content as in the original scenario. But if we can achieve a higher contentment, why not (or why yes)? It's all up to us, nobody can force us to gain our personal joy and happiness because everyone's different. My wife and I personally choose to have the ever improving contentment, we personally try to better up all the time. If we achieve our higher level of contentment, that's great! If we never achieve it, we will still be thankfully satisfied with all that we have and do. I also believe that change is not always for the better, it could be for the worse, but it's impossible to be better if we never change.

Here is a good example of the benefit of having an ever improving contentment. In my own family, even though we always have a great lifestyle (at least for us ☺) under our carefully made budgeting system, we have also faced financial downturn in our lives and we believe someday, somehow, we will face them again for some reason, even the ones we never think of. Our own personal experience was the year 2012, we were forced to spend an incredibly high amount of money for our income level. From March until July of 2012, we had some problems with our hail damaged roof and car, kitchen sink, garbage disposal, two of our cars, the cell phone and home phone, TVs, DVD players, and on top of all that, we also got tricked by some professional scammers on our car (I'll also show you how to avoid scammers at all costs later in this book). All in all, it cost us about $13,000 out of pocket during those 4 months. My wife also had to change jobs from her workplace at which she has worked for about 10 years because of the financial and schedule pressure caused by the 2008-2012 recession. That meant she had to start all over again from the beginning at another job or field. It's financially the toughest year we have ever experienced so far. But yet, we were still content and able to accept the reality with a big heart and mind instead of crumbling down spiritually, mentally and physically. We still chose to enjoy every other little thing, to love rather than focus on the worsening financial condition we faced. We still kept moving forward, trying to do our best until we found the "daylight". Never quit or whine too much (a little is fine, I called it sharing, not complaining/whining ☺) We just focused all our heart, mind, energy, skills and time for enjoying and bettering up our quality of life, although it wasn't easy at the time! Usually most people use most of their heart, mind, energy, skills and time to whine and blame themselves or others when hardships come. It just doesn't work that way! Whining, complaining or blaming here and there (even to ourselves!) will not fix anything! I emphasize it one more time, complaining and blaming people will not fix anything!! Just use all our time, energy, skills and all other assets to fix the problem and better ourselves instead of using all of them for whining, complaining or blaming people. Trust me, if we use all our resources that we usually use to complain or blame, toward our effort to fix the problem and move forward, our quality of life will be much better off, I guarantee!

e) How to Manage, Not Only How to Get Money or Things

Most people or institutions teach us very well how to gain then master the knowledge and skills necessary to be able to earn money, but there are way fewer people or institutions which teach us how to use the money since it's all up to us. It's personal, it's free will and it's a sensitive thing to talk about. All the reasons above are true, but because of that truth, we never really talk or check whether what we've done so far is the best fit for us. I don't say right or wrong, that depends on how we look at it, but certainly we can see where we are right now and where we will be in our future in spite of right or wrong.

Example, X makes $100,000/year and Y makes $35,000/year. I'm pretty sure that all of us will agree if I say X is going to have a higher, or as most people say "better" lifestyle. X will have a newer and nicer car, a bigger and nicer house, he can buy a lot more fancy stuff or gadgets, have more expensive vacations. etc. All that is very true, but will X definitely have more net value than Y? Will X will definitely have less debt than Y? That's not always the case! If we can make more, why not spend more? I totally agree, on one condition, as long as we can afford it under our budget safely (which I will explain in subchapter 2 point c. Budgeting. Budgeting is like our filter, whatever financial level we are in right now or in the future, if we always have the correct way of budgeting, then we'll be alright. The bottom line is our income relates proportionally to our lifestyles but good budgeting (managing) relates proportionally to our real net value (wealth). Just like in some sports, let's say in boxing, someone has very good upper cuts, hooks, jabs and crosses, all executed with perfect motion and great explosion so that pretty much anyone he hits will get knocked out. That seems pretty intimidating, right? But if this guy has a very bad footwork, that'll make him unable to make himself close enough (in punching range) to be able to land his killer punches. So, despite of his perfect and powerful punches, when he doesn't have a good footwork, he'll never have that chance to land his awesome punches, except when the opponent comes to him. Usually their opponents aren't stupid enough to come and bang with a boxer who is known for his great punching power. Their opponents usually want to keep moving to give the great puncher a hard time with adjusting their positions and postures to be able to throw their best punches. In this analogy, the great punches are our income and the footwork is our budgeting and the stupid opponents who will come and bang square on, is our luck which is very rare and I personally suggest never relying on luck! Just work hard all the time with the right attitude and it'll surely pay off! Trust me, I've been there, done that, seen some, and confirmed most! Same in tennis, too, if one has a superior stroke but has bad footwork, he'll never be able to position him/herself to land great strokes....... again, the strokes are our income and the footwork is our budgeting.

We will get used to everything we practice on a regular basis, in sports, at school, at work, in a relationship, and our financial life, too, of course. For example: if I was a playboy when I was younger, had a lot of girlfriends and easily switch from girl to girl. On top of that, I never felt that it was wrong, so that's like double trouble just like I said in the earlier point a: be different, don't get caught by trends. Later on, it's gonna be really hard for me to stick with one woman for the rest of my life and that'll ruin my marriage big time. Except I'm willing to realize and admit that I was wrong so I can change my way of thinking, then my way of acting or behaving, then after a progressive repetition I will change my lifestyle. So, if one has already decided and done the wrong thing and still denies that it is wrong, that's lost! It's just like a blind guy who's heading toward a cliff and being stubborn that he's heading the right way whenever others try to remind him. We have to fix our wrong way of thinking by admitting that we're wrong then having a turning point of view and put it into action before our wrong way of thinking might already be rooted in our habit or even worse, lifestyle!

So if in the beginning we already know that something is wrong, don't even think to ever try doing it! Seriously, once we get the taste of doing the wrong thing which usually is great (if the wrong thing tastes yucky, then nobody will do the wrong thing), we might get addicted to doing it. It's gonna be our habit, and before we know it, it's gonna be our lifestyle, the wrong and bad lifestyle! So, please be aware in your decision for your lives, especially in finance. Always make it a good habit to live within our means, or the easy way to say it is "our outcome must be smaller than our income". Basically don't spend more than what we can make.

What is the best way to manage our money? The three most significant ways to do it that I can't emphasize enough are:

1) Always put aside some portion of our money for other people and another time.

What does that mean? Why? Let's say if we have a family of four, just like me, we should think and care about our spouse and our children at the present time and in the future, too. We should not think and care only for ourselves and only for this present time. In our case for example, we are married and are both working so when we spend money for our hobbies or things we want, we should think that the money we're going to spend is our family money, my wife's money and my children's money, too, not my own personal money. What if we are the only bread winner or income earner in our family? That's even more serious, we will have a bigger responsibility for our family since we are the only one in our family who can generate income! Some might think that it's not fair, well, if we choose to get married and have a family, it's our responsibility to provide for our family. In addition, usually our spouse who isn't working will take care all of the household things, like cleaning, cooking, washing, ironing, dusting, sweeping, vacuuming, taking out the trash, beautifying our home, taking good care of our kids, planning, shopping, trying to get great deals, budgeting, etc. That's why it's called marriage. We have our own share to show our love in our marriage. We only get married if we really love one another and as I explained earlier in the book, love means joyful sacrifices :) We can spend some of the family money for our hobby, of course, as long it's in accordance with our proper budget.

This way of thinking to care about other people and time will make us think about the happiness of other people and at another time, too. If we think only about ourselves at the present time then nobody else will think about us and our future, either. How can we expect anyone else to do it for us if we never do it for ourselves and others? So we better exercise our way of thinking that whatever we want to spend must be under our agreed budget since we ourselves are the ones who have to generate and manage our own income for our family and for another time (the future). It might sound like paranoia and too much of a sacrifice, right? No! It's called responsibility and planning. Will that kind of thinking make us stingy? No! It will make us frugal, not stingy. Being frugal with ourselves but generous to others is actually noble. On the other hand, being frugal with others and over generous to ourselves, now... that's the really stinky stinginess, or we can even call it worse, selfish!! All these, I will discuss later on in the next subchapter (f). Just remember, if we really love somebody, then we should joyfully sacrifice for the ones we love and their future, too. That'll make us become a noble person, too.

Basically, we need to discipline ourselves to care and prepare for our significant ones (spouse, girlfriend, boyfriend, child, parents or whoever else are significant to us) and other times (time of need, lay offs, recession, future, retirement, etc.). You owe it to yourself to pay the two things above and you'll be happy you've done it. Some might ask," What if we are single and plan never to get married or have any kids?" In that case, if they are really sure and they make a pact with themselves, then they should at least care about their own future or time of need! Even some people that might think they're going to be single all their lives, still sometimes they may meet their soul mate in the strangest time and place, we just never know. Anyway, always put a portion of your money aside for you and your significant(s)' future and for other times of need. Some other people might ask, "What if we die early and never be able to use all our savings?" Well, we'll be better off anyway, right? Since we're going to heaven, that'll be a much better place, if not the best place (which I'm sure it is) for us to live the best life forever except if we're planning to go to hell (which I don't think so). If we believe we'll go to heaven, then it's good if we get called home by God earlier than we expect. If we don't believe in heaven and hell, well... there will be another LoVE (Lee on Vital Evolution) book series about life and belief which could help others who don't believe in heaven and hell and got my later book sold, too (I'm trying to kill two birds with one stone here, just kidding.... Or am I? ☺). Please just think about it, if we only live here in this world for this short period of time then die, what next? Nothing? That kind of thinking will usually make us live our life for granted! Life is too short, so have fun! That's a double edged sword. If we take it the wrong way (which most people do), then we'll abuse our right to live our lives. Only if we take it properly, we will have the ever improving contentment like I explained earlier. By being conscious of the reality of heaven and hell, it'll give us some awareness in our life, just like the check engine light in our car's dashboard. So, please go ahead start to save some portion of your money for your own future and potential significant other(s). Just do it and make a habit out of it. Trust me, the hardest step is always the first step and after the first few months of adjusting ourselves to it, it'll be easier when it's started rolling. Before you know it, you'll have the great feeling of having extra money set for you by yourself later on! And since you already taste the great feeling of it, you'll want to keep saving some more and the positive cycle will continue.

2) First things first (what we need, not what we want, first)

This motto is one of my favorite mottos, too. It actually applies to all other aspects of our life. We have to be concerned about first things first. We have to do first things first. We have to get, finish, pay, make, go, call etc. first things first, because if we don't, then we start wandering around using our energy, time and money for second, third, or even worse, useless things first!! And that's totally messed up! And don't worry, I've been there, too, before. Fortunately, I realized soon enough that it doesn't (and should never) work that way.

There is a funny joke which is kinda true to some extent (I don't mean to offend anyone by this at all), it said," A wise person will pay $20 for a $10 thing they really need or want, a fool will pay $10 for a $20 thing they don't really need or want". In real life, we should always go by getting (consuming): 1) what we need first, I mean really need them, without them, we might jeopardize–our life, health, relationship, future, and all the important things in our life, then after getting things that we need, 2) what we really want, even though we don't really need them but we really want to have them as our rewards for working hard and living smart. If you get the thing(s) you really want first before getting what you need, that's not right! That means you already violate the meaning of the rewards for working hard and living smart because that's not smart at all! That's what spoiled people do, always get/do what they want first not what they need, just like a little spoiled kid. Mature people get/do what they need to get/do first, then what they really want to get/do. One of the great Christian based financial teachers, Dave Ramsey says, "one of the signs of maturity is the ability to delay pleasure", I agree with that and my own motto is "sign of maturity is always doing what we need to do first before doing what we want to do" or just like what Spiderman/Peter Parker (Marvel's superhero character) has for his luck "bad always comes before good".

You will be surprised (at least I am!) by how many people think that they can:

1. Regularly get out to have fun with their friends, buying their niece/nephew a nice and very expensive toy, buying the newest technology for their leisure or entertainment first before paying their debt

2. Have money to eat out while having a hard time paying their rent

3. Keep exchanging their car for a newer and higher class car while they still have a couple thousand dollar loan for their old car

4. Go on a luxury vacation while they still have $5,000 in debt or more

5. Have a nice blackberry or iPhone while requesting a grant or support from our government

6. Have cool rims and a luxurious stereo for their car while using food stamps

7. Got paid under the table (cash) and then enroll for low income benefit

And there are many more examples.

The last three examples really make me mad because it's not just their fault, but ones who approve their grant, food stamp, and benefit requests are also responsible for their stupid decision or careless action! The worst thing is that they're using our tax money to do so! It's just like the authorities (who approve them without detailed investigation or with a bad decision) grab some money from our pocket and give it to those who use their money for their unnecessary luxuries rather than their needs. While, we, the ones whose money was taken don't always live that fancy ourselves!! People like that are people who don't understand the meaning of first things first. Their motto is logically "useless things first" as far as they can show off their fake condition. Yes, I said fake, since they try to look good while they really aren't that good, right?

That really upsets me, but I still think it's better to get upset seeing people like that, than we become one of them and others get upset because of us.

First things first, use our energy, time and money or privilege for what we need first. Be logical and honest in assessing what you need! Don't ask others (government aids, loaning company, bank, friends, family, etc.) for money or things if we ourselves misuse our money for secondary (good to have) or luxury (nice to have) things. That's just selfish and dumb!

The most important filters for our spending are these two basic questions respectively, the questions are, "do we really need it?" (primary need/need to have) then "do we really want them so badly that we've worked for it and won't hurt ourselves or others?" (secondary/good to have). Don't worry about what we want (tertiary/nice to have) that's because we, as a human being, always want more and more. If we are offered limitless things, we are never satisfied. That is our nature and that nature will convert to our mentality which is really bad if we apply it only to our emotional desires without seeing a logical plan (our priority order and ability to get it).

Do we really need it? We really have to be honest and seriously think about it before we answer this particular question. If we fail to do so then it's the beginning of the end. Seriously, if we are dishonest with ourselves and always take any important matter lightly then that'll become our habit in life. For example, one said, "I really need that ice cream, I have to get it because it will satisfy my need of taste", if you are this kind of person, then you are either being dishonest with yourself or don't think about any matter seriously. C'mon, you really need to buy that ice cream?? Or shirt, dress, watch, cell phone, iPad, etc., even when you'll be fine if you don't get it?? Another example, one might say, "I have to have that newest iPhone or Android, all my friends have it! They'll make fun of me if I still use my old phone!" Okay..... first, if everybody does it or has it, that doesn't always mean that it's the right thing to do or to have, it's just simply a trend or fashion. Remember, we could be a trend/fashion follower (which most people are) or a fashion promoter. It's all up to us. If we are afraid to be made fun of by our so called friends, then they're not good friends anyway. It means that our so called friends only want to be friends with our tools, gadgets, brands, and our overall lifestyle. They don't really want to be friends with us. They are only looking for a friend based on what we have, not based on who we are. Do we really want friends like that? I certainly don't! "But what if everybody is like that? I won't have any friends..." If we can prove that with our steady and simple lifestyle we still can be truly happy, enjoy every moment in life, always perform our obligations at our best and can accomplish better than them, then I guarantee they will bow down before us! No... Not really, they won't literally bow down (we wish, don't we?) but they surely will have respect for us even though we have a much simpler lifestyle and things. Our family has been there and done that, in two different sides of the world, USA and Indonesia, and it is proven that respect is not earned by what we have but mostly by what we do and how our characters are.

If we do have extra money after we pay all our obligations and debts then it's totally fine to get what is good to have (secondary) and even nice to have (tertiary) things. If you read this book, I assume you might want to learn how to be able to achieve the financial peace first so that later you can spend with more peace when you are already financially peaceful. Actually later on, you won't need to be taught how to spend your money if you can become financially peaceful from scratch or from the middle class, since you've learned to earn and spend wisely to get to that level.

So if we really need it, meaning we can't live without it, then, of course, go ahead get it.

Do we really want it so badly? This one also needs our honesty and serious thinking. We all know that we want a lot of things, but again we need to get our priorities straight. We need to be honest just as if we only can pick one of all the things we want, which one will we choose?

When we have made our choice, we better be content with that decision whatever happens later on because we might not have another opportunity to trade it. Let alone get "what should've been the right choice" and still keep what we already chose....that's cheating and kinda greedy since we are the ones who made the decision.

If we still have extra money after fulfilling all our obligations, needs and higher priorities, then we can get the next thing in our list and keep going like that. I hope all of you someday can fulfill all your obligations, needs, and wants, both the selfless and even the selfish ones, too :)

3) Maximize your money value (shop around!)

I learned from Dave Ramsey that money is active; it's always flowing in any kind of way and time. For example, I got a paycheck from my employer, then I cash it and gave it to my wife, she used the money to do our grocery shopping, the grocery company paid their employees, the employees used it to pay the bills and keep going on and on. The crucial thing is how to maximize our money's value. Just like in our life, we want to use our life, our time, energy, intelligence and skills to their maximum potential, right? I really do hope so because if any of us say "no", then we won't have the willingness and patience to read this book this far, or even if we open to this page of the book by accident, then we still have to choose whether to continue reading, understanding (and agreeing), and then applying the concepts in this book to reach our own maximum potential or just put it down and move on with whatever trends/fashion drifts towards us.
We need to decide whether or not to maximize our potential in any aspects in our life, including money, too.

Most people, realizing it or not, don't maximize their

money value. Here is the simplest and most common example: when they have some savings and just put it in any "free" checking or even in any "saving" account without any desire to understand what benefits and requirements are attached to them, then we might be missing a lot of opportunities to make some extra money for ourselves. What are the costs and what are the benefits? Is there any monthly or annual fee, any other hidden fee (ATM, online or anything else)? Is there any rate of return (interest)? What are they? 0.2% APR?? 2% APR? 4% APR? Basically if we choose a bank or any business institution to save some money, we absolutely have to choose one which gives us the most benefit and the least cost! I know it sounds selfish but it's not! If we apply this concept to our family, friends, church, colleagues, etc., then we're totally selfish since it means we only want to gain the most benefits from our family, friends, church, colleagues, etc., without giving too much on our part! But if we apply this concept to our bank or any business institution, that's called business!! The bank/business institution won't plan to lose some money in their regulations, requirements and offers. They usually offer things that are beneficial for us, along with their requirements which will be beneficial for them, too, in the short or long term, in a small or bigger volume, it depends on what kind of company they are. We just have to understand the rules they offer, then use them to our best benefit and least cost, that's the most basic principal in how to handle our economy (economy 101).

If we are too lazy or too "busy" to check around and understanding them or even worse, are too lazy or "busy" just to listen to good information and do it, then we really don't deserve to gain any benefits. We should wake up, open our eyes and use all our mind and energy to be diligent and smart enough to maximize our money value. We need to get the most out of our money that we earn with our sweat and hard work (at least that's how most of us earn our income/money ☺).

If we can get the exact same thing or service for a lower

price, why wouldn't we get it? If we can get a better thing or service (or both!) with the same price, why in the world wouldn't we choose that?! Except if we are violating some laws or morality then that's a great reason not to choose or get them, but if the products or services that we need (or really want) are open to everyone, then let the ones who sell their products or services compete their best to make us want to use theirs. The same exact thing applies to everything. For example: if I am a high-school boy who has an interest in a girl in my class, I will try really hard to get her attention and do my best to impress her. If I can get her attention and she is impressed by me then it's way easier for me to ask her out for a date, compared to if she never even recognizes me, let alone impressed by me! Why should I do that (get her attention and try to impress her)? First, because I am truly interested in her! Second, because she has a lot of choices to choose from! Why should she pick me? How am I better than other competitors for her? What can I do or am willing to do that no one else can/is willing, that will impress or benefit her? That's why we should do it! Same thing if a girl wants to get a boy's attention. Some of us use the aggressive approach and others might use the passive aggressive approach and they have tons of ways to do it. Same with businesses who sell products or services, they should do their best to get our attention and impress us. We have a lot of choices to choose from. So we better choose wisely. Make the best out of our money! Let our money be appreciated more by them, so we really should choose the best out of all the offers they made!

This shopping around is really important, or I should say crucial, especially for highly priced things or services (ex: buying a home, automobiles, roof, vacations, etc.) and long term routine products or services we use (ex: cable, phone services, internet services, clothing, foods, insurance, mortgage company or banks, etc.). So it's not only about what we have that matters, what matters the most is what we do with it. It's not only about how much we make, what really counts is how we handle/manage them.

f) The 4 quadrants of income-outcome usage

This is important since people usually get mixed up between being financially efficient/frugal and being stingy. How we spend our money shows what is important to us and thus also shows our personality and character.

1. Tight with ourselves and tight with others

This is simply being stingy. These kind of people usually don't really enjoy life because they always worry about being too careless with their money. They never have the heart to spend more than what they think is its real worth. Usually these people are the ones who are too smart/logical and overly prepare for their future or any emergency event with almost all of their earnings. But be careful, even though I strongly suggest for all of us to think about other people and times, I also suggest to put aside a portion of our money, not all (or almost all) for recreation. We still need to make memories, too, while making money (for both the present and future). If they always worry too much about their future and any emergency, then even when they really want to get something, they'll sacrifice their heart's true longing/passion because of their overly logical planning. That will make their life unbalanced. These people will have a lot more preparation for the worst, but they won't enjoy the journey getting there. They usually are the nerdy kind of people, not always, but mostly.

Examples from this group are people who never eat out, only buy clothing when the older one is totally unusable, never give for any good deed or donation (charity), always ride the old sputtering car even when they can buy a Lexus easily, never really tip for other's services (that is if they ever use others' services ☺), never really care about any fundraising, etc.

2. Generous with ourselves and tight with others

This is simply the worst group! Again, I repeat, this group is simply the worst group! It's simply called selfishness or being self-centered! These kind of people usually enjoy themselves way too much while ignoring, or even worse, ruining other people's rights or happiness. They have all the heart and mind for indulging themselves the best they can while clenching as tight as possible whatever thing or service they can/should share with others. They only follow their hearts for the passion/desire to fulfill their own hobby or liking but when the time comes to think or care about others, they will shut their heart and start thinking "That's not my problem", "That's their problem, they bring it upon themselves", "Well, it's optional, right? It's not like it's an obligation", etc. These people are the worst kind! So if any of us fall into this category, please open your heart and mind and be more humane or even better, be a more Godly person. One of my favorite writer/teachers is Dave Ramsey. He said once that us, human beings are like a pond of water (The pond represents the person and water represents the money), he said," If the water just flows in and never goes out, there will be no flow! What would happen? The pond will become stinky!" Hahahaha... I really like that metaphor! It's very funny and yet, true. This group stinks, because they only want to get the income/benefit for themselves but never want to present some outcome/good deeds to others.

One of my Christian best friends, Johan Luhulima said, "People who only learn about the Bible but never apply what they learn is just like getting fat not fit." I found that illustration to be very funny and yet, also true. It applies to any other aspect of our lives, too, actually, including financial. Let me break it down: What goes in must go out in the proper way so that we keep our health in balance. If we keep getting food, drinks, vitamins, proteins, carbohydrates, sugar, fat, and salt all the time but never exercise to burn all the calories, we'll be fat! Not fit! I never mean to offend anyone who might have some eating disorder, a digestive system problem, or different genetics, because they have no choice. But for people with choices, I believe we all, deep in our heart, want to be fit not fat. It's the same thing here, we want to be financially fit (could be in any income level as far as we don't have any debts) not just financially fat (rich but may have a lot of debts).

Examples from this group are people who like to eat out at an upper class restaurant but don't tip or tip really badly, people who have a million dollar home and all the fancy equipment and gadgets but never care about the people they know around them, people who always seek for a blessing/benefit from the church but never tithe (10% giving back to God), employers who make all the profit out of an illegal worker because they can pay much lower than paying a legal worker, people who abuse our country's welfare system while they're healthy and capable of working but are just being lazy and good at pretending or acting incapable, etc. Yes, they all are selfish and stink!

3. Generous with ourselves and generous with others

This group is basically the happiest group. It doesn't necessarily mean that it's the best; it depends on how disciplined they are with their budget. If they can be generous with themselves and others with a proper budgeting system, then they are the best group! But if they do that on their messy irresponsible budgeting, then they are just financially careless while really having fun and enjoying life until they go broke or even worse, bankrupt. They usually are compulsive or spontaneous people. They are strongly moved by their feelings/emotions, not their logic. They usually are the contemporary or free spirited kind of people.

So, if one can do both, the logical/nerd way and the contemporary/free spirit way with good balance, they will be the most secure and happiest people! They will fall into this category if with their properly planned budget they are generous with both themselves and others. These people are the best! If someone is just being generous with themselves and others without a properly planned budget then sooner or later they will find themselves short financially. I guarantee that's not going to be the best feeling you ever get. On the contrary, it might be the worst feeling we ever get! It's just like in all other aspects of life, when we feel we're good but suddenly we realize that we are short or worse, we don't have the capacity to do what we think we can and we really can't cancel it out! What a mess! Just picturing that feeling even gave me goose bumps!!

So be careful if any of us fall in this category because if it's done properly, great, if not, it can be really bad!

Examples of this group are people who always buy or update to the newest, cool technology even if they don't need it, people who always enjoy life all the time by using a lot of money for their vacation, lifestyle, hobby, etc., yet they also like to give some donation when needed, like to treat their family or friends out for dinner or a treat, are always touched and support any humanity or good deeds program, give the tithe/commitment to their God or church, and beyond.

4. Tight with ourselves and generous with others

This group is basically the noblest one since they don't use their possessions for themselves much but mostly for others' needs. Yes I said needs, not wants! If it's for others' wants then this group is really not smart and being used like a slave, how ironic... The noblest one? Yes, but this also doesn't necessarily mean the best. It depends on whether they do that from their own will and how joyful they are with this kind of lifestyle. If they really are willing and have great joy in living this lifestyle, then they live their fullest, noblest way. There are only a few people in this world who fall into this category and I really mean a few...

Examples of this group are the people who enjoy their life to the fullest by living simply and humbly but are greatly active in helping others and making lot of contributions for good deeds, church, etc., with pure (genuine) intention. These people will use the simplest cell phone but everyone respects them as an elder of the church or community association committee. People who drive a reliable standard minivan but rarely mind helping their friends and families who need to haul big things. People who have a simple average size house, but already paid it off and open their home for Bible study and fellowship, a warm gathering for families or friends or any other good deeds meeting/occasion. They also will use their extra money to help families, friends or church, etc. This group is simply the noblest; I might even dare to say that this might be the best group out there. How come? Here is the breakdown: If there are two people with the same amount of wealth, the first one is joyfully generous with himself and with others, while the second one is joyfully tight with himself and generous with others, logically the second one will have a bigger percentage of his wealth to be shared with others who need it. Therefore, I confirm that this group will be the best out of the other four groups, as long as they enjoy their lifestyle genuinely.

So the last two groups with the generous-to-others characteristic are actually both the best, but the greatest one is the-tight-with-ourselves and generous-with-others group since they are the noblest one by giving their part more to others. There is nothing wrong with any of these two groups, on the contrary, they are both great people! It's just that the last group is nobler since they joyfully sacrifice more for others. But, please stay away from tight-with-others and tight-with-ourselves group. You will hurt yourselves and others in the process, with or without your consciousness. And last but not least! Don't even think about being generous with ourselves and tight with others. This last one is the worst group by far, hands down!! And nobody likes people who are in that selfish group except if they're in the same group or they need a favor from the selfish group! That's a fact!

g) Quadrants of the Income Earner

There are four quadrants of the income earner:

1. Academic Based Professionals

This quadrant is the one that most parents usually want us to be in. We go to school to study hard and be smart then get a good job and be wealthy steadily. Usually the better we do at school and college, the better we do in our work field, knowledge wise at least! But it takes a lot more than GPA alone to be successful in this quadrant. It takes social skills, communication skills and hard work, too! And believe it or not, in some cases, it even takes what people call luck! Luck here means chances, for example our social class or how much money we have, how many friends we have or more importantly who we know and also how other people see us.

Most parents love for their children to be in this quadrant of income earner because they are usually well respected, known as the smart and helpful one in building and protecting our community or nation. Examples of this quadrant are doctors, engineers, lawyers, attorneys, CPA and the like.

It takes serious dedication of mind, energy, skills, time and responsibilities to do well in this quadrant, particularly in being a doctor, especially a specialist. It will take a lot more energy, time and even money, too, to be one. After we successfully graduate all the schools and programs needed for our knowledge and experience, we have to start our more serious and intense internship for a few months or in some cases, years, then we can reap what we have been sowing very hard. We can soon pay off all our debts for learning and sacrificing that much, then we can all build wealth step-by-step in a pretty decent amount, and the pace is much more steady than other quadrants.

In this quadrant, there are a few professions that are totally academic-based that don't necessarily make good money. For example: pastors, evangelists, preachers, etc. Some might make a lot of money but most don't.

2. Non-Academic-Based Professionals/Employees

This quadrant has the biggest percentage in the US and actually in all the world. About 60% of our society don't work in the field they studied at school. That's just a wowing fact. Why does this quadrant become the most occupied by our society? Here are a few good reasons for this:

a) Going to school without considering our passion, abilities, and chances

  Many graduates are just going to school because of someone else's passion, persuasion or even because of their own wrong motivation. They don't really know what they really want to do for a living, what they're capable of doing, and what their chances are, they just go study and finish that particular degree because of their parent's dream, wife's request, friend's inspiration, chasing their significant other, money they can earn if they got that degree, etc. without really considering whether they have the heart/passion (or at least willpower), talents (abilities), and conditions (chances) to do it.

  For example: to be a great boxer, we need all three main factors. Let's say we are really good at it (abilities/talents) and we have the physical prowess (chances/conditions) but we don't want to do it, we don't have the heart (passion/willpower) to do it, then we'll never do it. If we have the heart (passion) to do it and we have the physical prowess (chances) but we're not good at it (abilities), then we might be a boxer still, but not a successful one, or even worse we might get serious or long lasting injuries which might not be worth the income we make out of it, the juice is totally not worth the squeeze. If we have passion (heart) and are good at it (ability) but we have a bad eye and acute asthma (chances), then we better not be a boxer or we might get a tragic result. So, we need all three, passion, ability, and chances, to be great at anything we want to achieve. We always have to look at all those three main factors.

So by going to school without knowing our real passion, abilities and chances, most of us won't be as great as we should in our study field; we'll be just an average graduate. So even though there are a lot of vacancies but most of them want the few best of the graduates, how about the rest? Well... there are three choices: The first choice is to be one of the few best on that particular study field by redoing their school. The second choice is to redefine what our passion, ability and chances are again before returning to school. The third choice is to work in another field just to make a living. Most people choose the third choice with whatever reasons they have. It might be not enough money, time or passion to redo their schooling or they might want to invest their money, time or passion for something other than career, etc.

What about us? At that time, we personally chose to join this non-academic-based employees quadrant since we couldn't use our engineering degrees from Indonesia. And we didn't want to go back to school again with both our engineering degrees just being thrown out of the window like that. We really wouldn't like to spend more of our time, energy, and money right after that vain experience, especially with the $1.00 = Rp.10,000 currency at that time. But if by not going back to school, we can't improve our quality of life and become stagnant, then we have no choice. Fortunately, we are so blessed by God that we can improve continuously and get a better quality of life gradually.

b) Shifting job description

The percentage of this quadrant is very big caused also by many companies having a shifting job description for their needs, such as combining two similar (or not too similar) jobs, transferring one's skill set to another department, etc. for budget saving or cutting, even sometimes that's the requirement for climbing the ladder, and many more reasons. Many of us who originally want and are able to work in our study field, slowly (or suddenly) we start doing the shifted job descriptions (which actually makes us more versatile ☺) to fulfill the company's needs or our desire to progress.

c) Straight to work or unfinished school

Some of us go straight to work without enough formal education. Some also don't finish school for whatever reason. This group usually will work for a particular job they've always wanted and know that particular job can make a way better use of experience than a formal education, or will get whatever job they can get and try to be great at it! What about the ones who work either at their well-planned job or whatever job they get and are not trying to be great at it? Well.... in this case, as long as they are content with their life, joyful and useful to others and their community, I don't mind. But I really hope that we all want to do our best to be great at something, anything. Why? Because if we have that particular area that we really want to be great at, we will make that our vision, a realistic dream, we will have a mission, and plan on how to reach that dream of ours. And when we have a goal in life and the discipline to do it, it will mold our character better and stronger. I really believe that if everyone has their own dream and the discipline to make it happen, it will make our lives much more beautiful.

Just think of Walt Disney (the amazing Walt Disney Mega

Company), the late Steve Jobs (Apple personal computer and technology), Bill Gates (Microsoft personal computer and technology), Anderson Silva (UFC Middleweight Champion, 17-0 in 2006 – 2012), George St. Pierre (UFC Welterweight Champion, 11-0 in 2007 – 2013), Fedor Emalianenko (one of the greatest all time MMA fighters, 30-0 in 2000 – 2010), Floyd Mayweather Jr. (one of the greatest all time boxers, 44-0 in 1996 – 2013), Michael Phelps (the greatest Olympian ever, 22 medals, including 18 gold medals in three different Olympics), Roger Federer (the greatest all time tennis player, 237 weeks as no.1 ATP ranking in 2004 -2008), Jackie Chan (I believe you all know who he is ☺), Alexander Graham Bell (credited as the first inventor of the practical phone), Thomas Alva Edison (phonograph, motion picture camera, long lasting practical electric light bulb), Albert Einstein (developer of the general theory of relativity), Michael Jackson (King of Pop), etc. I don't necessarily say that none of them have finished any formal education or went straight to work because some of them have finished some basic formal education and some haven't. I just mentioned them as the greatest examples of people who have a dream and commit themselves with great discipline to achieve their dream!

Since this group usually work separate from their study field, they can be really good at what they do by experience and also their overall skill sets that might be different than what the school curriculum can teach us.

Examples from this quadrant are: secretaries, entry level clerks, office managers, servers, retail, department stores, grocery stores, sales people, administrations, franchise store managers, retail managers, restaurant managers, mail carrier company employees, etc. They usually make a pretty steady income but still way less than the curriculum based professional's steady income. It's called no pain no gain. :) The academic based professionals have to spend energy, time and money for their school and they really have passion, skills and chances, so as a result, they'll most likely gain more money than this non academic based employee quadrant.

3. Business Owners, Entrepreneurs, or Job Order Based Professionals

This group could be made of former other quadrants members, actually it should be made of the ones from other quadrants, using a lot of experience, knowledge and creativity and maybe getting courses here and there along the way, but basically this quadrant could be made of anyone at anytime and anywhere, as long as they have enough passion, skill sets and chances.

There are so many entrepreneurships and businesses of any form in this world that can be started by anyone, anywhere and at any given time. It just requires a really big passion (just like in any other thing we want to do), knowing a lot about our big passion and the business side of it, such as: all the regulations, laws, techniques, etc. We also have to have enough money to start it since this quadrant is the only quadrant that requires us to do all the work and pay all the costs first until our job or services are appreciated by our customers. So we don't make money right away for all the work we've done but also we have to risk our finances, too. It could be from our hard earned lump sum savings or even from a loan (which is more likely) but then later on, if the business works well, we will surely reap all the profits ourselves, not our employer, association or the like. So basically, entrepreneurship usually will cost all of our resources (knowledge, experience, skill, energy, time and money) in the beginning and will benefit us the most later (in profit, work schedule, reputation, etc.)

Here are some examples of this quadrant: a hairdresser opening their own salon, a financial advisor might open their own financial company, a chef might open their own restaurant, an engineer might open their own design company, a former athlete might open their own training center or their own themed restaurant, a fiction writer might have their own title franchised to movies, vanity toys or merchandise or amusement parks, an MBA or even a server might open their own frozen yogurt shop, a mechanic might open their very own auto repair shop, a movie or pop star might open their own clothing line or restaurant, an engineer turn into a professional poker player, an accountant might open their own gas station and convenience store, an engineer or part-time performer who builds their own event organizing company, a high school graduate who opened their landscaping business, automotive body repair company, Heat and Air repair company, etc.

This quadrant will get us a lot of money and satisfaction if it really works but if it doesn't work, we who don't have a good enough plan and financials will suffer badly, and the worst, file bankruptcy, since we put all of our sources on the line for chasing our dream. Again, I said if we don't have a good enough plan and financials, we'll be in trouble. But if we are passionate about it and do it properly, plan every single step with a humble heart yet an enthusiastic spirit, we'll be fine.

The hardest part of having our own business or being an entrepreneur is usually the first couple months, or even years, after we open. That's when we need to really connect our products or services to the consumers and give them good reasons why they should try and trust ours. It will be really hard if nobody ever knows our product or service at all. The juice will be worth the squeeze only if we squeeze the right fruit at the right time and the right place. But again, if we prepare our best and carefully pick the right products or services that we believe we are really good at, offer them at the right time and place, we'll be okay at least, at most we'll be great at it. Tailoring all that is hard part but the hardest part is the low consumer response for the first couple months, or even years, after all the effort (energy, time and money) we put in. That kind of challenge and hardship usually would melt anyone's spirit. But if we get good consumer response, then the bright future is getting nearer, just keep up the good job and make it better all the time.

4. Professional Athletes, Artists/Entertainers

This quadrant, if people do it as their main job professionally and are successful, will usually make really good money for their job order they have and I mean really big pay, like jaw dropping figures. None of the other quadrants make as much money during the same amount of time they use on the job, not even close, except a renown business owner or entrepreneur quadrant. They might be closer or a few even gain more, but overall, every other quadrant will make much less compared to this professional athlete/artist quadrant for the same amount of work. These professional athletes/artists usually get from hundreds of thousands to millions of dollars to do one work project or contract that might take a few months or up to a year!!

I know it sounds super awesome but people who are successful in this quadrant are usually born with particular gifts, special skills, awesome or uniquely built bodies, ever improving talents and they are committed to use all those gifts to make their living!! They get up in the morning, eat breakfast, shower and prepare themselves for the day. It could be performing, filming if they are actors/actresses, singing in concert if they are pop stars, training if they are professional athletes, get lunch and have a short break, then continue their performing or training, get their dinner then continue performing or training again, just like that. Every day most of their lives, just a little break here and there in between contracts. For some athletes, when the tournament season arrives, they'll be in tournaments and competitions all the time, no more practicing or training but time to show and test their training results, what they honed and sharpened all that time and to keep improving in every tournament and competition. That very same intense journey also applies to almost every actor, actress, pop star, rock star, and entertainer.

You won't believe their schedule, it's crazy tight!! And they usually are always in the spotlight, much less privacy in life! People usually think that this quadrant gets paid way too much but the ones who say that usually can't make it to that professionalism as an artist or athlete. I guarantee, if they were in that same position, they will say the total opposite. "The grass is always greener on the other side", right? But personally, I don't think that they can handle the intensity of that crazy tight schedule, plus the pressure of being in the spotlight all the time, anyway. It's always easy to talk about how other people have better luck and comfort but try to be them or beat their accomplishment? It's always harder than it looks! :)

This quadrant's members usually dedicate their lives to their profession and we can easily distinguish the levels between the performance of a world class athlete and others. We will literally drop our jaw just from seeing what they can do or achieve. Same thing with the world class actors, actresses, directors, and stuntmen, most of us can see the difference between them and the average ones. If any of you can't see the difference then it's too bad. Next time you watch any sport, show or movie, just watch anything available since you can't really tell the quality difference anyway and you will save money, time, and even energy by doing so. I personally can see the wowing factors that make this quadrant extraordinary and world class. Many people will try hard (at least they think so ☺) to be in this quadrant but only a very small percentage can really make it to their dream level. I really mean a very small percentage, just as small as the tight-with-ourselves-and-generous-to-others percentage in our previous 4 quadrants of income-outcome usage topic. You know exactly what I'm talking about if you've ever watched American Idol, American Top Model, etc. Trust me; it's not that easy to be one of this quadrant. I've been there trying, too, actually. Oklahoma Idol, martial arts stuntman, singing competition, etc. but God doesn't seem to approve of what I dreamed of at that point of my life. But that's a long time ago about 2004. No more dreaming about stardom now except if God has another plan, ahahahaha... :)

Some make it to stardom but can't handle the pressure or hardships. Their life starts to fall apart even when they're already at the position that they've dreamed of, just like in the movie "Rock Star" with Mark Wahlberg and Jennifer Aniston. We've heard the saying "Born to be a star" which is true, but I think it is also supposed "Born to be able to live like a star" since not everybody can handle it. Even the real super stars themselves who are well known and have been in the business for a while sometimes can't handle the pressure to be themselves, too. Examples: Elvis Presley (the king of rock 'n roll), Michael Jackson (the king of pop), Bruce Lee (the king of kung fu), Heath Ledger (the Joker in "The Dark Knight" movie), Whitney Houston (one of the greatest singers of her time). I really respect all of them for all their talent and dedication, all their contributions to our world, the inspiration they provide us, the quality entertainment they display, and a lot more, but unfortunately, they all passed way from unnatural causes. Bless their hearts.

This quadrant's examples are: all the world class actors, actresses, directors, performers, rock or pop stars, super models, football players, tennis players, basketball players, boxers, etc.

You might want to ask about the non-world class artists or athletes. They will have to have another job since the income they make from the entertainment or sport fields aren't enough. If not then it's too bad, they might live in a fantasy world..... I believe most of them realize that, so they will have another job to support themselves and their families.

In the world class athlete category, no one will be able to perform better than when they're at their peak! At some point in time, they will have to retire. Unlike the world class artists, who still can do what they are passionate about and great at, but in the less physical form. Let's say an actor/actress can still act really well, but in less physical roles. Some still do what they did as great as when they were younger, especially in the recent years (starting in about 2007). Names like Tom Cruise, Bruce Willis, Sylvester Stallone, Harrison Ford, and Jackie Chan, spanning from almost 50 to over 60 years old but they still act in action films (Knight and Day, Mission Impossible 4, Jack Reacher, Lives Free or Die hard, Red, Rambo, Rocky Balboa, The Expendables series, Indiana Jones and the Crystal Skull, Rush Hour 3, Robin B Hood). For singers, take Madonna, she's over 50 years old and still sings and dances with high energy. Those are the best of them. Unfortunately not in the world class athlete category, they will usually have to train and coach, or have another kind of job or business later on, and it could be in any quadrant of the income earners I talked about before.

Where are we in all these quadrants? It doesn't matter where we are right now, as long as we have enough passion, abilities and chances for any of these quadrants, we'll be fine. And don't forget that it's not about how much we make but more about how we manage what we have. There are so many great examples to confirm this principal. Here are some true stories of historic battles. Let's take "The Three Kingdoms", one of the most famous wars that changed the face of China. The three leaders (Liu Bei, Kong Ming, and Zhou Yu) with a smaller amount of soldiers and supplies, won the battle with their intelligence and perseverance, all by using their inferior supplies and number of soldiers because they could not get more. You can watch it in a movie called "Red Cliff". In the "300" movie, the Battle of Thermopylae (Gate of Fire), the Spartan king, Leonidas, did the same exact thing, with his and his team's heart, loyalty and skills, Leonidas lead his small group of 300 warriors to win the battle against the much more numerous Persian soldiers. In the movie "Troy", the Trojan's king Priam and prince Hector also did their part to show that heart and ability can beat some chance if we persevere and are intelligent enough. There is a lot more proof in many inspirational true stories like in the movie "Defiance". It's about the Bielski brothers, three Jewish partisans whose parents have been killed brutally in the Holocaust. They then escaped, survived, strived, and eventually saved and lead over a thousand other Jewish escapees for about 2.5 years in the East European forest!! In the movie "The Pursuit of Happiness", Chris Gardner, a father who could barely make ends meet for him and his son kept on trying, thinking outside the box and working hard passionately, so later on he became a Wallstreet legend. In the movie "The Social Network", we see how Mark Zuckerberg from Harvard, a poor nerd became a truly successful founder of Facebook and the youngest billionaire.

The most important thing is to always work hard with what we have while trying to get better all the time. Never be idle! My wife and I did it, too, as we mentioned in the About the Author chapter when we worked at fast food restaurants (working with what we had) while we kept looking for a better job that we desired (trying to get better all the time).

And always remember that how much we make relates to our lifestyle, but how we manage it relates to our real net value (wealth). So what matters most is what we do with what we have, not what we have itself!

h) Studying/Working

There are two important factors that will determine whether we can be successful or not in our job. First one is school or (academic) and the other one is experience or we call it "flight time". Some work fields required the academic performance more than experience and training and other work fields required the other way around. According to csmonitor.com in January 28, 2013, about 48% of the college degree holders, are in work positions that the US Labor Department classifies as requiring less than a four-year college education. As in January 2013, in the three most commonly filled occupations: retail sales person, cashier, and waiters/waitresses, there are more than 1.7 million college graduates employed," says the study by CCAP (Center for College Affordability and Productivity) researchers Richard Vedder, Christopher

Denhart, and Jonathan Robe. At the same time, 15 percent of US taxi drivers have a college degree, rising up from less than 1 percent in 1970. The overqualified worker is much more prevalent today than in 1970. The share of retail clerks who had college degrees back then was less than 5 percent, and has risen more than fourfold (20%) since then. According to the Bureau of Labor Statistics, fewer than 40 percent of the nation's largest and fastest-growing job classifications require four-year diplomas.

Unfortunately, recently, especially in the last decade, employers are mostly looking for a college graduate to hire simply just because of the prestige of having college graduate working for their company. It doesn't really matter whether the applicant's major is fitting their job description or not. That is one easy way to sort out the qualified applicants. They will surely hire the applicant with a college degree even though the ones without any college degree might have the same work experience and credibility. I totally understand why they do that, though. It's just like the "shopping around" method I explained earlier in the book. Actually, we all should do the same method in our lives, too. So, if we are an employer, we'll get a better quality for the same price, too, right? :)

Since between 48% – 60% of our society fall to the employee quadrant of income earner, at least about half of our society benefit more from training and experience than from their academic in their jobs. As for them who fall to the academic based quadrant of income earner, then they will surely need to perform well in their academic journey. With the exception of the academic-based professionals quadrant, honestly, it's about 80% of the theories and knowledge we learn from school either can't be used or is not applicable in our real life jobs. Usually most of the knowledge and skills we need to do our job are gained from training and real life experience. In addition, we usually can also use our degree(s) and experiences in multiple different fields and positions. Again, these are not the curriculum based professionals jobs like doctors, engineers, lawyers, accountants, pastors and the likes. They do need their knowledge and training from their study field!

Our parents usually want us to go to school, study well, get great grades, get a degree so we are well respected and can make good money. By doing so, we also bring up (and in some cases, keep) the family honor. Most parents want us to be like that (about 90% according to futurereadyproject.com). The most common dream of parents for their kids is usually that their kids will fall into the "academic based professionals" quadrant of an income earner. It is well respected, they are always needed by the work field, and has a pretty stable and decent income, more than average Americans which is between $20,000 - $40,000. Unfortunately, that's not always the case, just like I explained earlier in subchapter c. Learn to Love Working Hard, Whatever We Do. Not every person wants the same thing in life; the truth is actually quite the opposite! Most people think differently, despite what's right or wrong, they want different things. They want to be successful in different areas than others. Not everybody wants to be a doctor, not everyone wants to be an attorney, not everyone wants to be an engineer, and not everybody has the ability to be a doctor, attorney or engineer, either! Not everybody has the chance to be ones, either, sometimes. So there are a lot of factors, at least three main factors: what we really want, what we are capable of and how our conditions/chances are.

Most parents don't realize that and usually the kids are the ones who realize first! But it's better late than never realize it at all, right? Still, most parents, including ourselves, would like for our child(ren) to go to school for a better future, better opportunities in a line of work which usually offers better income and respect. What do I think about school? I think it's a must! Even though there are some great and very successful businessmen or scientists out there who never get their degree or never finish their 12 year education, they are a one in a million gem! They are geniuses and I am sure that they work really hard and under deep pressure from their families, friends or even the media before they all are big names, which I believe none of us, the ordinary people, want to or are able to handle anyway. So they are a one in a million gem! Don't shoot for that. Most of us are not a one in a million gem in this particular case. We have to work hard to be one in a hundred, and then keep getting better to be one in hundreds, then one in thousands and keep going. Even the one in a million gems I talked about, they, too, have to work really hard to be where they are (or were). We might be one in a million, too; we never know until it's proven, right? But why risk it if we have a choice? So if we can, meaning we have the money (or at least, a reasonable loan ☺) and time then we better have the desire to go to school! Find our dream first, what we really love to do and what we are really passionate about, what skill set and talent that we excel in, how we want others to remember us in our career, wisely check the prospect of it, then shoot for that study field!

The main reasons why I fully support and even suggest people to go to school is that schools will prepare our logic, discipline and perseverance through all the time we are there. How can the schools prepare our logic? Even though we won't necessarily use the exact knowledge and theories we learn, we will learn the basic logic of the relating field and at the same time we train our overall way of thinking to be more logical. Schools also teach us about discipline since we have due dates for tests, papers and any kind of task. So, we learn to prepare ourselves for a particular due date or season in our life. We have to understand properly what our teachers and lecturer require, just like later with our employers and supervisors: Do what is required in a proper way and a timely manner. How about perseverance? If we can't hang on through the basic 4 years of college time then how can we expect to survive the much harder and longer period of life? Except if any unexpected event occurs, like we won't live long after college, win the lottery, and that kind of stuff. But honestly, if we think like that (about unexpected events) then we'll never do anything useful with our life. So, always be prepared for the worst for the longest time, just like the Batman. :) So, yes, I highly recommend that everyone goes to school. We have to choose the one college major we are passionate about the most (will we love to do it for a long period of time?), can do great and advance in it (will we be proud of how we do them?), and that can fit our chances (will we be okay financially if we choose to do it?), too.

Can we learn about logic, discipline and perseverance outside school and college? Sure! But school and college are the most organized place there are. And there are other benefits also for being in school, like: socializing, communicating with different kind of people in different positions from different backgrounds, working as team, etc. If we can sharpen all those skills at school, then we'll be better off when we need to use them later in life when it's time to generate income for ourselves and our family. Sometimes, we might even meet our other half there, too, just like me. ☺ There is a funny joke (and truth, too, in some extends ☺) from one of my former college lecturer, he said," For you, boys, I believe your parents (and you should, too) really want you to be an engineer. For you, girls, I believe your parents (and you should, too) really want you to be an engineer …. or get an engineer." :) Of course, the best is both, being and getting an engineer!

Anyway, if we can, always prepare ourselves and our next generations our best! Our children must be motivated and supported to go to school and perform well there despised of what they really want to be or what they are really passionate about. Why? What if our children want to be a businessman who need more creativities, experience and non academic knowledge or an employee who need more dedication and diligence to be able to keep climbing the ladder or a movie star or an artist? My answer is still "yes", do our best to motivate and put them to school. Here's why:

Going to school doesn't necessarily mean that we will learn and use all the theory and simulation there in our real life (which most likely will be different since there will be so many non ideal conditions in real life) but it's more like stimulating us to use our heart, mind and attitude the best we can so that later, we can use our heart, mind and attitude properly in the real world that we are passionate about. It's about mimicking the real life their best so that we can be ready for it in the matter of the logical way of thinking and the discipline. The theory and simulation will not guarantee us to be able to do in real life exactly as we learn but at least we can think, practice our best the closest to the real world we are about to face. That will make our logic and discipline sharpened. Again, it's the habit of thinking logically and systematically that is most important gain we can get from school. Then the habit of the being discipline in doing all the home works, exams in particular due dates is the second most important gain from our years in school (except if we rarely do our home works or mostly fail our classes ☺). And the last gain is our perseverance in finishing our 4 year college degree (except we dropped out from our college and never finish them any at any point of time in our life).

So, always motivate and support ourselves and our children to go to school for whatever passion we/they have. It's good for us, building and molding us become a better person overall, except if we (or our children) really hate school even though we promote them in the proper way, then don't stress over it since we/they are going to fail the school or at least we won't excel at all since we are under pressure doing it. Before any of us hate it, please see and promote all the best things school/college could give us and make sure we choose our major wisely according to our passion, skill set and talent, and our prospect. If we still hate them from the bottom of our heart, then use our energy, time and money for something else useful (not useless!) that we are passionate about.

2) Preparing or Fixing Our Way of Doing (and Committing to It So It Will Be Our Habit and Mold Our Lifestyle)

a) Immediate Term (All Of Us Should Do All the Below as Soon as Possible, Between 2-12 months):

1. Budgeting (Always Make it the Worst Scenario for Cushioning)

I really hope that none of you skipped the "Preparing or Fixing Our Way of Thinking" section and just go right at this "Preparing or Fixing Our Way of Doing" section in order to save time, because you actually do the opposite. Just like building a nice house on a weak foundation then it's just a matter of time before our nice house will crumble. It's also like going into an MMA fight without the proper warm up, we will be more vulnerable to any serious injury. So please make your way of thinking, your basics strong first, then build on it so that your "nice house" and "body" won't fail you later. :)

Okay, after we start generating income for ourselves (and our family), now is the time to get to the meat and potatoes, time to have fun with our facts and planning!

Here is the basic financial statement or budgeting sheet that I use for my family:

Financial Statement or Budgeting Sheet of the _____ (ex: Smiths)

Made on ____/____/_____ (mm/dd/yyyy)

Now (in our current condition), we have $_____

It could either be positive or negative, depending on our current condition. We should add together all the savings we have, except property. Let's say the sum is A. We also should add all debts of any kind in the amount that we currently owe from any credit card to school loans. With the exception of a mortgage, let's say the sum is B. After that, we have to subtract B (the total debts) from A (the total savings) then put the end result in our current condition space, let's call it C. C is our real net value!

Our average monthly income is $_____ minimum, let's call it X. We have to use all income generated for the whole household. If we are a family who has more than one job then add all the incomes, but again it must be in average.

How can we do the average?

1. If we get paid routinely and the amount is roughly the same in every check, then we just have to make it the monthly average:

    If we get paid weekly, the monthly average is going to be the net amount (after deducted with all the taxes), not gross amount (before tax), in every paycheck, times 52 weeks then divide it by 12 months. For example: if we get paid $400.00 weekly, then our monthly average is going to be ($400/week x 52 week/year)/(12 months/year) = ($20,800/year)/(12 months/year) = $1,733/month net.

    If we get paid biweekly, the monthly average is going to be the net amount in every paycheck times 26 bi weeks then divide it by 12 months. For example: if we get paid $725.00 bi weekly, then our monthly average is going to be:
    ($725/bi weekly x 26 bi weeks/year)/(12 months/year) = ($18,850/ year)/(12 months/year) = $1,570.83/month net.

    This will calculate our monthly average more accurately compared to if we just add two of our biweekly checks or four of weekly checks for our monthly average.

If we get paid monthly and it is roughly the same amount in every monthly paycheck, then just use that number!

If we get paid quarterly, every 3 months (which is very rare now), the monthly average is going to be the net amount in every paycheck times 4 quarters then divided by 12 months. For example: if we get paid $8,000 quarterly, then our monthly average is going to be:
($8,000/quarterly x 4 quarter/year)/(12 months/year) = ($32,000/year)/(12 months/year) = $2,666.66/month net.

By adding the total amount for the whole year and divide it by 12 months, it will cover our paid holiday, paid vacation, sick pay and the fifth week in a month that might affect our total income.

2. If we get paid routinely but the amount is not the same in every paycheck, then we just have to record the different amount every time we get paid. After that, sum the total payment for the whole year and then divide it by 12 months. For example: a server or salesperson.

3. If we get paid routinely with the roughly the same amount in every paycheck but we also receive bonuses, commissions, etc., whether it's routine or not, then we just have to sum all the extra income through bonuses and commissions. Then add the total sum of all those extra income with the total sum of our steady paychecks, then divide the total income for that year by 12 months.

This will take real commitment to do, especially in the beginning. The first step is always the hardest one, but once we pass that first step, we will roll. That's why it is very important to understand and agree with the way of thinking I explained in previous chapter as your foundation. If our foundation is strong then we can move on with peace in mind and get a better result. If you have kept reading until this part of the book and are still interested then I believe that you are ready to make the commitment. ☺

Here is the general budgeting sheet. Some people might add more to their list and some might not use all of the list I listed below. The important thing is that we have to know our honest priorities and have peace with whatever the result is later.

Our average monthly expenses:

A) Food:

a. Primary (need to have)   : $_____
(Basic groceries)

b. Secondary (good to have)   : $_____
(Fancier groceries and eating out)

c. Tertiary/luxuries (nice to have)   : $_____
(Fanciest groceries and eating out)

B) Accommodation:

a. Rent/house payment   : $_____
(Rent/mortgage per month)

b. Property tax   : $_____
(Only if we own a property)

c.   Property insurance   : $_____
                                           (Only if we own a
                                           property)

d.   Property owner association fee   : $_____
                                           (Only if we own a
                                           property)

e.   Property maintenance/repair   : $_____
                                           (Only if we own a
                                           property)

f.   Luxuries   : $_____
                                           (All extra
                                           features we
                                           want)

C) Utilities:

a.   Electricity   : $_____
                                           (Average per
                                           month)

b.   Gas   : $_____
                                           (Average per
                                           month)

c.   Water and waste management   : $_____
                                           (Average per
                                           month)

d.   Telephone (home & cell)   : $_____
                                           (Average per
                                           month)

e.   Internet   : $_____
                                           (Average per
                                           month)

f.   Cable/satelite (luxuries)   : $_____
                                        (Average per
                                        month)

(We may combine phone, internet and cable if we have
that kind of deal)

D) Transportation:

a.   Our vehicle   : $_____
                                        (Car payment per
                                        month)

     OR
     Public transportation cost   : $_____
                                        (bus, subway,
                                        etc. per month)

b.   Auto tax   : $_____
                                        (Only if we own a
                                        vehicle)

c.   Auto insurance   : $_____
                                        (Only if we own a
                                        vehicle)

d.   Auto maintenance / repair: $_____
                                        (Only if we own a
                                        vehicle)

e.   Auto luxury   : $_____
                                        (All extra
                                        features we add)

E) Health & Beauty:

a.   Vitamins, bath & oral supply, etc. : $_____
                                        (Any regular
                                        things)

b. Specific doctor and treatment   : $_____
                                       (Any occasional
                                       incidents)

c. Health, dental & vision insurance : $_____
                                       (If we have any)

d. Luxuries   : $_____
                                       (Fitness,
                                       massage, etc. per
                                       month)

F) Clothing:

a. Primary   : $_____
                                       (Need to have)

b. Secondary   : $_____
                                       (Good to have)

c. Tertiary/luxuries   : $_____
                                       (Nice to have or
                                       seasonal things)

G) Children's Needs:

a. Day care   : $_____
                                       (When both
                                       parents have to
                                       work & don't have
                                       any choice)

b. School & education   : $_____
                                       (Only if they go to
                                       private school)

c. College fund   : $_____
                                        (529 plan,
                                        UTMA/UGMA/
                                        custodian fund)

d. Fun and games/toys   :$_____
                                        (Whatever the
                                        kids want that we
                                        allow)

H) Good Beliefs/Deed:

a. Primary charities   : $_____
                                        (Tithe to God,
                                        charities, food
                                        banks, etc.)

b. Luxuries charities   : $_____
                                        (Charities not for
                                        primary needs)

I) Retirement/Saving:

a. 401K   : $_____
                                        (Employer's
                                        retirement plan, only
                                        if they match)

b. Roth/Traditional IRA   : $_____
                                        (After we have
                                        maximized our 401K)

c. Mutual Fund/other   : $_____
    investment   (Non retirement
                                        saving)

J) Hobbies/Fun:

a. Family   : $_____
                                    (Family fun and
                                    hobby)

b. Personal   : $_____
                                    (For our personal
                                    fun and hobby)

                                                      +
_____
Total expenses per month   : $_____
                                    (Total expenses,
                                    let's call it Y)

So our potential monthly balance is (let's call it Z): our average monthly income (X) subtracted by average monthly expenses (Y).

We always want to shoot for a positive potential monthly balance (Z). Why? If our potential monthly balance is positive, that is great! It means we live within our means! The bigger the number the better, it means we have a bigger potential savings. The smaller the worse, it means we have a smaller potential savings. What if it's negative? That should never happen!! That means we live way beyond our means, and we spend way more than we should. That's childish and very not smart!

Remember at the beginning of the book when I talked about how we should only get something if we have something to trade it for? It's a very simple logic we've learned since we were children. We only got rewards if we behaved well, we got treats if we helped our parents with chores, we got to go somewhere fun if we got good grades, etc. That's logic everyone can understand, even kids. So now, as an adult, we should follow the same principle. We can't just enjoy our rewards without earning them.

So to make our potential monthly balance better (as big of a positive number as possible or fix it from negative to positive) we either increase our income or decrease our expenses. We can always do both of course for the best and fastest result. :)

Below are 3 ways to make our balance better:

As the first option, we want to keep our current lifestyle even though it is higher than we can afford (as indicated by our negative potential monthly balance). In this case, we just have to work smarter and harder! If our income is based on individual commission, tips or bonuses, work smarter by mastering our knowledge about our products or services and hone our communication skills. Work harder by providing great follow ups and getting extra shifts. The most important keyword here is to do more than others, quality and quantity wise! If our income is based upon hourly wages without any individual rewards based on our performance, we still have to do all of the above since God and our supervisor will see our performance and we might get promoted. But we definitely have to work more hours!! And if our main job doesn't allow overtime, get a second or even a third job!! Do whatever it takes to increase our income since we don't want to change our lifestyle, right?! By doing all of the above, not only will it increase our income at that time, it will also increase the chance for a promotion since we become a more hardworking person and passionate about our job! And that will increase our pay rate (quality), too, on top of all the extra income we already generate by getting more shifts and doing more than others (quantity). So that would be a good (positive) cycle. :-)

For the second option, we don't want to or we can't work more than we do now, so the only way is to cut our budget. Look through our budgeting sheet, cross off all the luxury (tertiary) things or "nice to have" areas. Those are usually the things only for spoiling ourselves or for showing our class, which we actually don't deserve since we don't (or can't) work hard enough to be able to afford them! If it's still not enough to balance our budgeting sheet, then start cutting the "good to have" or secondary things. Those are usually the things that we won't get hurt if we don't have them. If it's still not enough, then we just aren't working hard enough! Work harder to get more income to support your life!! If you really can't work harder (not just don't want to), then work harder to get disability benefits! That's simple! I never ask you to cut your basic or primary things since we really need those things to live our life. So if we have crossed off all our tertiary and secondary things and still are not able to support our life, then we either need the disability benefits or are just being lazy and aren't working hard enough. Sorry for the harsh truth but I prefer to have a true friend who really cares about me and will tell me the truth even though it might hurt but will make me better, than have a fake friend who always sugar coats the truth and will make me handicapped in my life.

The third option is the hardest one but it will be the most satisfying accomplishment in our financial condition! Work smarter and harder, and still budget ourselves mainly for the primary needs and a little bit for the secondary needs. By doing so, we'll be well off. If we get that simple and smart lifestyle first, it will be way easier to switch to the more luxurious and fun lifestyle later. On the other hand, it will be harder if we have to switch our already luxurious and fun lifestyle (which may not be necessary), to the simple one, trust me on this! If we work hard and live simple, we will have a lot more savings and peace of mind, but if we work okay and live a luxurious lifestyle, we will have a lot more debt and we should worry about our life. When we have the power to choose to live simply or luxuriously, we will feel awesome. But when we don't have the power to choose but are still choosing the wrong one then it's so not smart and just plain selfish! There's a good movie about it, called "The Joneses" with David Duchovny and Demi Moore in it. If we can afford it after all our primary needs are fulfilled then why not? But if we can't afford it, then be mature enough not to live that lifestyle, that's plain and simple logic. If we don't work, we don't eat. We should always spend less than what we can make. It applies to everybody in any kind of healthy environment: businesses, banks, companies, schools and of course families and individuals, too. What if all our friends have all that cool stuff and we are the only ones who don't have it? Do we really want friends who will make fun of us if we don't have what they have? It's pretty obvious that our "friends" we choose actually want to be friends with our "cool stuff" more than with us as a person. I prefer to have real friends who will share the ups and downs of life with each other, who encourage one another, who share the joys of life with each other and who appreciate us as who we are, not based on what we have.

Budgeting is the best tool for checking where we are right now financially, whether or not we are on track. The funny thing is that most people don't do budgeting, especially the written one. They think it's way too much trouble and too complicated, but then they ask," Where did all my money go? It just seems like we are always short of it!" Hmmph.... Let me think...How come? Mystery? No! It all goes to our lifestyle. If our lifestyle is right and simple then it'll go to our savings, etc. But if our lifestyle is wrong and way too luxurious for our income then it'll all go there, and the worst part is that we might be in debt!! So please do make a budgeting sheet, it's just a little intimidating for the first time but you'll get used to it. The first step is always the hardest one, but remember: "every hero starts from zero" and budgeting will be the best tool we'll ever have for checking our financial standing.

A few tips to make the best budgeting:

1) In your average monthly income:

   Always put about 5% short on your budgeting sheet (ex: you make about $2,500 per month so put down $2,375) just in case you get less hours or a pay cut or if anything else happens. Always hope for the best but prepare for the worst.

2) In categories of our expenses:

a. For most utility bills, just like how we calculate our monthly income, sum the total bills for the whole year then divide them by 12 months so that you include every high and low amount of bills since the usage of electricity, gas, water, etc. will surely vary depending on the season. The same principle applies to any other monthly, quarterly or semi-annual bills or payments you have.

b. Always put about 5% extra on your budgeting sheet (ex: you have about $2,000 for our monthly expenses so put down $2,100 monthly expenses) just in case the worst scenario happens. It's always better to be safe than sorry.

Andy, what if the worst case never happens? That will be even better for us since by putting all those extra cushion, we will have extra money saved for that particular month! From the example above, with our budgeting we will have $275 (from $2,375 - $2,100) to save monthly, but if in that particular month the worst never happens, we will actually have $500 (from $2,500 - $2,000). That's almost double our potential monthly balance to save!!! Yayy!!

3) Always make the proper percentage in your budget.

Our primary (need to have) things should have the highest percentage. Our secondary (good to have) things should be the next highest percentage then the last, tertiary (nice to have) things should have the lowest percentage.

11. Saving (Percentage)

Saving may be the biggest challenge for most of us, especially in America. It sounds weird, nerdy or abnormal since our world is moving way too fast! All the nice and cool lifestyles, all the comforts and conveniences they offer (or promise) us with all the advertising and commercials representing movie stars, celebrities, and sport stars, really lure us to spend more money to enjoy whatever they offer. And when most of our friends and families have those cool things and make it common in their life, we feel weird, abnormal, nerdy, or outdated since we don't have what they have, even though we might not need it anyway. On top of that, our community also lacks introspection. Altogether, those are a great formula for disaster. Most people say, "Save?! I barely have enough money to pay my rent!" but they smoke a pack a day and dine out twice a week. "Nah, I'm gonna enjoy my life first. After I've lived my life then I'll start to be serious about making money and saving a lot." Yeah right! Ever heard of habit? If the habit of living fun and luxuriously is instilled at an early age without learning the responsibility needed to earn the money to pay for all that first, then it'll be a really fast turn toward debt, even faster and scarier than the fastest and scariest roller coaster you've ever ridden when your friend kept persuading and forcing you!!

Actually having fun using money we don't have yet is like a tornado. It might make you feel hot and moist but after it's all done, it'll leave you dry and messy. We might feel like we're "hot" or "on a roll" in our lifestyle, because it's easy to do, but after a short time we'll be in trouble, our savings, wallet, pockets, even our credit limit will be dry! That'll surely leave us in a messy financial condition, whether or not we realize (or admit) it, it won't change the fact that we are in a heap of trouble financially. And to make the matter worse, some people start paying one debt with another debt, loan etc. Just please be careful...

Anyway, we have to earn more than we spend, then the

excess will be saved for another time or even better, for other people and events, too! The key to success in saving is strict discipline, it's just like the key to success in perfection is practice. And discipline needs real commitment, not a half-hearted one. Discipline will go a long way in every aspect of our lives. It doesn't really matter how much our income is or how much we can save. The first and most crucial thing is the attitude and commitment to do it which is discipline. Always have the heart and mind of a person who cares about the future and others.

There is a saying, "what is behind us is the past, what lays ahead of us is the future but what lays in front of us now is a gift, that's why it's called the present." These wise words mean "life is short, enjoy!" or "live for this moment" or "live our life to the fullest." It's a great motto if the right person applies it but if the wrong person applies it, it might make things worse. So it all depends on who applies that motto, and how they interpret that motto. Whoever has a good filter can filter that motto in the best way possible, if not, they'll just take it as it is, whatever situation they're in, which may endanger themselves and others. Here are a few examples: a sharp knife can be used to cut a lot of stuff to prepare a great meal but it also can be used to kill somebody. Drugs can be used in many great ways in medical field but yet the very same thing can be used to get high. Great social skill can be used both to inspire people to be better or to manipulate people to follow whatever we want. The list could go on. It's just like a double edged sword. Basically, it is not about the tool but it's all about who uses that tool. Don't just trust any popular saying. There is another popular saying which I prefer:" Plan as if you'll live forever, live as if this is your last day to live, and give as if this is the only chance you can give." This saying I categorized as wise words. ☺

One more important thing, even if most people do it, it doesn't necessarily mean that it's the right thing to do. Remember the 80/20 law, basically 80% of the success in our life will be enjoyed by 20% of society and the other

20% of the success will be enjoyed by the rest of society which is 80%. It all depends on our willingness and commitment in deciding which 80/20 group that we really want to be a part of. Remember that what most people think and do is the 80% society, right? That means they (80% of society) are sharing only the 20% of success happening in our life. So most of the successes in our life (80%) are shared only by the few of us. I don't know which one you really want to join but I personally want to join the few and the proud, just like the marine's motto which is very inspiring and good. :-)

Most people say that they really want to be the few and the proud but they never really reflect it through their actions. People who only want the rewards without the work are either living in their own fantasy world or are just plain lazy! C'mon, how can we eat if we don't even want to open our mouth and chew? How can others know how we feel and what we want if we never express ourselves and tell them? How can we can be wealthy if we never really want to work hard and save hard?

Enough said about how to prepare our mind and heart to save effectively, now we'll talk about the tips on how to save effectively itself. So do you really want to save money? Go ahead! Just do it! No excuses, no postponement, no everlasting failed attempt, there's only one way, just do it!! Just like one of my favorite promos for Pierce Brosnan's first James Bond movie "Golden Eye", it said, "No fear, no limit, no substitute, there's only one James Bond". Fear represents excuses, limit represents postponement, substitute represents an everlasting failed attempt, and James Bond represents our action of saving our money. :)

These are 3 practical steps for saving effectively:

1. True discipline in doing it, not just trying to do it. Like the quote in the first Matrix movies, Lawrence Fishburne's character (Morpheus) told Keanu Reeves's character (Neo),"Stop trying to hit me and hit me!!" or

the Nike brand's motto "Just Do It." It's very true, most people are just too busy "trying" to accomplish something but never really accomplish it since they lack finishing spirit and energy. They have the dream but do not follow up, or they might follow up for a little while, but not until they complete it and get their dream. I'm sure that you know someone around you who's just like that. :) Only a few people really accomplish what they really want to do in their lives. Sadly, only a few people really finish what they have started or promised. The rest, which unfortunately are the majority, haven't finished what they've promised or started to do, let alone accomplished what they really wanted.

So again, I can't emphasize too much that the most important key of saving is true discipline. There's a really awesome motto that I live by personally: "If anything is worth doing, it's worth doing properly" meaning never do anything half-heartedly! Why even waste our focus, energy and time doing something that we don't think is worth doing anyway? By doing so, it will make the end result suffer from bad quality! When we don't get a good result, we will say," See? I knew it wouldn't work!" It's not working well because we do it half-heartedly! Then our poor result will make us want to quit. Even though we might still have the willingness to try it again, it will be without enthusiasm and passion (quarter-heartedly, maybe. ☺) It's just a negative cycle!

Instead of wasting our focus, energy and time for that and producing a bad result, just let others who think it's worth doing do it. They will have the passion and enthusiasm to do it properly with eagerness. They usually will get a great result so others can enjoy the most of it, and they can be proud of themselves while also getting their rewards. On the other hand, we can do something else that we're passionate about and produce our own great result and get our hard earned rewards, too.

If we are a new saver, we still have to remind ourselves all the time about our total commitment to save. It means we have to always save as often and as much as possible and don't spend anything (don't worry, I'm not done with the sentence yet ☺) on luxury (nice to have) things, spend a little bit on secondary (good to have) things and just spend basically on primary (need to have) things. Someday when we have financial peace and a true freedom, we can get all the secondary and tertiary things we want without hurting ourselves figuratively and literally. Usually people who gain financial peace from ground zero or on their own hard work, will never think or act like people who are under the bondage of debts. They are too wise to want to go back to that under-bondage feeling again. They will be wise with their money even though it's their time to enjoy their lives with secondary and tertiary things all they want. On the other hand, someone financially wealthy without any hard work or any considerable efforts, usually don't have appreciation for their wealth as much so they might still be kind of reckless while using their wealth. Just like the motto "no pain no gain," it always works. Well.... at least most of the time. :)

2. Always shop around for the bank or financial institution with the highest rate of return (interest) you can get, and the lowest cost/fees if you want to save your money there.

So after we establish the great habit of saving, we should maximize the rate of return of our money as our next good habit. But still, the first priority is the habit of saving since it won't mean a thing even though we have a bank or financial institution which will give us a 20% interest for our return but we never save. It's way better to get only a 2.5% APR but save diligently in a regular basis. And of course, the best plan is that we save diligently and get the highest rate of return (APR) as possible. Yayy!!

3. Always have your income direct deposited to your bank (with the highest benefit for us) whenever that feature is offered by your employer.

Why direct deposit? The first benefit is the emotional benefit. If we don't see it, we don't really think about it, then it will be easier for us to not use the freshly earned money we have. Our eyes will tempt our heart and mind at times, and for some people, all the time. The less we see our hard earned money in our hands, the less desire for us to spend it. Trust me! I've been there and done that. We still need to get the print out, though, so we know how much money we have saved and also whether we got paid properly for our work (clock in system, bonus, etc.) And if you really need the money, you can get some cash through the ATM, through banks or use a debit card, etc. It may sound like too much trouble just to get the money but that is actually good because we won't be willing to go through all the trouble just to have fun. When we really need the money for our necessities, then we will make it happen since we really need it.

The second benefit is the practical benefit. It is much easier for us to save our money without having too much trouble. We don't have to drive all the way to the bank after a long working day or week, we don't have to beat the time before the bank closes, etc. If we have to go through all the driving and whether we beat our bank's closing time or not, then we will get discouraged and get lazy to save money. We will lose the chance to save our hard earned money and to earn interest from it and we will be tempted a lot more to use the money at hand.

If there is no such feature offered by our employer, we still have to go right away to the bank and save our paychecks and cash. We have to make it a habit as the first step. When we need the money we can use debit cards, checks or get some cash first at the

ATM or bank. By doing so, it's guaranteed that we feel the sacrifices needed anytime we use our money. But isn't a debit card the same thing as credit card? No! They both are convenient plastic cards that we can put in our wallet and just swipe them whenever we need it, but the most important and main difference is that we have to have money in the bank to be able to use our debit card while we don't necessarily have to have money to be able to use a credit card, that's why it's called credit. So a credit card will give us the opportunity to be tempted to use money that we do not have yet. Some people call it a privilege. If the credit card user is a wise one, it will be a privilege, but most credit card users are not wise, then it'll be a privilege to fall into a trouble!

So, always save all our income, paychecks and cash, as soon as possible so there will definitely be less chance for us to be tempted to use our hard earned money! The less we see money in our hand (wallet, secret box, save box, money jar, etc.), the less we want to use it. At the same time, we build the habit of saving and earning interest, too! Yayyy!!!

III. Deal Hunting or Shopping Around (for the End Cost)

Deal hunting is not as hard as saving in our culture. I saw a lot of people already using coupons or special membership cards that give them discounts at multiple establishments (restaurants, stores, etc.), and a crowded store when there is some kind of big sale, especially on Black Friday. Despite all the proof that people chase better deals, there are two crucial things to remember before we go crazy hunting some deals. First: "Do we really need it?" "Do we really want it?" and "Do we have a budget ready for that without hurting our higher priorities (mortgage, bills, payments, loan, etc.)?" Second: We really need to know the standard price for the things we hunt. Don't be easily fooled by the big signs like "The Biggest Sale of the Year!!," "Now 75% off! Hurry while it lasts!" "Blowout Sale," "Grand Opening Sale," "Only $40 Flight to Vegas," "Lowest Price Ever on This Three Day Only Special!" "$100 Free Walmart Gift Card" blah blah blah... Very few of them are truly great deals. Most of them are pretty much a gimmick! Trust me, been there, done that unfortunately. :) But that's great since I can pass the knowledge on to you! Everything happens for a reason, I even believe that everything happens for the best reason even though sometimes it's not easy! But later in life when we are wiser, we'll realize and admit that.

We already discussed how to answer the first crucial thing to remember "Do we really need it?" earlier in the book. Now let me explain how to achieve the second crucial thing to remember "We really need to know the standard price for the things we hunt." We always have to see the end price of the item we want to get. For example:

Let's say we are looking for an Under Armor compression tee and we know that the price is around $34.95 - $39.95 depending on where we shop. And then someday when we walk around the mall, we see a store that we're not quite familiar with putting a sign up that says: "30% off on any workout apparel". We might want to check them out if we're into workout apparel especially the Under Armor that we're looking for. We check the price tag for the same exact Under Armor compression tee (always compare apples to apples) and we'll see the tag which was originally priced for $54.95. So with the 30% off it'll make it $38.47. If we don't know the standard price, we would pay almost the highest price there is ($39.95) since the store has already marked up the "original" price to $54.95! And the bad thing is we still feel like we saved 30% off of the "original" price, and we might want to save more by stocking up on workout apparel. So we would pay for all of that stuff at almost the highest price possible and still feel good! Then if we are nice guys, we will tell our family, friends, colleagues and usually they truly trust us, while in reality we are unconsciously dragging them into that particular store's marketing scheme! The store will make tons of profit from people who:

a. Don't know enough about the items' standard price
b. Have a compulsive buying habit (easily get excited about something that looks/sounds good and then buy it)
c. Nice people

Isn't it bad that a person or company profits out of people who are lacking in knowledge or willingness to research, people who easily get excited, and people who are nice?! They may be smart by exploiting others' weaknesses just like a credit card company but they're bad! Bad in a bad way! The first group of victims might deserve it since either they lack knowledge or the willingness to research, but that doesn't mean it's okay to exploit it. Just like in most of the true heroic movies, truly good guys usually don't kill the bad guys even though the bad guys might deserve it. But a person or company who preys on the second and third group of victims are pure evil, they make profits out of other people's enthusiasm and kindness. But again, we as consumers are also as responsible as them, the marketing schemer. Let's be diligent and smart. Let's be composed and collected. Let's be kind and yet be aware. If we do all those, we won't only be a wiser consumer, we will be a wiser person, too. Killing two birds (being a wise consumer and a wise person in general) with one stone (by being diligent, smart, and aware)! And the second bird is even bigger! :)

Here is another example: a really cheap plane ticket deal. The deal is usually only for a one way trip so that will require us to buy the other half of the round trip at the "original" price which is pretty high usually. Most people don't purchase a one way ticket except if they are moving to another state and have all their stuff shipped or taken care of by professionals. If that's the case then it's a great deal to grab but most people don't do that. Most people plan to buy a round trip ticket since it's cheaper and easier that way, especially with all the websites available right now, such as Cheaptickets.com, Hotwire.com,

Expedia.com and a lot more. If we only buy a one way ticket, we usually will have too much unnecessary stress later like whether we will get a seat or not on the particular day we need (or want) to go back, how much the price will cost, etc. Usually the price will be high since we need a ticket on such short notice, but with all the stress we face, we might be willing to pay whatever price just to get it done. Trust me, don't do that! Don't buy a one way ticket except if that's what you really intend to do. So, only if we ever need a one way ticket then it's okay to check around for those special deals.

Here is another example of other gimmicks/scams. A company promises us any kind of tempting "rewards" (a $100 Walmart gift card, a $200 Best Buy gift card, or sometimes even a more ludicrous offer like a $1,000 gift certificate of a big company!) when we do something "easy and fast" on their terms. Those "easy and fast" things include but are not limited to: applying for a credit card, listening to a presentation, buying a particular service, etc. Most of the time, it's the scam company who tries to trick us by using all those big companies' names just to make us fall into their trap to buy some kind of product or service from them that we originally never needed (or even wanted). Usually we don't do research for things we don't originally need or want, so we are more vulnerable to all those products/services. On top of that, they use a professional salesperson who can play with our emotions so we feel we need or would really love their products/services! They will try to stimulate our compulsive buying. Those scam companies haul tons of profit from people who easily fall for their trap just to get whatever they promise in the beginning. Usually their products/services are not good since they don't have the guts to try selling them in the normal way without framing or tricking us into it. Just like in any sport, whoever tries to cheat are the ones who usually don't have confidence in themselves so the only way to secure a win or victory is by cheating, right? Please be careful! Never fall for any kind of scam or gimmick! Scams always make us pay a higher price for a mediocre or even worse, bad quality product/service, and on top of that, they usually give us a lot more stress compared with getting those very same products/services in the normal way. We could actually get a better product/service with a lower price and with less trouble and stress. In my personal experience, I once tried one presentation of a water filter system. After all that time wasted listening to them which didn't even make any sense, we politely refused to use their product. They kept persuading and pushing their ridiculous water filter, we kept saying "no, thank you," just like trying to get a dried gum off our pants. It was really hard but finally we were successful in refusing their product. Then they tried to just leave without giving us what they promised us in the beginning! I asked for it, and they gave us a coupon with online access to redeem our gift card. And after all that trouble, the code or password they gave us was already expired or not even valid!! Trust me, I've been there and done that myself a few times. What a fool (and kind of greedy) person I was at that time!! It's a total waste of our time, energy and even money if we fall into their trap. Fortunately we only fell three times into their traps during our ten years living on this lovely US soil. We have learned the hard way, so we promised not to fall for any more scams! So please don't ever fall for scams! If it's too good to be true, it's usually a scam or gimmick!

So again, two crucial things to remember when you are hunting for a deal:

1. Make sure you hunt for the things/service that you really need or want without hurting your budget. Make sure you will use them. If not, why even bother to go to so much trouble hunting for deals for stuff you don't really use?

2. Make sure you do your homework, research the standard price for the stuff we're about to hunt for. Then always look for the end price of any offer, it doesn't matter what they say about how much of a discount they offer us or how hot a deal it is, if at the end we pay more than we should, it's a rip off!

If we already established the understanding of the two crucial things above and really believe it, then it's much easier to talk about the real deal hunting. The most important thing is that we have to be willing to sacrifice our time and energy a little bit for further benefit later. Just like the life lessons I mentioned a lot already in the previous chapters, no pain no gain and hard work pays off! We have to do our job at our best so that we can get our recognition and rewards. In this deal hunting case, we have to shop around to get the rewards of paying a lower price for the very same thing or to get a better thing for the same price.

The more money involved to get what we need and really want, the more we have to do some serious shopping around since it's gonna be a big loss if we get the wrong deal. The right order from the most costly to the least costly thing in our life usually goes like this:

1. Buying a house and finding the mortgage company: the biggest investment most people make in their lives

2. Finding an apartment, studio, choosing a cell phone, internet service, and all other monthly necessary living costs

3. Finding what to eat and where to get it from: most people spend way too much in this category, sometimes even more than their mortgage/rent payments!!

4. Finding the proper vehicle and how to pay for it: most people fall into the trap of buying the one they desired the most even though they can't afford it yet, then they use the credit system and make payments. With that unhealthy way of thinking and habit, I assure you before they even pay off their payments, they will have already gotten tired of that vehicle!!

5. Finding the right insurance and the right price, too: whenever I ask people I know how much their insurance premium cost and what the coverage is, most of them (about 90%) usually answer like this, "Hmmm... good question. I never really know how much I pay or what the coverage is, I really should look it up." (and they never do!) or "Yeah... I trust all that to my company, they take that stuff from my paycheck automatically so I don't have to worry about it at all." Yeaaah... right... They don't have to worry about the automatic deduction from their paycheck alright, that's good and all. But they should worry about how much they are paying, and what coverage they are getting for what they pay. And is that even what they really need or want? Is that really the best deal they can get? It's actually a lot to worry about! I don't mean to burden any of us with extra stress, it's just that we need to know how much we are paying, what it is used for, if we even need or want it, and whether we have the best deal or not. If people don't know the exact policy and cost of their insurance, then why spend money for things they don't even understand? And to make it even worse, they might get overcharged for it, too??! Most of them also buy the one with the best coverage; do we really need that? The main key for buying insurance is to first check our condition, let's say for health insurance, the happier and healthier we are, the less we need insurance since the less likely we are to go to a doctor or buy medication for our emotional or physical condition. For auto insurance, the safer we drive and the cheaper or older our vehicle is, the less coverage we need in our auto insurance. It's actually the same way with life, property and any other kind of insurance, too.

6. Getting all the secondary and tertiary stuff: most people fall into the trap of "competing with the Joneses" or "let's get what we deserve" mode. By doing so, they usually spend way too much for things

that they don't need.

7. Shopping for regular simple groceries or daily needs:
   We need to go to different grocery stores for different
   items based on availability, quality, and price, too. Of
   course we don't have to drive 10 miles just to save 30
   cents, we have to count the gas money, too. :)

So the bigger the money involved, the more effort and
time we should put in to shop around and find the best
deal for what we really need and want. Things that involve
a lot of money could be something occasional that is
expensive or something that requires us to pay a decent
amount on a regular basis since it all will add up.

Deal hunting is all about being determined to know
whether we have a great deal or not for a particular
product/service. We need to compare which one is the
best way to get the very same thing with the least cost
from our pocket or how to pay the same price for the
highest quality product/service that we need. Do not
forget to calculate all the taxes, shipping and handling
fees and any other fee included. For example: I am
looking to buy UFC MMA gloves. I can find them at one
online store only for $45 while I can get the very same
gloves for $50 at a local sport shop. At first glance, I'll be
jumping up and down excitedly since I could use the $5
(10% off) difference for something else. But if I'm not
careful enough, I might forget to add the online store's
shipping and handling fee which is $15.95. That'll make
the online total price of $60.95 ($45 gloves + $15.95 S&H
fee) while the local store here in Oklahoma, will only
charge the tax of 8.375% that'll make the gloves price at
$54.19 (($50 gloves + ($50 x 8.375%) tax = $50 gloves
+ $4.19 tax = $54.19).

So with the example above, the online store seems to
save me $5 (10% discount) while actually if I'm being
careless and make the wrong decision, I'll pay $6.76 more
on a $50 item!! That's 13.52% more!! That's just one
thing at a $50 price. Imagine if this is my habit and

lifestyle for making decisions for my home buying, mortgage, payments, cell phone, insurance, food, etc. It will cost me a lot of money for being not careful enough in making my decision. Some people are lazy and ignorant, "Ah... it's okay. It's only a few dollars," but with that kind of habit, it will all add up, trust me!

Shop around! It is worth our time and effort, trust me! It's the number one principle in deal hunting, always open our eyes and ears and also be proactive and do some research on the particular thing we seek and its price, especially for the big or continuous money involved.

Just do some research, call around or surf around (if we have internet access). Find out what the options are, what we get for what we pay. Call (or surf) a few more trustworthy (especially for online) places, then compare all of them, which gives us the most benefit with the least cost. It's basic economy 101: get the most benefit with the least cost.

Let's say we have a company or business to run, will any of us choose the get the least benefit with the most cost? That will surely bankrupt us in just a matter of time, right? So why don't we make it simple like that in any aspect of our lives? Keep it simple, it's not rocket science like most people think. There was one joke (and also a good lesson I learned) from my former choir conductor while he trained me when I was a 20 year old: he told me "KISS" and I'm like "What?", "Keep It Simple, Stupid! KISS" with a smile on his face hahaha... That's very true though, too many people are too scared (or lazy), thinking that those things (budgeting, saving, and deal hunting) are just way too complicated to do or even to think about! No! It's actually pretty simple. It might be a little bit hard at the beginning but that's just because it's new to us, not because it's very hard itself. It is supposed to be in everyone's arsenal of knowledge. Embrace ourselves and have the willingness to know and understand those simple basics and we can enjoy the benefits in our life for life.

IV. Giving (Percentage)

This is usually the hard part especially when we think we don't have enough for ourselves. Fortunately, though, despite that logic, our country, the United States of America where most citizens live paycheck to paycheck, really amazed me because it is one of the most compassionate and generous countries in the world. We are always compassionate about other people and other countries and are always generous in giving to others in need, locally, domestically and internationally. I am really proud to be part of this compassionate and generous country. Not everyone is like that, of course. Most of us are like that but some are just thinking about themselves all the time. But it's okay, I always believe that what goes around comes around, with interest! Hahaha!!

The only problem with our giving habit is that we may do it compulsively, spontaneously, if we are moved by what we see, hear and feel. Why is that a problem? First scenario: if we are not very good in managing our money, and we are a compulsive giver based on what we see, hear or feel following a trend after any particular disaster or need, then we really might not have enough for ourselves since we are careless. We are not using enough logic. We could say we use more heart than head, which is noble but sometimes stupid. Second scenario: let's say that we are good with managing our money. It shouldn't be a problem to spontaneously give based on what we see, hear or feel of any need, right? Right! But only for that moment! How about the rest of our lives? If we don't keep up with the updated news then we might not see, hear or catch that there are more needs which we can fulfill as our good deeds. There is always need somewhere at any given moment, we just have to be proactive in finding it. In this case we use more head than heart which sometimes could be a selfish lifestyle. We should use both, our head and heart.

In the movie "300", in the beginning scene, young Leonidas's mom gave him advice after his training session: to use his head first then his heart in a fight. In Donnie Yuen's version of the "Fist of Fury" series, the legendary kung fu master and hero, Huo Yuen Cia, also taught Zen Chen (another legendary Chinese hero) to train properly and plan his strategy before his fight against another great kung fu artist. He taught him to learn his opponent's strengths and weaknesses so he can prepare better, not just to prepare himself without knowing anything about the opponent. We need to use our head first then our heart. Nowadays mixed martial artists, in organizations like the UFC, Strikeforce, DREAM, and Bellator, all the champions and top contenders who prevail usually have a training camp which tailors their training and strategy differently depending on who they will face. They don't just say and believe that their fighter is great at everything, great in striking, takedown, submission, have awesome stamina, or a super fitness level so that that they don't need to worry tailoring their training and strategy when they prepare for a fight against different fighters. That's just heart and no head. They always need to know who they will fight, even though their fighter is a very good fighter. They still need to know how good the other fighter was in the last three fights, what the other fighter's strengths and weaknesses are, their tendencies, etc. We need to use our head first then our heart in preparing for any kind of fight or battle, especially war. If we use our heart first then our head in a fight, that means that we will fight our heart out and never quit a fight first, then adjust the proper strategy later…. We might be willing to die (in a battle) together with our opponent if it's necessary, but what if our opponent doesn't want to die with us and they prepare for us properly? Then we will most likely die (in a battlefield) or lose (in a fight) respectfully, but again, we will still die or lose! If we have the proper training and strategy first, then we have heart as big as a lion, we will prevail, brothers and sisters!

Even though it is supposed to be in that order (head then heart), we truly need both of them in our life just like in a mixed martial arts competition. Fighters who only use their heart with less head will draw fans, they never give up and they like to bang it out, but they might lose or get injured worse in the end. On the other hand, fighters who only use their head with less heart might always go for the win or be too safe which could be boring. They might just focus on scoring points but not take any risk for finishing the fight. They might give up relatively easily or go on the defensive when they know they can't win the fight, so they don't get further injuries.

The same thing applies to our financial life. If we only use our heart, we will draw other people's gratitude and compassion, since we are always genuinely compassionate concerning others and are generous in our actions, too. We give our time, energy and treasure for others' needs. It's all good but with if we don't use our head that means we don't manage our financials properly so when we keep helping others, we might end up hurting ourselves, just like in an MMA fight. So, we can't just use only our heart, we need to use our head, too.

On the other hand, if we only use our head without heart that means we only think about ourselves since we only want to be safe and get to our own goal without caring or being concerned about others at all. Never giving or helping others, just wanting to get the most for ourselves, that's called selfish. Just like an MMA fighter who only goes for the win but never takes a risk to finish the fight, or one who easily gives up to avoid a bigger possibility of getting injured (a possibility is different than a risk) and doesn't even try to give a fight and entertain the audience and supporters.

These are the three keywords for saving success: discipline, discipline, discipline! True discipline is rooted from real commitment. Once we understand and believe in something, we can start making a real commitment then become disciplined to do it so that it will be our habit which we can do as easily as breathing air. But first, we have to change our way of thinking before we can change our actions. Then we need to keep doing it repetitively so soon that'll be our lifestyle.

There is a wise saying, "Giving is better than receiving." Is that true? Actually it's very true, but why? The one who gives is usually the one who is either in a better position or has more compassion than others who don't give. Those who have more money can give to others who need more money, those who have more time can help others who need more time, those who have extra energy can give to others who need more energy, those who have more kindness and compassion in their heart can give to others who need more kindness and compassion, and the list could go on for almost every other aspect in our life. The giver is usually better off, in a better or stronger position, more peaceful, more relaxed, basically just in a better position than the receiver. It's really awkward if the one in a worse position is willing or capable of giving to another who is in a better position, except if the one who gives knows something we don't know or is simply dumb. :)

So the giver is usually the one in a better, stronger position. I believe that every normal person wants to be in that position. Only some weird or mentally impaired people have the really bad mentality of enjoying receiving all the time, meaning they enjoy being in a worse or weaker position all the time. Sounds weird, right? But some people think that it is to their advantage to always receive or be in the worse position, or even worse, sometimes they pretend to be in the worse position just to be able to receive stuff or services from others out of pity. That's totally heartless even though they might use their head but once again, definitely no heart. On the other hand, if we don't manage our financials wisely and always give just to look good or be compulsive (spontaneous) then we don't really use our head, just our heart (or worse, our ego). That will put us in a big heap of trouble. It's a financial mess waiting to happen. Always keep our life in balance, use our head and our heart.

The best way to give wisely to a noble cause or belief is

just by percentage. It doesn't matter how much we make, big or small, the percentage will follow in the right ratio, the more we make the more we give, the less we make the less we give. Yes, that simple. Just like in spending, the more we make the more we can spend, the less we make the less we can spend.. :)

Here is an example: Let's say we make $2,000/month and we commit to give 10% for our beliefs and/or as a good deed to others, then we will have to give $200/month. If we make $10,000/month, then we have to give $1,000/month. People will start saying," What??!! Giving or donating $1,000/month?? Are you crazy??!" Hey! Wait a minute! We make $10,000/month anyway! It's still the same percentage/ratio we committed to at the beginning, duh? The more we make, the more we can (and should) give to others and spend for ourselves, too. The less we make, the less we can (and should) spend for ourselves and give to others, too.

It's simple. What goes in must also go out for good circulation, just like anything in our life. All we eat must go out somehow in a proportional amount, if not, we will have health problems, right? All water ponds that have water flowed into them must have a way to circulate it in a proportional amount, if not, it'll overflow and stink. I'm sure that there are some people out there really believe that our body or pond can hold all the intake without giving any out (usually they're the selfish or unrealistic type), then their body or pond will surely stink from the gas or odor it might produce and it'll get really messy, too. :)

Remember, what goes in must go out proportionally. What we make we must give out or share proportionally to what we commit, which usually is 10%. The bigger the percentage, the better since it is noble to give as long as we can handle all other responsibilities and appropriate areas in our life.

b) Middle and Long Term

After we get comfortable with all the immediate term habits above and have no debts at all, then all of us should really think about doing the below; the earlier the better, between 12 months and unlimited years since everyone starts and enjoys the result at different points of time in their life.

I. Accommodation:

1) Shopping Around

We should always shop around for the best value in every aspect of our lives and make it a habit. It will make us more diligent and smarter, and that's good for our life. Some people might say, "I don't have time to shop around", "Nah, it's too much trouble", or "Only women do that." It's just their excuse for being too lazy to do it. Trust me, it's much easier to do it when it has become our habit and the first step is always the hardest one. But the amount of effort and time spent is very small compared to how we'll benefit from it, especially in the big or routine buys, like property, autos, insurance, etc.

Lower price items (cabbage, carrots, peppers, beans, juices, etc. except if we use them a lot or routinely) might not be as influential, but if we hear or find out about the best place to buy those items with the same quality but a lower price, why not use it? All the excuses above will only be fine if the ones who say them have a lot of money. In that case they don't have to worry about shopping around for the best value for their money since it won't impact their financial stability much at all. If we are not there yet, don't act like we are already there. That's a fantasy and denial, double suicide like I said earlier. We will only get hurt spiritually, emotionally and financially by doing so.

Shop around with an apple to apple system. The first way is to find the best/lowest price for the same quality of product/service. In this case, the apple is the quality of the product/service. The second way is to find the best product/service for the same price. In this case, the apple is the price. But always shop around for the things that we need or really want without hurting our budget!! If they offer the best products and services even with lower prices but we don't need them, never accept it! It's just a waste of money that only makes us feel good in the beginning but we rarely, if ever, use the benefit!! Some people say that they will use the product/service if they already have them, that's the same thing. Actually it might be even worse since they will spend the extra money and will make more time to use the benefit (that they didn't need originally) since they already paid for it!!

I can't emphasize enough that we only should only buy things we need or really want without hurting our budget. Never compare two different product/service's quality with two different prices, since logically the higher priced ones are supposed to be the better product/service, if not then they are totally a scam and they are "trash" for us as a consumer. So it's our own fault if we fall for it!

Always shop around before we buy something, especially for something expensive or routine expenses since they will add up, too.

In this subchapter, we have to shop around for the house, apartment, condo, duplex, mobile house, or whatever kind of place we plan to live in. Make sure you get your (not someone else's standard) best property at the best price and also make sure you can afford it with a maximum of 30% of your monthly income.

2) Renting vs. Owning

Renting is always the best way to start but then after we do our research and homework to make a bigger decision for our future, we have to start considering buying our own property. Why? Here below are all the major advantages of renting and owning a property.

The advantages of renting a property:

1. It usually has a cheaper monthly cost than buying

2. It usually gives us easier access to move in and out

3. It is more hassle free.

   If something goes wrong you just have to report it to the owner and usually they'll take care of it as long as it's reasonable

All the advantages above are really good reasons for people who:

- Don't have enough money for a down payment so the interest rate will be higher and have to pay a PMI fee to make up for it
- Are just starting to look for a place to live and are not sure how long they will stay in that particular area
- Don't want to or aren't used to handling all the hassle of being a property owner.

If the advantages above are not beneficial for us when we rent a property, then we might as well buy a property so we'll own it, because renting means we are just borrowing, right? Can you imagine that you have to pay a higher price to rent than to buy for the same thing? Or get stuck with a 10 year contract to rent something? Or have to do all the repairs by ourselves but we have to pay rent? Seriously, we might as well just buy it and own it ourselves if we have to deal with all that stuff anyway. If we have to deal with one of those things when we rent, make sure we get compensation of some kind from the property owner that benefits us, if not, then don't even bother! We should always look for an apple to apple comparison with the best value or price, whichever we need it the most.

The advantages of owning a property:

1. We own it! All the money we spent to pay the monthly payment is not wasted. It's just like paying car payments. Logically most people would prefer to pay monthly for their own vehicle than pay monthly for renting a vehicle. If we rent instead of own the same vehicle for the same amount of time, it will blatantly cost us much more money! Actually renting a car is way worse than renting a property since renting a property usually will cost us less monthly than buying it, while renting a car will cost us more monthly than buying it! But the main point is that we are supposed to prefer to pay for owning something than to pay for borrowing something for a long time and never owning it.

2. We can do any repair, renovation, or modification however we want and whenever we want it done as long as we are not violating any property ownership law or rule.

All the advantages above are great for people who want to settle down in one particular area and especially (which I strongly suggest) have a pretty decent nest egg (a lump of money) to put into their down payment.

If we are not sure whether we should settle in one particular area at least for a solid couple of years, we shouldn't plan to own any property since it is way too much hassle to deal with the property owning process. We have to shop around for the property itself, may be use realtor, deal with a bank or mortgage company, do all the paperwork. And after all that, before long we already want or have to move somewhere else and have no choice but to try to sell the property. And when the economy is down, it's really hard to sell except if we sell it for a cheaper price and lose some money or we have to delay our plan to move, in order to wait for a better economy so that we won't lose money on our property. The latter option only has a very slim chance, though. So, only buy a property when we're sure that we will settle in that particular area for at least a solid couple of years so it'll be worth all the hassle we have to go through. But again, do not be uncertain for too long! Some people are always unsure whether they will settle or not for 8–10 years, meanwhile their money keeps being wasted paying all the rent money for those 8-10 years and they still never own a piece of property!

Let's say we are pretty sure about settling in a particular area for a solid couple of years. We still need to save and have enough to put down for the down payment. What is enough? At least 20% down on the price we agree to buy, since if we put down less than 20% we will have to pay PMI (Private Mortgage Insurance) fee, an insurance to protect the lenders against losses should the borrowers default.

So it all comes back to our perspective and condition. If we are pretty sure that we'll settle down and have enough money for the proper down payment so that we don't have to pay PMI or other extra fees, then we are ready to buy a property. And don't forget to always shop around for the best value in an apple to apple comparison.

3) 15 vs. 30 Year Mortgage, Fixed Rate!

Most people don't have enough money to pay off their newly bought property right away except if they are already wealthy. Some people get another really big loan from somebody else just to pay off their newly bought property, something I strictly forbid! That's just like covering one hole by digging another hole! Believe it or not, I know some people who do just that! Not necessarily to pay off a property but more to pay off one credit card with another credit card or loan. I don't even understand how they think. Some people even think that they do the right thing by doing so! Again, it's just double trouble, the first trouble is because they did the wrong thing and the second trouble is because they are in denial. People like that are in deep doo-doo.

So if we still have a lot of debt of any kind and have a lot of savings or a high lifestyle at the same time, then there's something totally wrong with the picture! If we have a lot of savings, then why in the world don't we pay our debt(s)? It's just like I owed $600 to you who are a hardworking and simple yet content person. Then I bought the newest PlayStation Video Game console and dine out every weekend at a nice restaurant and brag all about that stuff in front of you and yet, I haven't paid my loan or debt to you. Won't you get upset or more likely, pissed off?? I would get super upset for sure, and I believe most people would, too.

Again, remember the previous Giving subchapter. The one who gets help is usually the one who's in the weaker or worse position, not better!! Even though the one who we receive the loan from lives a much higher lifestyle, that's normal since they are the one who are lending us money. We don't have any right to have fun before fulfilling our obligation! Just like with little kids, "If you want to get a treat, you better clean your room first."

That's the simplest principle we learn as a child and we want our child to learn that, too. How come adults don't understand that? Or actually, why are they trying to ignore that principle? Anyway, if you have extra or a lot of savings yet you still have debt, you have to go ahead and pay your debt first. Why? First, to avoid the interest, penalty or any other kind of fees (for our own sake), second, to make us a better person (for our own and others' sakes, too).

So, since most of us will likely get a loan for our mortgage, there are usually two basic options: a 15 year or 30 year mortgage. There are a few more options if you really want to know, but most likely there will be these two popular and logical options. There will also be some other options about the flexibility of the rate, in this case, always choose the fixed rate! That's the absolute best choice for everyone! Whoever the lender is, if they offer you a flexible rate, they will most likely offer you a pretty good rate or at least slightly better than other rate, but again, the word "flexible" really means flexible or varied. So after we got lured into getting it and signing the contract, they will most likely increase the rate sooner or later and we will end up paying a lot more than the initial deal which is usually also a lot more compared to the fixed rate overall. Trust me, the fixed rate is something certain that you can predict, the flexible rate is like a temporary little sweet temptation and usually the sweet part is only for a short period of time and the bitter part will be a lot longer. So, always go with the fixed rate!

Usually, we will have to pay more per month for our mortgage if we choose the 15 year contract and pay less per month if we choose the 30 year one. That's common sense, if they ever offer a lower monthly payment mortgage for our 15 year contract and a higher monthly payment for our 30 year contract, then who in the world would choose the 30 year contract? Every person in their right mind would love to pay less monthly and yet finish paying off their mortgage in half the time rather than paying more monthly and still have to pay for twice as long for the same property! So the shorter the mortgage contract, the higher our monthly payment will be! But how much higher? And the most important thing is what are we going to do with the difference? That is the most important matter! Remember that we are creatures of habit and tend to spoil ourselves too much if we're not careful and disciplined enough, and yup, that's including me, too. That's why I have been and am still trying my best to discipline myself so that someday we are able to do whatever we want and spoil ourselves as much as we want. :)

Usually, people think that by choosing the 30 year contract, they only have to pay a couple hundred dollars less a month! They think that they only can afford it that way or by doing that they can have an extra few hundred dollars each month. Wow!! That's great, right? No! By choosing the 30 year one instead of the 15 year one, they will have to pay 15 more years which means 180 (15 years x 12 months/year) more monthly payments!! And not just that, the interest rate is usually higher by 0.25% to 0.5%, for a 30 year contract, so they'll end up paying more interest and have to pay it 15 more years (180 more months!!) to own the very same property. To make the matter worse, usually they don't even save the difference or put it to good use, usually they use it for dining out, having fun, doing something they "deserve", or paying their "emergency" needs, etc. Trust me, we all would most likely use the difference for temporary luxuries, like food, movies, etc., since we tend to spoil ourselves too much. So let us not tempt ourselves. Just go ahead and pay that difference as our dues for our own great future in much bigger and longer lasting things, like property in this case. After we pay off our home mortgage, then we can have fun with much less stress since we don't have to pay that big mortgage payment every month. Now that's what I call real extra money. :) So, always get the 15 year contract at a fixed rate at all costs and make it happen (work more and/or spend less)!! Trust me, it's worth it!

I'll give you an example of our own real experience:

When we bought our home in 2005, the agreed price was $125,000. We put down $31,000, which means we owed $94,000. After we shopped around with various trustworthy and decent companies, we finally got the best rate we could get at that time, a 5% fixed rate. If we chose the 30 year contract, we would have paid about $703.57/month and had a total interest of $87,660.44 during the course of our 30 year contract. After proper calculation (now we can access tons of trustworthy mortgage calculator websites and tools), we chose the 15 year contract with the same fixed rate, so we paid about $942.30/month with a total interest of $39,802.28 during the 15 year contract!

Sure we paid about $238.73 more per month and that means we paid $42,971.40 ($238.73/month x 180 months of the 15 year time period) more for the first 15 years. But by then, we would have paid off our mortgage, meaning we owned our home 100% and had no more payments to make for the next 15 years. While on the 30 year contract, we would still pay $703.57 per month for the next 15 (30 -15 year contract) years and that would cost us $126,642.60 ($703.57/month x 180 months of the next 15 years we were still in contract)! So, actually we saved $83,671.20 by choosing the 15 year contract! That $83,671.20 that we saved (avoided paying) is 89% (from $89,671.20 divided by $94,000) of our $94,000 original loan amount!! And once again, we already own our property with no debt at all in half the time!! So by choosing the 15 year contract, we saved serious amount of money ($83,671.20) and a huge amount of time (15 years) to own 100% of the very same property we call home. After that, we can use all that money and time we saved for doing tons of other things, good and fun things since we already finished our obligation. :)

How do we find a trustworthy and decent mortgage company or bank? It's just like finding any other trustworthy company, the trustworthy one will usually welcome you with warmth and humility and is usually willing to passionately make us understand how it works, what options we have and the benefits and loss of each option. If they are arrogant and not willing to make us understand, they usually throw this kind of line: "Don't worry, man. We'll take care of you." "Just sit back and relax, you're in good hands." "Don't worry, we'll handle the hard parts, you just sit back and see the nice result." "Don't worry, man. We'll fix you up." or any line that has the same color and meaning. We don't have to ask them to explain to us. Just see if they will do it on their own to make us understand what's going on, how it works, and what options we have. If they don't do that, they are either hiding something, too lazy to explain to us, or they just don't really know what they're doing. None of those are good for us! So, always see whether they are passionately trying to make us understand or not. See if they are humble or just talking big. See if they only suggest the options that will give them the most benefit (money) with the least work. If they are humble and try their best to make us understand and let us decide for ourselves, they're great. If not, they're bad! It's very simple logic but most people forget this most of the time. Even I forgot this concept, too, in the past and I really had to pay for my mistakes! I hope none of us will have to go through those bad experiences in the future.

How can we afford the difference? Actually the real question for all of us is how much we will sacrifice our (mostly) luxury lifestyle temporarily for much better benefits in the big picture and long run! If we really want to gain the benefits in the big-picture and long run badly enough, we will make a way to afford the difference. We could cut our living costs; especially the luxury ones, or we could gain more income! We could choose from a lot of options available for all of us. For examples of our monthly costs: cut or have simpler cable or satellite television service (could be from $99 to $0 if we use antenna, depends on how fancy the service we have now and where we live), use simpler cell phone service (from $99 to $6.69), simple internet service (from $55 to $33), eat out less frequently (from once a week to once in three weeks, that'll save us 66.66% of our dining out cost right away!!) and in less expensive places (this really depends on how badly we spoil ourselves, from $60 or more to about $7/person meal), buying less expensive clothing (this is the same as our dining out taste) in less frequency, be an energy saver which we all should do anyway (turn off anything you don't really use as long as it won't ruin anything), bring our own lunch instead of going to the cafeteria or food court every day, drink tap water (which might be healthier anyway ☺) instead of buying soda pop or something else from a vending machine (this could save unbelievably a lot, from $182 to $52) and there are a lot more ways to live frugally.

The other option to help us afford the difference is by working harder and smarter, getting a second job, increasing our productivity and enthusiasm, etc. If we can, the best option is working extra and living more frugally (increase the income and decrease the spending). :)

For my family, since we already committed ourselves to the right way of thinking about managing/handling our finances, that commitment gives ourselves the discipline to sacrifice all non-basic needs temporarily to gain much bigger and longer lasting real benefits for us. So, we haven't had any of those secondary and tertiary things mentioned above since we came to this great American soil in May 2002, anyway. That way of thinking has already become our habit since then. So in February 2005 (less than three years), that frugal habit (not stingy! They're two different things) has already turned into our lifestyle. We just stay simple and enjoy every little beautiful thing around us without having to spend a whole bunch of money to do so, unlike what some people might say or believe.

Again, there's a wise saying that money can't buy true happiness, and it's very true! Money can buy a house but not a home, money can buy a bed but not a good night's sleep, money can buy companion but not love, money can gain a lot of things but not everything is about money. It takes humility and wisdom to be able to enjoy a simple life. How so? Only people with a humble heart are willing to live simply and under the radar. Only people with wisdom can see beyond what our eyes can see. Don't we all respect a person who is wise and humble? Don't we all love to be around people who are humble and wise? People who are always talking about themselves or showing off what they have are usually self-centered. I don't think any of us like to be around that kind of person. And if we don't want like to be around them, then don't be around them, and most importantly, don't be one of them! So it truly takes a humble heart and true wisdom to be willing and able to live simply and enjoy every beautiful little thing without having to spend a whole lot of money. Money can't buy true happiness. So why is the wisdom pearl forgotten nowadays?? Go figure: bad examples, trends, intimidating marketing, greed, lack of self-assessment and self-control, ignorance, etc.

Anyway, back to our real life case. We got the difference covered by working better and more. But mostly, we covered the difference by being more aware of what we spend. And yes, we chose to be alert in all the areas above and we saved even more than we needed. Once again, that's called frugal not stingy! Stingy is when we spoil ourselves and never want to spend money for others, for example: always dining out at fancy restaurants but always tipping below 10% or sometimes just a few cents!! Always buying the newest gadgets and equipment for our own indulgence but never really giving to any noble or good cause, etc. Frugal is when we are watching our spending for ourselves but always respecting and being generous to others who are due too. And that is fine especially when it is a temporary must so that we all can achieve much bigger and longer lasting benefits.

How about the tax deduction? It's way over rated, especially by people who don't really understand how it works. Let's say we are in the 28% tax bracket (most of us are in that or a lower tax bracket), the government will give us a 28 cent deduction for every dollar we pay toward our interest. So do you prefer paying the bank $1 interest and get a 28 cent deduction back from the government, meaning that 72 cents total is out of our pocket for every dollar we spend toward interest? Or just pass the 28 cent tax deduction potential but also not have to pay $1 toward our interest, so we're saving the 72 cents. The simple way to say it is whether we want to save 72 cents right away for every dollar we put toward our interest for 15 years or not! In our family's personal case, we preferred to save $47,858.16 ($87,660.44 interest of the 30 year contract subtracted by $39,802.28 interest of the 15 year contract) right away compared to getting a $13,400.28 ($0.28 for every dollar we pay our interest) tax deduction back from the government but having to pay $47,858.16 for the interest itself if we chose to pay the extra 15 years for our 30 year contract!!

I believe everyone in their right mind would prefer to not pay (save) $47,858.16 right away compared to paying $34,457.88 ($47,858.16 extra interest we would pay for choosing the 30 year contract deducted with a $13,400.28 government tax deduction). Tax deduction will only benefit us if we really can't afford the 15 year contract's monthly premium at all costs. If it is in our power and we don't choose the 30 year contract, for my family's case, we wouldn't be able to save $83,671.20 in the first 15 years in total payments difference between the 15 and 30 year contract (refer to the real number above) and at the same time, we would have to pay $34,457.88 more interest for the rest of the 15 years! That's 36.66% of our original mortgage amount just for the extra interest if we chose the 30 year contract ($34,457.88 extra interest already deducted with government tax deduction / $94,000 original mortgage amount)!! The real savings we got for choosing the 15 year contract was $83,671.20. That amount of money will grow amazingly well if we put it in the proper investment for the same 15 years extra period of time!

So, always choose the 15 year contract, not the 30 year! Some of us might ask, "What if we can't make up the difference even though we've tried our best to increase our income and cut our spending?" Honestly, it means that you live way beyond your means. We need to earn everything we want, remember? If you can't afford it that means either your demands are too high (too expensive of a house to buy with your financial condition, too luxurious of a lifestyle to live, too high in speculating our uncertain income, etc.) or you are too weak to gain what you want (not enough willingness and/or power to work extra, not strong enough to control ourselves not to wanting stuffs beyond our capabilities, etc.) or the worst, both!

So work harder (or at least more) and/or spend less to make up for the monthly payment difference between the 30 and 15 year mortgage! Always get the 15 year and make it happen, you'll find it most beneficial for you, trust me!

IV) No Pain No Gain: Hard Work and Sacrifice Now for Later Success or Superiority (Biggest Reasonable Down Payment and Frequent Extra Payment)

We all have heard wise sayings such as "There's no gain without pain" "There's no peace without a war" "There's no freedom without fight" or such through books, movies, mottos, etc. Basically, the main message is that we all have to work hard and sacrifice before we can gain any success and great achievement. We have to do something that we don't naturally like to do first, and then we can do something that we naturally like to do. If we don't want to experience the pain then there will be no gain. If we don't want to work hard then we won't have enough money for how we want it to be, if we don't do any workouts then we won't have a fit body like we want it, if we are lazy to study for a test then we won't be able to pass the test. We need to show great effort and make some sacrifices to achieve greatness. Well, actually to achieve anything we should do something, even in the simplest example like when we feed a baby, the baby has to at least open their mouth. :) Here is another important fact: hard work usually pays off later and in the long run while laziness usually pays off that particular time and for a much shorter run. It applies to everything in our life, our study, our work, our family, our health, and of course, our mortgage, too.

When buying a property, I suggest you put down at least 20% down payment on your mortgage to avoid the unnecessary PMI (Private Mortgage Insurance). Actually, we don't have to stop there if we want to keep the benefits going our way. Basically, the bigger the down payment we put for our mortgage, the smaller our interest rate will be since it shows our good intent to have the least amount of debt as possible.

Just think as a lender, if someone wants to borrow a very large sum of money, there will be more risk for us to cover should the borrower fail to pay us back later on, right?

That's why as a lender, we will surely increase the interest rate so that we can get more rewards for taking that risk. If the same someone wants to borrow less money from us, the risk will also be less for us to cover should they fail to pay us back later on. So, usually we would lower our interest rate, wouldn't we? And remember, a little difference in our interest rate will go a long way for the 15 year period which is equal to 180 months of payment! In our personal case above, let's say we got a 5.25% interest rate instead of 5%, so we had to pay 0.25% more for all our mortgage payments. We would have to pay $2,214 more! That is 5.56% ($2,214 more in interest, divided by $39,802.28 original total interest) more interest than our total interest we had to pay during the 15 year period with a 5% interest rate! Do you see how it works now? Even though on the APR we only see 0.25% difference, after 15 years (180 months), the real number we pay would be 5.56% extra money!! And don't forget that it's only in my personal case. Everybody will have different scenarios depending on how much they are willing to spend for their mortgage and how much interest rate they get. The more expensive house we want to buy, the more amount of money we have to pay since it's a percentage. And even though it seems like only a slightly higher interest rate (0.25%), it will make about 5.56% difference in 15 years! Let alone 30 years! It will be multiplied so much worse that you don't even want me to show the calculation here!

So, we have to always aim for putting down our down payment as big as possible as long as it won't hurt us. Why? Because the bigger the down payment we pay, the bigger the chance we'll get a smaller interest rate, even 0.25 % difference will make 5.56% difference in the total amount of 15 years. The bigger the rate difference the better, but remember not to get tempted and put down way too much down payment while you can't meet your end need. Always have some emergency fund (for real emergencies! Not an "emergency" like I talked about in the beginning of the book). Do not hurt yourself just to chase a better interest rate, but if you can get a better interest rate without hurting your other obligations and responsibilities, why not? Just do your best!

What if the lender won't give us any interest rate discount even when we put down more money? Still do it! Why? Because that will make our debt less and we can pay them off faster, right? Remember? Why wait to pay if we do have the money? That's a bad habit! Just a disaster waiting to happen! A disaster to our finances if we have to pay any interest, fine or penalty in any kind and it could be worse, it could be a disaster to our morality, too! If we still think that not paying our debt to others while we already have the money is cool, that is wrong! Always pay as soon as possible and as much as possible if we are ever in any kind of debt!

So always put the biggest possible down payment on our mortgage or any kind of other huge loan! That's the first important hard work and sacrifice we need to do to achieve greater and long run benefits, in this case, paying our biggest (or at least one) loan faster since we put down more, we will have less debt.

The second important thing is that we should try hard to put down extra payments on a regular basis for our principal only. At this point in time, I believe you all already know why. Alright, for those who haven't paid attention (just kidding), this is why we should want to put down more money on a regular basis for our principal only: It is really good to pay off our mortgage as soon as possible and save a fortune of money from the interest for our own investment or benefit. Again, I'll use our real life case as an example:

We bought our home in February 2005 and paid it off in September 2008. Our first original (without any extra money we paid) mortgage monthly payment was $942.30 but $198.95 was actually for the escrow payment. Escrow payment is a great feature they offer so we don't have to worry every year about paying our property tax at the end of the year and paying our property insurance (house hazard insurance) at the beginning of our mortgage loan anniversary. They just add the total amount of our property tax and property insurance for the year and then they divide the total by 12 months. So our monthly mortgage payment already includes the property tax and insurance. By doing so, the first benefit is that we don't have to worry about forgetting to pay two more important and more obligations in our life, and the second benefit is that we don't have to worry about saving for those two big lump sums of money for their anniversary.

So, after our original mortgage payment, the $942.30 was used for our property tax and insurance ($198.95), it left us with $743.35. This amount would go to our real mortgage payment. The first month's monthly payment was broken down like this: $391.67 for interest and $351.68 for our principal, so it was (and still apply to all kinds of payment until now!) 52.69% of our payment went to interest and only 47.31% went to our principal! Our monthly payment breakdown (composition) will slightly change as we go along our way to the end of our 15 year loan period. And yes, we always talk about 15 year, ladies and gentlemen, don't even think about a 30 year mortgage, that's an absolute sugar coated destructive option! If we can't make extra money or spend less money to make up the payment difference between 15 and 30 year mortgage, then we're not ready to buy that particular house yet! Seriously! It's that simple!

So in the beginning, our monthly payments will be used more to pay our interest than to pay our principal. Then every single payment after that, the portion of our monthly payment that is used to pay our interest will slowly get smaller while the portion used to pay our principal will slowly get bigger. In the last few months of our original 15 year period, we will see that most of our monthly payment will be used mostly toward our loan principal and only a little portion will be used toward our interest. Again, this is how it works so that the lender gets some benefits for taking the risk should the borrower fail to make a payment. So the more we put down as extra payment only to our principal on top of our monthly payment, the more money and time we save while we enjoy our home sweet home.

Since we came to the US in May 2002, we both have always worked hard and saved hard, too. We had some fun too, but not as "fun" and as frequently as others, of course. :) And the good thing is we could enjoy our life while doing so. We had fun and were content without necessarily spending too much money. We still spent money, of course, but not a whole lot. What a content frugal couple we were (and still are ☺). Remember, money can buy a lot of things and even happiness (external factors: surroundings, materials, belongings, "fake" friends, etc.) but not joy (internal factors: a good heart, a noble and pure mind, peace, contentment, an uplifted spirit, pleasant and peaceful thoughts, etc.). So we were able to save up a lot of money. We saved about 50% of our income after about 10% for God, about 4% good donation or help families or friends, about 30% living cost, about 6% fun, what a nerd I am, huh? :)

Actually, it is all true, though. With both of us working multiple jobs, our combined net income (after tax) was about $38,000/year in those early years we just arrived in the US (2002 – 2005). So we saved about $19,000/year. So from May 2002 (actually early June was when we started to be productive) until February 2005, we saved about $52,000. In that point of time, we had sent about $7,000 to my wife's parents back home in Indonesia (my father is a dentist, so my parents understood that we mainly supported my wife's parents since my parents were better off at that time), that left us with $45,000 savings still. :) We put $13,000 of it toward a great rate-of-return mutual fund which I will explain later.

So, when we bought our $125,000.00 house, we decided to put down $31,000 for the down payment, so we owed only $94,000.00. If we always paid our mortgage's monthly payment for 15 years without missing or adding any payment, we would have to pay $94,000 plus the $39,802.28 interest for the whole 15 years. With our proper way of thinking and lifestyle at that time, we tried to liquidate (cash) our great return mutual fund so we could put some down toward our principal only. Why principal only? Because you want your money to pay what really matters which is the principal, not the interest!

So soon enough, in about a month, we put down our $13,000.00 investment money toward only our principal which cut our loan down to $81,000. By doing so, it saved us a lot of time, about 3 years or 36.6 months (from $13,000 extra payment / $355 monthly principal allocation) shorter time than the original 15 year plan and saved us a whole lot of money, $14,200.00 (from 36.6 month x $388 monthly interest) from our mortgage interest!! It also helped us with the break down for our $743.35 monthly payment, it changed to the better, $407.32 (54.79%) toward our loan principal (which used to be only 47.31% in the beginning!) and $336.03 (45.21%) toward our interest (used to be 52.69% in the beginning!). And here is our true history of the extra payments we put down, the balance left and how the monthly payments' breakdown changed along the way:

06/10/05: $3,000.00 ($76,831.99 balance left, $409.01 principal, $334.34 interest)

07/26/05: $2,000.00 ($74,408.77 balance left, $423.22 principal, $320.13 interest)

09/06/05: $1,985.24 ($71,555.10 balance left, $433.31 principal, $310.04 interest)

09/20/05: $1,890.97 ($69,664.13 balance left, $435.12 principal, $308.23 interest)

10/18/05: $2,194.46 ($67,016.59 balance left, $453.08 principal, $280.27 interest)

12/13/05: $3,279.00 ($62,807.43 balance left, $466.05 principal, $277.30 interest)

03/03/06: $5,000.00 ($56,356.45 balance left, $485.67 principal, $257.58 interest)

07/10/06: $3,500.42 ($50,809.16 balance left, $514.91 principal, $228.44 interest)

01/18/07: $4,750.00 ($42,835.88 balance left, $542.81 principal, $200.54 interest)

04/17/07: $7,600.00 ($33,534.21 balance left, $569.58 principal, $173.77 interest)

07/27/07: $6,000.00 ($25,715.79 balance left, $608.66 principal, $134.69 interest)

09/11/07: $6,000.00 ($18,440.74 balance left, $638.85 principal, $104.50 interest)

12/11/07: $1,036.16 ($15,396.70 balance left, $672.08 principal, $71.27 interest)

04/30/08: $3,607.00 ($9,055.88 balance left, $687.72 principal, $55.63 interest)

09/16/08: $6,258.02 (PAID OFF)

And yes, I checked our own record, it's not a made up number. You can check it, too, in any amortization table. For the same scenario as mine, just put in all my numbers and you should get the same detailed payment breakdown from month to month. :)

The total interest we paid during those 3.5 years of hard work and hard paying is $7,776.14. That's much better than the original interest which was $39,802.28!! A saving of $32,026.14 in 3.5 years!! Not bad at all, right? It was actually super awesome since we earned that $32,026.14 saving on top of the $83,671.20 we already saved for choosing the 15 over the 30 year contract! That's a total saving of $115,697.34 during that 3.5 year period of time!! We actually put $58,101.27 extra toward our principal only during that very same 3.5 years! And also, as a bonus joy, we received a $1,473.99 check from our lender after everything settled down. It was for our overpayment since the lender usually calculated it a little higher for us just in case we bailed on them. But of course, it never happened since we really wanted to knock the mortgage payments off ASAP because we always try to avoid any unnecessary interest, fees or penalties of any kind.

Remember: always pay your debt as soon as possible if you have the money. That's the most important lesson to be a decent human being and to be decent financially, too. I called it financially fit, not just financially fat! :) If we live a fancy lifestyle but we have a lot of debt, that's just financially fat but not really fit (having a lot of health problems behind the grand surface). We want to be fit, not fat! The same with our finances, too, we want to be debt free, not only look fancy!

The beauty of it is in that 3.5 year time period (Feb. '05 – Sep. '08) we were as average as everybody else. I worked as a server at a Japanese restaurant and taught martial arts while my wife worked as visual staff at a retailer in the mall. Our combined net annual income had been averaging about $38,000 up to 2005 (the year we bought our house), and kept climbing until finally hitting its peak in 2008, soaring to about $46,500/year. But before long, the economic crisis which started in late 2007, started to plant its gritty sharp teeth into our state, Oklahoma, too. My income has dropped about 15.4% and has stayed steady at that rate ever since. Fortunately, my wife's income was increasing pretty decently, especially with her great work ethic and solid effort working at multiple workplaces. So altogether from 2002 to 2008, our annual income was averaging about $42,600 ($21,300 average/person). That's like a person who works 40 hours a week, 52 paid weeks in a year and earning $10.24 hourly wage. What if our hourly wage is lower than $10.24? Just work more (a second job or overtime)! And it'll be even better if you increase your skills or talents that could be appreciated by others (trust me, everyone has their own!) and you can earn more because of it! Just in case, the worst scenario (which I highly doubt), you still can't make that $10.24 hourly wage by working more or better up your skills or talent, then you better cut down your secondary and tertiary things in your life. We did all three: work more, better up our skills and mainly just live simple and enjoy every beautiful little thing that God created around us without the need of expensive tools or equipment. Happier, healthier and wealthier, yayyy!!

If with that income level we could do it, everyone can do it, too! Just by living frugally and more efficiently for a couple years, we can save a fortune of money and also we can pay off our home mortgage in an incredibly fast time. Just remember our case, paying off our mortgage in 3.5 years and saving $115,697.34 plus getting an extra check for $1,473.99!! On top of that, as icing on the cake, after those 3.5 years of living a simple and disciplined lifestyle, our way of thinking and discipline stayed like it was in those years. So, even though we can (and do ☺) enjoy our life more with a bigger percentage in our "good and nice to have/do" area, we still have the proper mind set of being responsible with our money.

We can enjoy all that by putting about 65.51% of our net annual income toward our home mortgage in those 3.5 years! Here is the calculation: in those 3.5 years, with a $42,600 net average annual income, we put money averaging at $27,907.96 [from ($58,101.27 extra payment / 3.5 years) + (12 months x $942.30 monthly mortgage payment)] toward our home mortgage annually!! And that is 65.51% of our after tax annual income!!

Some of you might think that we broke our own rule of thumb in this book about not putting more than 30% of our monthly income towards our monthly mortgage payment. But again, we were maybe one of the very few who are so passionate to pay off their home mortgage and as I explained above, the result was truly worth the sacrifice. And the most important thing is that we have enjoyed our lives to the fullest while doing so. For most people, I believe the 30% limit is the way to go since there will be less risk of them having a hard time paying their mortgage. But actually, we didn't break our own rule of thumb since our mortgage monthly payment was $942.30 and our net monthly income was $3,550 ($42,600 average net annual income since 2002 – 2008 divided by 12 months). Our real monthly mortgage payment is actually only 26.54% of our monthly income, it's not more than 30%. We just made an extra payment whenever we really had the extra money after all the obligations and basic needs were fulfilled and we still had our emergency fund at ease, which is $5,000 in our case. The rest we put down toward our principal as soon as possible since the earlier we put the extra money in, the more interest and time we will save. So our obligation to pay our monthly mortgage is actually on the 26.54% but through our own willingness (totally depending on our own abilities and time), we put an extra 38.97% of our income toward our principal only! We would have broken that rule of thumb if we set up an automatic withdrawal for our extra payment toward our principal only (never put your extra money toward the monthly payment, let alone interest only!). Yes, they offer such great feature but be careful, I really don't recommend it at all since it will require you to pay more than 30% as your monthly obligation, then it will get you stranded every month.

After 65.51% went to our mortgage intensive plan, we only had 34.49% left for our living cost and hobbies. That 34.49% is $1,224.33/month ($14,692.04/year). Basically, we just work hard and smart, and then live frugally! We just lived as we needed to, not like we wanted to.

Here are some examples of what we did and didn't do, and we still apply some of them now:

- When we didn't have any children yet until May 2006. We always worked hard and smart by working at one main job from which we can earn the most income with our skill set and our second job usually was very beneficial toward our own living cost. For health reasons, restaurants will throw out their unused food by the end of the night. We asked the supervisor if it was okay for us to take it home, and most of the time it was okay. We refrigerated it then re warmed or re cooked them for the next day. Some might say," Eww... That's very unhealthy and nasty." The most important thing is that I can guarantee you will never see those characteristics in us when you meet us in person. We're healthier and cleaner than most people, at least we are average. It's not what goes into our mouth that defines us but what comes out from our mouth. Also, it's better doing that by our own will, early in our lives so that we can eat what we please later in life than doing that because we have no choice later in life (like the main story of Les Miserables, it's not who we were that matters but who we are now and what we choose to do in the future ☺).

- When we had children, my wife's second job was (and still is) a teacher at a child development center (child care) where our children go. It's great to work (earn money) and be close to our children and at the same time, we save money with the employee discount for our child care costs. In addition, it's great to be knowledgeable parents, too.

- We never had any cable/satellite service for our TV since we didn't really have time to watch TV anyway. If we really wanted to watch a particular show or sport, we just went to that TV station's website and searched for the particular program. It wouldn't be as good quality and might not be as complete and updated as the real TV showing, but that isn't our priority in life anyway. Even if it was, I personally don't think we could ever watch all the shows or sports on all those channels they offer. So, if we cramp them into what we really watch, it would only be a total of five channels or fewer maybe. Is it worth the cost to get cable or satellite? As long as we follow our proper budgeting, it's fine. But don't watch just because you already paid for it!

- We just used the simplest high speed internet service as long as we could download or stream some basic stuff at a decent time. Just in case the download time is kind of long, just do something else (either for productivity or fun ☺) while you are waiting for the download.

- We didn't use a regular phone company, we used a computer phone as our home phone. Most computer phones have better features for less money. The quality is fine for me, especially for the price, but again, everyone is entitled for their own opinion.

- We used pre-paid cell phones so that we paid only for what we used. Having a smart phone will make us want to use it more since we have all those awesome features. If we don't use any of those features, then why pay for it? The less we talk with our cell phones, the less we use data (mostly for games, texting and browsing), the more likely we only need pre-paid cell phones and vice versa.

- We ate out only about once in two weeks and mostly ate at middle class restaurants or buffets, not the highest class or fanciest restaurants, except for really special occasions (I mean really special, if you make everything really special just to give yourself an excuse to eat out, then nothing is really special in your life, it's just self-spoiling lifestyle). Again, it's not what goes into our mouth that really matters, but what comes out from our mouth.

- We didn't drink alcoholic beverages. We might drink once in every 6 months and that's like one serving. We saved our money, health and lifestyle (money for sure, health and lifestyle, again, it works for us but everybody is entitled for their own opinion).

- We didn't smoke. This I'm sure saved our money, health and lifestyle. ☺

- We prepared our lunch boxes ourselves for our break time at work. Preparing means cook, assemble or just go from a bigger value size to our smaller lunch box size. We might buy our lunch once every three weeks. When we worked in the food business, we usually got a free lunch from them. Even though sometimes we might get tired of, or not like what they have to offer for our lunch, we were just grateful that we still had food to eat. Just remember the "Survivor" reality shows from CBS TV station or other people who have a hard time getting food. We can do it! It's just mind over matter. :)

- We didn't have HDTV, let alone the newest technology or biggest screen with the highest resolution. We only had a regular TV box with an antenna and a decoder box since all TV stations changed their signal digitally in 2008. We didn't watch much TV anyway. We have a lot of obligations and higher priorities: church, Bible Study, choir, family, work, martial arts and workout, reading and studying about the proper way of life, about parenting, about finances, about martial arts and health etc.

- We only bought used cars as long as we can test drive and bring them to our mechanic that we really trust. Up to 2008 (the year we paid off our mortgage and had no debt at all), we bought an 11 year old 1991 Honda Civic with 187,000 miles on it in 2002, a 10 year old 1992 Toyota Corolla with 95,000 miles on it in 2002, and an 8 year old 1998 Honda Accord with 124,000 miles on it in 2006.

- Our family rarely watched movies, maybe once every two months. And when we watched movies, we came mostly at matinee hours and saw the regular 2D format. If we wanted to experience IMAX, just go sit in the front row! Hahaha!! :) Just kidding, I tried IMAX and it's really different, not just bigger but better picture and sound quality, too. :) Still we only watch great action or adventure movies at IMAX once in a while but definitely not dramas, comedies or musicals.

- We watched DVDs more since we rarely went out for movies. Fortunately by doing so, we got used to waiting to watch some movies. So it's easier for us to wait a little bit more until the movies came out at the $1 something movie rental. :)

- We had our vacations every two years and they always followed our budget without hurting any other aspect in our life (California in 2004, Las Vegas in 2006, California in 2008, Florida in 2010, and California in 2012, yes, we have a lot of family in California ☺).

- We always did our research and shopped around before any decision we made involving a lot of money (anything more than $100 for us) in the likes of roof company, heat and air company, termite and bug company, sprinkler system complete installation, handyman, hospital, doctor or dentist, computers, vacations, newer used cars, etc.

- We always do our research and shop around before any decision we make involving paying on a regular basis in the likes of home insurance, auto insurance, health, dental, and vision insurance, phone, internet, any kind of membership, auto mechanic, etc. In addition, about every two years, we usually do more research and shop around just to make sure we still have the best choice. If yes, that's great! If not, it's time to change companies. It's just like a baby's diaper, we should check it periodically. If we wait too long to check it, we might be too late and the mess will be worse and stink more. If we check properly in a timely manner, we will find either it's still good and clean or it's a light mess with less stink to handle. :)

There's only one thing that involved a decent amount of money and on a regular basis that we didn't shop around for. We only did our research and shopped around twice for this since we came to the U.S. It is our tithe to church, that's a must for us (if you don't go to church then please give to a worthy or noble cause). We just simply checked our previous year's after-tax income then 10% of that divided by 52 weeks. That's the amount we need to tithe to our home church, other good deeds above that (to parents, people in need, military support, breast cancer association, etc.) is up to us.

- We didn't buy things from vending machines. If you really want something from vending machines, then you better prepare it yourselves when you get home that day. Go to your neighborhood grocery store, buy the things you really wanted from the vending machine earlier in value packs, and then prepare it as you need/want it for the next day from the value packs. We save a lot of money by doing so especially if we consistently do that. In a year, you won't believe how much money you'll save with that habit.

- We didn't drive our car like racer/movie star wannabes by accelerating and stopping quickly, or turning sharply/quickly until our tires screech, etc. All that will totally ruin the gas efficiency and also wear out the engine, brakes, and tires, way faster than it should. That will already cost us more money for sure. On top of that, our collision/accident and traffic violation risk will be higher if we keep driving like that. If we ever get one, the ticket will be decent and our insurance's premium will go up, too. All that will cost us a lot of money and respect from other drivers, too.

- We don't play games like PS 3, XBOX 360, Wii, computer, etc. We bought a PS 3 game console complete with the PS Eye and PS Move Controller in 2011 (at that time, we already paid off our mortgage, were debt free, and had started saving for our retirement and children's future) for our first son's birthday and also for the ultimate reward for our family since we hadn't played let alone had any game consoles since year 2000. It is such an amazing entertainment equipment! We all had tons of fun! Unfortunately, it is so much fun that it is addictive. And anything addictive will make us get hooked and always want to do it too much. As I said in an earlier chapter, too much of anything is not good, even studying or working out, let alone playing games! Despite the addiction, it's really not good for our social skills and health, either. The more we play with the screen games, the less we play with others with the real things in real life. I personally don't prefer that. On top of all that, those games also cost us a lot of money, too! So basically, being addicted to playing games will cost us our money, time, and maybe social skills and health, too. I'm not against it, just do it in good balance.

The list can go on but those are the things that most people have or do but we choose not to have/do. By doing all of the above, we actually can appreciate our life and surroundings more. We also appreciate the awesome technology even more even though we don't really have/use them. The more we see and use them, the less we appreciate them while at the same time, it costs us more. I am always in awe seeing others' cool and high tech stuff but I don't really need them anyway, at least for now. :)

The good thing is that we will be happier when we can appreciate more every little thing in our life and surroundings. And when we can appreciate the little things, we surely will appreciate the bigger things (upgrade). If we get used to all the big things, I guarantee we won't be able to appreciate the smaller things when the big things are gone (downgrade), at least we will have a harder time doing so. So by living simple, we are more appreciative and that will make us happier and save money at the same time. That's what I call "killing two birds with one stone" Woohoo!!

So don't forget "no pain no gain!" Always work hard and sacrifice first for longer lasting success later on! In the case of having a big loan or home mortgage, always choose the 15 year plan, put as big a down payment as possible, then always put extra money to your principal only. I really do wish that our personal story will inspire all of you who read it. And yes, you all can do it, too!! Just have enough will to do it and then do it! Trust me, the bigger the will, the more likely anyone will be successful in gaining anything! Just like the DC Comic's Green Lantern story, the power of will (green) not fear (yellow), right? If we really focus all our might and energy on our will, we can do anything we want. That's what the Green Lantern Corps motto is and it'll be awesome if we can adopt that very same motto. But again in the Green Lantern story, the ring will choose the individual who deserves the Green Lantern ring, so if we have a strong will to scam someone or steal money, then we don't really deserve to get the power of will, do we? Yes, if we have an evil will then the power of our will won't work! Well, at least that's how it works in the Green Lantern graphic novel universe. :) Anyway, in real life, I always believe that whatever goes around, comes around, with interest!! So if we use our will for evil or bad things, someday, somewhere, somehow, it will come back to us in worse ways. Fortunately, that also applies when we use our will for good and noble things. Remember "What goes around comes around, with interest!" :)

II. Mutual Fund

MoneyCrashers.com defined mutual funds as investment vehicles that pool money from many different investors to increase their buying power and diversify their holdings. (This allows investors to add a substantial number of securities to their portfolio for a much lower price than purchasing each security individually).

A mutual fund is usually managed by a professional investment manager who trades (buys and sells) all kinds of assets and securities for the most effective growth of the fund. Therefore, we don't have to worry about learning, analyzing, deciding, and diversifying our investments ourselves. But that doesn't mean that we can just buy some mutual funds and then be completely ignorant about them! I strongly suggest not doing that!

When we already do the right thing that doesn't mean that we don't have to do anything at all after that, right? Remember the baby diaper analogy above? Never be lazy or ignorant like that! We also shouldn't obsessively check the market and our portfolio's growth every hour. We just have to check it out every few months, at least once a year, we have to see how our mutual funds grow and how well our portfolio (sheet plan) matches our goal.

As mutual funds investors, we are the shareholder of the mutual fund company. We will earn dividends when the company makes profits and we will lose our share value when the company suffers losses. We also can get our share value higher (return) when the company is doing well. The great thing is that all and every one of our gains (dividend and return) will be reinvested toward our mutual fund principal again to grow compounded.

The first important meaning of the word "mutual" here is that it we, as investors, will have much more buying power since there are a lot investors gathering the money together to buy a large scale price. It's just like an old Chinese wisdom saying "It's easy to break one single chopstick, but it's way harder to break the whole bundle of chopsticks" or the wisdom saying "United we stand, divided we fall". We will have a lot more buying power as a "mutual" funder (investor) than as an individual funder (investor). So basically, we share the burden together as "mutual" investors. Unfortunately, by doing so, we also have to share the gain, too. But don't worry; this is where the second meaning of the word "mutual" comes in handy. :)

The second important meaning of the word "mutual" here is that our investments are built of a lot of different investments which tend to lower our risk (avoiding the old "all of your eggs in one basket" problem). So the risk of our mutual funds (investments) falling all together is very small compared to that of individual investments which invest only in one or two particular company(s) in a particular category. Basically we will experience less impact in any condition compared with buying individual investments ourselves.

With the properly planned portfolio, mutual funds are the best vehicle for a middle (at least 10 year) or long term investment (unlimited time since everyone starts and enjoys their result at different points of time in their life ☺) because it's based on mutual (gathering) of investors and funds, meaning it will be less risky yet still gaining a great return as long as we let a decent period of time work for us.

Mutual fund investments work more like a slow cooker (takes a long time but tastes better) than a microwave (instantly done but won't taste as good as slow cooking food ☺), more like the humble and constant pace of the tortoise than the arrogant and much faster pace of the hare, more like slowly but surely rather than fast but fading, more like running a marathon than a sprint. Mutual fund investment is also like love. To love someone means we want to spend our energy, time, and even money, joyfully for that particular someone without expecting anything back instantly. Remember how we feel when we fall in love for the first time? We always make time to be with them, learn more about them, do our best to make them happy and give anything to show that, right? Mutual fund investment is like a long lasting marriage. We don't know what the future will have for us but we are willing to commit ourselves to the long term and make it official! Not worrying too much about "what ifs". We just have to work it out as our commitment to our first love. Be true and faithful, be disciplined and patient and we will reap what we sow in the long run. Trust me! Basically it takes faith which shows in our discipline and patience (kinda like a mature lifestyle) to be successful in mutual fund investing. We don't have to worry about the ups and downs of the market, just keep our discipline of putting money in them regularly and patience enough to not worry too much. Individual investments are more risky but may get a faster and bigger result or loss. It takes guts, a lot of time and energy (more like young people/children's lifestyle), like keep researching, checking, then buying and selling individual stocks, bonds, securities, gold, property, automobiles, gambling, etc. more frequently. Believe me, most people will find it much easier to be a mutual fund investor than to be an individual investor. They will be better off investing in mutual funds than in individual investments if they have limited money, time, and knowledge about investing.

The Advantages List of Mutual Funds for Middle or Long Term Investments (Based on Wikipedia and Investopedia):

1. Great diversification (fairly spread): so it is safer. Remember the wise saying, "Don't put all your eggs in one basket?"

   One important rule of investing for any size (big, small or anywhere in between) of an investor is an asset diversification. Diversification is the mixing of investments within a portfolio which is used to manage risk. For example, by choosing to buy stocks in the retail category and balancing them with stocks in the industrial category, we can reduce the impact of the performance of any particular security in our entire portfolio. To truly achieve diversified portfolio, we may have to buy stocks with different capitalization (current value) from different categories and bonds (our loan investment to a particular company or institution for a defined period of time at a fixed rate) with varying maturities (dues when we will get paid back for our loan and the interest) from different issuers. For the individual investor, this can be quite complicated and expensive! By purchasing mutual funds, we are provided with the immediate benefit of instant diversification and asset allocation without the large amounts of cash, knowledge, and time needed to create individual portfolios.

   Each mutual fund company has many kinds of funds serving different purposes and goals. Each fund has multiple categories of stocks, bonds, short term money market instruments and/or other similar securities, such as financials, industrials, consumer staples, information technology, consumer discretionary, telecommunication services, health care, energy, utilities, materials, etc. And each category has multiple companies, too. So it is very diversified and very well spread, therefore it is very safe compared to other kinds of investment vehicles should any company or category fall apart.

I'll give you this simple example: let's say we have $10,000 to invest. We want to invest it in a very strong and reputable company, so we do our research, checking many companies' past performance, their rate of return, their growth, etc. Then we find one match, the most reputable company with the biggest rate of return, fastest growth and internationally well known. So we use our $10,000 to buy its stock or whatever form of security we would like to have in that company, thinking that it is the best decision we could ever make with this $10,000 investment. In life, though, something always happens. I'm sure we all know that and some of us have experienced it more than others. Just like the wise saying: "life is like a wheel", "prepare an umbrella before it rains", etc. Somehow, someday, even the biggest company, the richest people, the strongest man, the most successful person, etc., will have their off days. That downturn can always happen to anyone, any company, anything at a certain point of its life. It always does. So when that happens to our best company that we put all our $10,000 in, all our investments will suffer, if not worse, be gone. So what will happen? Usually if one leading or famous company/person is down, the other (usually the competitor) will rise up to keep the balance of that category. In that case, we will lose a lot of hard earned money just because we thought we knew what we were doing but instead we didn't. We thought we had it under our control and could gain way faster but instead it's beyond our control and we might lose our investment very quickly. Meanwhile, others who have chosen the other competing company will rise very well. Unfortunately, that's not how our healthy mind works. Nobody will invest their money in the second rate company when there is also the first rate company available for us to invest in the same category. Yeah, most of us, including me, will invest our hard earned money toward the first rate company even if we know what will happen to our money if someday "the rain" pours beyond our control. We usually are greedy enough to take the risk, that's our human nature.

In mutual funds, our $10,000 will be invested in very diverse categories and multiple companies (usually the top 10 companies) in each category. So when one (or even two) leading companies from the same category hit their downturns, the next strongest company (or companies) will rise up to balance that category and we also have our money invested in them, too. So it is very safe! What if all the good (yes, there are some bad ones, so never just pick any mutual funds company! Always do your research and shop around!) mutual fund companies fail altogether? Well... that means that our world will fail altogether, too, since all the categories in our life are failing, right? It is a possibility but when the end of the world comes, I think we all have higher priorities than our investments, at least we should. :) And if we are good people, the end of the world is just the beginning of the greatest journey we'll ever have anyway, so yay!! Win-win solution! We always win if we're truly good people. If we're not good people or even worse, evil people….. Well, we better change and make things right before it's too late! It'll make our lovely world and life much more beautiful anyway if everyone is trying their best to be good hearted people, don't you think?

Just please make sure to choose the proper mutual funds not just a mutual fund. If you simply purchase one mutual fund, it might not give you enough diversification. Check to see if the fund is category specific. You want it to be multiple categories mutual funds. For example, if you are investing in an oil and energy mutual fund, it might spread your money over thirty companies. But if oil and energy prices fall, your portfolio will most likely suffer, too. So a good mutual fund–portfolio is one that has a balance of many categories and includes the top ten companies from each category, so that they will balance each category and the whole portfolio overall.

2. Ability to participate in investments that are available only to larger investors because our and others' investments are being pooled/gathered to make it large enough to invest.

It's just like volume discounts. In most companies, the more of one product you buy, the cheaper that product becomes. For example, when you buy a dozen donuts, the price per donut is usually cheaper than buying a single one twelve times. Another example, when you buy a double pack ink toner, the price per ink toner is usually cheaper than buying a single one twice. This also applies in the purchase and sale of securities. If you buy only one security at a time, the transaction fees will be relatively large.

Mutual funds are able to take advantage of their buying and selling size, thus they reduce the transaction costs for investors. When we buy a mutual fund, we are able to diversify without the numerous commission charges, too. Imagine if we had to buy the 15-20 stocks needed for diversification. The commission charges alone would eat up a good chunk of our investments. And we will see the costs begin to add up. With mutual funds, we can make transactions on a much larger scale for less money.

Many investors don't have the lump sums of money required to buy round lots of securities, especially after deducted with all the commissions. Mutual fund investors can purchase smaller round lots, ranging from $100 to $1,000 minimums. Smaller round lots of mutual funds provide mutual funds investors with the ability to make periodic (monthly, quarterly, etc.) investment–purchase plans while taking advantage of large scale price. So, rather than having to wait until we have enough money to buy higher-cost investments, we can get right in with mutual funds. This is vital since sometimes when the time finally arrived when we have enough money to buy higher-cost investments, that particular investment's buying price might not be in our benefit (in their high price).

3. Professional investment management.

They have many professional fund managers who work for the mutual fund company, meaning they work for us, too, as an investor. These managers will use the money that we invest to buy and sell stocks that they have carefully researched. Since the fund managers' compensation is based on how well the fund performs, we can be assured that they will work diligently to make sure the fund performs well. Managing their funds is their full-time job (and income source)! Therefore, rather than having to thoroughly research every investment before we decide to buy or sell, we have professional investment managers handle it for us.

4. Daily liquidity.

It's relatively easy to access, to put or take some money, compared to other investments. We are usually able to sell our mutual funds in a short period of time without much difference between the sale price and the most current market value. Also, mutual funds transact only once per day after the fund's Net Asset Value (NAV) is calculated, unlike stocks and Exchange Traded Fund (ETF) which trade any time during market hours.

5. Extremely high return for the ease of having it.

Great mutual fund companies give us an average 10-12% rate of return, that's about 5 - 7 times higher (500 - 700%) compared to the CD or money market!

6. Convenience of service and features.

Mutual funds usually have great service and pretty simple procedures. They also have a lot of online resources, tips, and features for our convenience. You can sell and buy the same day with just a click of a button wherever you are as long as you have internet access.

7. We have relatively big control over our retirement plan.

It's all in our control. We are relatively independent from the government's program (Social Security) and employer-offered mutual funds company (401K) as far as the investment and retirement decision I mean, not the market. We all wish we could control the market, too, huh? ☺

We all hear that our Social Security fund will run dry by year 2033 if we don't do anything and that still sounds a little too optimistic for many economy experts. Anyway, we don't have to worry about that if we have our own savings, especially in a mutual fund investment, which will work very well for us if we allow a decent amount of time (10 years at least) to work for us and keep our discipline and patience. If the government somehow successfully manages to do something about the social security fund for us, that's great! It's an extra benefit for us, like icing on the cake. If not, we still have our main retirement secured ourselves; we still have the main cake! :)

By having our own retirement secured in the proper mutual fund investment, we can worry less when the mutual fund choices offered by the mutual fund company through our employment in a 401K program are not performing as well as great mutual funds companies can. Lastly, we can worry less about how and where to roll over our 401K if we have (or want) to change jobs.

So we, ourselves, can control from which mutual funds company we want to benefit the most, how much we can contribute, where and when we want to change jobs, and when we want to retire.

The Disadvantages of Mutual Fund Investment (Based on Wikipedia and Investopedia) :

1. Expenses

"You don't gain something for nothing" and "nothing is free in life" theories apply to mutual fund-investments, too. There will be some kind of fee, cost, and charge for what we can gain through mutual fund investments. They are needed to pay all the fund managers, the operation, transactions, administration, etc. Of course, we should try to find a mutual fund company who has the highest rate of return history and lowest overall expenses possible.

There are basically two kinds of expenses that we have to pay attention to most of the time: the trading charge (the popular term is loaded) like A shares, B shares, etc. and operating costs (annual fees). The trading charge or load can run from 1 percent to 8.5 percent of the funds being invested. Low-load funds charge between 1 and 3 percent. The operating cost usually has already covered the 12b-1 distributing fee (for annual marketing) and also paying the fund managers, etc. This operating cost usually runs from 0.25 to 2 point something percent of the funds being invested.

There are so many different kinds of trading charges in mutual fund investment but the two major loads are the front-end load (A shares) and the back-end load (B shares). The A share (front-end load) charges us when we buy the share while the B share (back-end load) charges us when we sell the share. Some funds also have C shares, D shares, T shares, and even no-load funds. The fees and charges on each class of shares differ, as explained in the prospectus. Which one is the best for us? It really depends on what our purpose is. But trust me, for any beginner, the least complicated and yet most beneficial are just the first two I mentioned, the A shares and the B shares. Different funds are designed for different investment needs. No-load funds don't charge any fees to buy or sell their shares, but no-load funds aren't free, they have higher operating expenses that reduce returns to investors.

The B shares usually have a back-end fee that disappears over time. For example, there may be a 5 percent back-end fee to sell the fund in the first year of ownership, but the fee may be reduced by 1 percent each year. Therefore, if the shares are held more than five years, there'll be no fee to sell it. Usually after B shares have been held beyond the specified time that the fees can be charged (5 years for the example above), they're automatically converted to A shares. But the B shares usually have a higher 12b-1 fees that relate to the cost of distributing (marketing) of the fund shares.

All those expense terms sound so intimidating and too much for anyone the first time. But, trust me, it's not as intimidating as it sounds. There are basically two things that you have to pay: the first one is the trading charge or load whenever we have a transaction (could be a front or back load) and the second one is the annual operating fee. And the most important thing is that both those charges or fees are a percentage of the initial funds that we invested. If we earn some dividend (portion of the funds' profit) and capital gain distribution (increase in the value of the fund itself) which will be reinvested toward our mutual funds automatically (compounding), they will not be charged any percentage for the trading charge or operating cost.

The great thing is, after the decent period of time we keep our discipline for, our gain will be built mostly by the compound interest and only a small portion is from what we really put into the mutual funds.

Here is an example: With the assumption that our mutual funds' rate of return is 12% and the inflation rate is 4%, our net growth will be at 8%. Let's say I myself, 35 years old, want to retire at age 65 (30 years from now) on an annual income of $40,000 for an unlimited time since I don't know when I'm going to pass away. The only way to generate that $40,000 for an unlimited time is by getting it purely from the interest without touching the principal (we have to adjust a little bit here and there but nothing major just in case the return and inflation fluctuate). To earn $40,000/year with net growth of 8%, we will need $500,000 ($40,000 annual income divided by 0.08 annual net growth already including inflation) as our principal. We can pass that $500,000 on to our children when we don't need it anymore and that will change our children's life! To have a $500,000 principal 30 years from now, I only need to put aside $335.5 monthly for my mutual fund investment (I'll explain the retirement chart later in this book).

So, we actually put $120,780 in along the way (from 30 years x 12 months/year x $335.5 monthly savings) but we will have $500,000 in our savings! It means that $379,220 (75.84%) will be generated from the compound interest and only $120,780 (24.16%) will be generated from our own money that we save! And the good thing is that the trading charge (load) and the operating cost only apply to the initial funds that we save ($120,780), they won't apply to the compounded interest ($379,220)!

So, I personally don't call this a real disadvantage, it's just the cost of our chance to gain all the benefits from mutual funds. :)

2. Less control over exact timing and amount of our gain recognition

Mutual funds are great for middle/long term investments since they will average out all the ups and downs for a much better return as long as we let a decent amount time work (10 years at least). Unfortunately, we might gain more or gain less value just because we take out our mutual funds investment at different time (era). We might gain more value for our money if we take our investment out by selling our shares (distribution) in the golden or great years when our economy is stable and great. We might also lose some money if we get our distribution in the unstable and tough years. Fortunately, the term "lose" above actually means "make less" since in our middle/long term investment, the mutual fund investment will absorb the ups and the downs in all those years and summarizes it as the average return of 11%. But we still might make more or make less depending on the market in that particular time when we get our distribution. If we want to maximize our gains all the way, then we have to be able to wait for the good years (or at least good timing) to get our distribution. If we can't wait at all, then we have to accept it as what it is.

Nobody knows what the future will hold, including the market. Fortunately, we can be prepared by learning from the past, analyzing it, and then planning our best to face what might come ahead. But again, nobody knows how the market will do 100%, because there are so many factors affecting it, including mutual funds. Fortunately, mutual funds have a lot of categories and companies so they will absorb less impact however the market performs. But still there's no guarantee on it.

That's not the case with CD which is FDIC insured for their agreed time contract (maturity time) and agreed rate of return. So we should know exactly when we can get our investment out which is the maturity time and how much we will get for the time we get it out since it's a FDIC insured rate of return. But the return is usually way lower (about 1/6 of mutual fund investment) and the amount the FDIC is insured is usually pretty low ($250,000), too. So in CD, even though the timing and the amount of our investment's return is clearer, you'll see that in the same period of time, your money will grow slower and you won't be able to reach your ideal retirement or nest egg amount that is still insured by FDIC.

So, it's just like anything else in life. If the risks are high and the returns are small, then who in the world will choose that? Anyone in their normal mind would try to get the most income with the least outcome and risk, right? But everything has a price.

3. Not for people who have a lot of knowledge, time, and money to do individual investments.

In mutual funds, the fund (investment) managers are the ones who manage the transactions based on what they study, research and monitor. For me, it's actually a good thing since I have faith in professionals who have done it for many years (decades for some) and still have decent overall history records. I know I'm not even close to being able to predict and prepare as they do. Unfortunately, for someone who already has good investing experience (meaning they have the knowledge, experience, time and access as the professional fund managers do), they won't have enough opportunity to customize for themselves. They have to rely mostly on the fund managers since it's a mutual fund not an individual investment. Unfortunately, to be as experienced as the fund managers is not easy. It's a full time job itself! We always have to study, research, analyze, sell and buy all kind of stocks, bonds, short or long term securities or all the combinations at the proper time and in the proper manner, etc. If we like to do all that stuff, we could be an individual investor or just be the fund manager. :)

I personally love mutual funds since the advantages really outweigh the disadvantages. But first, we have to have an emergency fund that is realistically decent for our own condition and comfort level, and we can get into it pretty easily and quickly (we personally always have about $5,000 in our checking account). Second, we have to clean up all our debts (I really mean all!!) except the mortgage. If we don't have any emergency fund and still have unpaid debt but we want to gain all the benefits of mutual funds then we are greedy!! As I have explained in the previous chapters, first we always have to prepare for our and our significant other(s) "rainy day". That's why we need an emergency fund! Then, to be a decent person, we have to take care of our obligations (pay our debts) first before we can start preparing for our own wealth. If those two things are done, then we deserve to think and prepare about our own wealth!

Personally I don't have the knowledge, experience, time, or access as any of the fund managers who manage our mutual fund investments. So I'm really fine with them managing the fund, I just manage the overall big picture, like what we choose between the Roth IRA or traditional IRA, when we should start, which mutual fund company we use, which financial advisor we trust, etc. I prefer to think like we are the CEO and let the experts run their own departments under our overall leadership. :) That's how the mutual fund investment is supposed to work anyway, we are the investor, the owner, not the employee.... Ahaa!!

I) Retirement

a) 401k :

Investopedia defines 401k as a retirement (qualified) account provided by employers where eligible employees may make salary deducted (deferral) contributions on a pretax or post-tax (less common) basis and they will only be taxed when they make a withdrawal from it. Employers offering a 401k plan may make matching contributions to the account on behalf of eligible employees. They may also add a profit-sharing feature to the account. Earnings grow on a tax-deferred basis which means it will grow tax free until we withdraw it. There are rules and restrictions on how and when employees can withdraw this retirement plan, penalties may apply if we withdraw before reaching the retirement age as defined by the plan.

IRS regulations and/or the plan usually give us the percentage limit (cap) of salary deferral contributions allowed. That's understandable since our employer won't or can't match whatever we want to contribute. There are plans that allow the employees to manage their own investments by providing a group of investment products from which employees can choose. There are also plans where the employer hires professionals to manage the employees' investments.

Important things to look for when we are deciding whether or not to join the 401k program offered by our employers are:

1. Will the company match our contribution to our 401k account?

   If they match, most likely we should grab that opportunity since we will gain extra money right away to put into our 401k account except if we just started the job and are not sure whether we will stay in the company for a decent amount of time or not. The better (bigger) ratio they match our contribution the better.

   For example: If our employer matches $1 for every $1 contribution we make to our 401k account, that means we get the 100% match or 1:1 ratio match from our employer! That's awesome! It's just like our money has double power going into our 401k account. If our employer matches $0.50 for every $1 contribution we make to our 401k account, that means we get the 50% match or 1:2 ratio match from our employer. The second scenario is not as good as 100% or 1:1 ratio but hey, our money still has an extra 50% of its original power going into our 401k account!

As long as our company matches us to a certain degree, it is wise to put money into our 401k account. The bigger the percentage they match the better. The examples above are the popular number examples of employer matching ratio or percentage. They might offer a different percentage or not even offer-to match our contribution at all. If they do not offer to match our contribution to our 401k account at all, most likely we shouldn't put money into our 401k account through our employer. That is not always the case but most likely. Why? Check the next point.

2. How has the mutual funds company performed and how long has it been around?

The better performance record they have and the longer period of time they have been around the better. If they have been around for a while and still perform decently, or even better, greatly, then those companies are proven to be consistently strong through all the history of ups and downs, such as in the 1929 economic crash, the 1973 down market, the 1999 downturn and the 2008 economic recession. If they have been through all those tough, bad, dark years or whatever you want to call them and are still standing proudly, that's the one we should trust. Just like in our life, workplace, appliances, automobiles or even spouse. :)

3. Learn and understand our company's vesting schedule and rules (sorry, this one is gonna be a little bit intimidating but it's all for our own sake though ☺).

What is vesting? A vesting system is a type of security feature for companies to retain (keep) talented and hardworking employees for a longer term. Usually, when our employer offers to match our contribution to our 401k, they also use the vesting system (kind of a catch). When we vest in our employer's matching contributions, we can only legally keep our fully accrued (full amount) matching contributions when we have reached a specific period of time of employment agreed to in the 401k rules.

Some (very rare) employers offer immediate vesting of their matching contributions, but it's more likely that employers require employees to vest according to a pre-determined schedule. So we won't be able to quit a job after just working for a short period of time with a particular company and still get the full amount of their matching contribution.

There are two kinds of vesting schedules: graded vesting and cliff vesting.

a. Graded Vesting Schedule

With a graded vesting schedule, we vest in our employer's contributions on certain anniversaries of our employment. According to the Pension Protection Act of 2006, our employer's graded vesting schedule will be at least like the one below, yay!!
After one year of service: 0% vested
After two years of service: 20% vested
After three years of service: 40% vested
After four years of service: 60% vested
After five years of service: 80% vested
After six or more years of service: 100% vested

b. Cliff Vesting Schedule

Just like its name, a cliff vesting schedule means that for a period of time you won't be vested at all, then like going off a cliff, you instantly become vested all at once. Again, your employer's cliff vesting schedule may be more generous than the one described below, but your vesting will occur as least as fast as the following schedule:

- After one year of service: 0% vested
- After two years of service: 0% vested
- After three or more years of service: 100% vested

Our employer will offer either a cliff vesting schedule or a graded vesting schedule, but not both.

Make sure you are aware of your employer's vesting schedule especially before making any major decisions. For example: you wouldn't want to leave your job voluntarily a week before you can legally obtain your employer's fully vested match which might be a big lump sum of money.

Remember, always shop around for the best end value by comparing them apple to apple for what we need! That's one of the basic ways to be prosperous (and be diligent and smart, too ☺) that I can't emphasize enough.

What if our employer offers to match us 100% for every $1 we put into our 401k account, but the mutual funds company they offer performs really badly? If they perform really badly, chances are they will be bankrupt soon. If they have been around for a while but still manage to always perform just well enough to stay alive then we might consider not putting any contribution towards our 401k. If their performance is only okay, it might hurt us in the long run even though we double our money power (100% match from our employer) at the time we put in our money. How come? Just like I mentioned in the mutual fund investment example above: the end value of our long term mutual funds investment for our retirement usually has a much bigger percentage by the result of the compound interest (which highly depends on the performance: average rate of return deducted with the all trading charges and operating cost) and a way smaller percentage by the result of our own contribution (which might be double if we get the 1:1 ratio matching from our employer).

Fortunately, our employer usually won't be too happy either if they use a really badly performing investment company. :) So, chances are whenever they offer to match your contribution, just go ahead contribute to your 401k account until you reach the maximum contribution allowed to be matched by your employer and make sure you stay at your work place long enough to earn the fully vested matching contribution from your employer.

By the way, there is one more thing to understand and remember. Usually our employer has a certain percentage limit (cap) on how much they will match your contribution. Example: If your employer offers 100% matching for any $1 you contribute to your 401k but it's only up to 5% of your paycheck amount, then just contribute 5% of your paycheck because any contribution above that 5% amount of your paycheck won't be matched by your employer.

So again, the three most important things we should really understand before we decide whether or not to put/contribute money to our 401k account are: knowing whether our employer will match us or not. If yes, go ahead contribute up to the percentage limit they will match. If we get a small matching percentage then we have to look and learn carefully about the mutual funds company our employer offers us. If they perform pretty decent and have been around long enough to experience all the ups and downs through history, then go ahead and contribute. Unfortunately, the mutual fund company our employer offers for our 401k is usually an averagely performing company. Why? I am not 100% sure myself why, but their average rate of return after all the fees, costs and expenses is usually weaker and they usually haven't been around for that long compared to other mutual fund companies out there. I think the bigger company and more strongly rooted company usually doesn't necessarily need the collective system to attract people to invest with them. But that's just my assumption, it doesn't really matter. The most important thing is that we check all those steps above. And the last one is to know how our employer's vesting program works and make sure we make it the whole period of time needed to be able to harvest our fully vested employer match. Check your likeliness (chance) to stay at your workplace for a decent amount of time so that you can legally obtain the fully vested matching from your employer. If you aren't planning to stay at your workplace so that you might not be able to use the benefit of the fully vested matching from your employer, then don't do it.

So just be diligent when learning and understanding those important things. Then combine all the information we get to make the best decision for our own sake. If we are too lazy to learn and try to understand them, then we shouldn't expect the best result for ourselves, too. One of the most important lessons in life is that our hard work will pay off. It's a give and take rule of thumb. In this case, the hard work is our willingness (which everyone should have anyway!) to research and plan our decision, then be disciplined as we plan. I really love (and apply myself to) these two awesome sayings "If you fail to make a plan then you're planning to fail" and "plan your work then work your plan". Yeehaww!!

b) Roth IRA vs. Traditonal IRA :

What is an IRA (Individual Retirement Arrangement)?

Christian PF.com explains that an IRA is basically an account that provides great tax benefits when used to save money for retirement. This might be a little bit confusing but basically IRAs are not investments themselves, they are only the account that holds the investments. Within the IRA account who gives us great tax benefits, we can choose to invest in money markets, CDs, stocks, mutual funds, and you can even own real estate through your IRA!

IRAs can be opened at brokerage firms, online brokers, mutual fund companies and most banking institutions. With that in mind, there are different kinds of bank or financial institutions, some banks (usually the smaller ones) will not give you the freedom to invest in stocks and mutual funds, because they do not offer brokerage services. Some other banks (usually the bigger ones) usually have that option for us.

We can open multiple IRA accounts at different places but keep in mind that there is a maximum amount that we are allowed to put into our IRA account each year which is $5,500 and $6,500 if we are 50 years old and older for 2013. If you open multiple IRA accounts, you have to keep track of how much you put in each one each year and make sure the combined amount doesn't exceed the IRS limit. I strongly suggest not opening multiple IRA accounts for ourselves so that we don't get confused and then violate the IRS law which will be really messy and bad for us. Some might say that they would love their retirement investment to be spread out just like I talked about in the previous mutual funds chapter. But again, if we really do our homework and research (as we should anyway!) then we should find that our best choice for our financial institution will be the one who already has spread out investment options for our portfolio without us having to spread our investments ourselves at other financial institutions! Another reason for not having multiple IRAs opened up is that there is an annual fee of $30-45 usually charged by the financial institution that you have your IRA with. Some are more, some are less, but this is a good ballpark figure.

Roth IRA or Traditional IRA?

Deciding whether to open a Roth IRA or Traditional IRA is a major decision with potentially huge financial consequences later in the future. Both forms of IRAs are great ways to save for retirement, although each offers different advantages.

The main advantages of Traditional IRA:

1. Available to everyone without any income restrictions
2. Tax deductible contributions (depending on income level, most middle class and below will get this benefit)

The disadvantages of traditional IRA:

1. Taxes are paid on earnings when withdrawn from the IRA
2. All funds withdrawn (including principal contributions) before 59 1/2 are subject to a 10% penalty (subject to exception such as extreme conditions)
3. Mandatory withdrawal by age 70 ½ (if we fail to do so, half of the mandatory amount will be confiscated automatically by the IRS!)

The advantages of Roth IRA:

1. All earnings and principal are 100% tax free if rules and regulations are followed
2. Principal (not earning) contributions can be withdrawn any time without penalty (subject to some minimal conditions)
3. No Mandatory Distribution (Withdrawal) Age

The disadvantages of Roth IRA:

1. Available only to single-filers making up to $110,000 or married couples making a combined maximum of $173,000 annually (up to year 2013)
2. Contributions are not tax deductible

There are two most common and basic IRA types: ROTH and Traditional. There are actually about eleven other IRAs but these two are the most popular and easy to have. A Roth IRA (The term Roth IRA is based on Senator William Roth who was the main sponsor of the idea through all the legislation) and traditional IRA both provide tax-free growth. The biggest difference between the Traditional and Roth IRA is the way our government treats the taxes. With a traditional IRA, our contributions are tax-deductible (depending on your income) but we pay taxes on earnings when we withdraw them. While with the Roth IRA, our contributions are not tax deductible but the earnings are tax-free when we withdraw them.

So if we earn $50,000 a year and put $5,000 in a traditional IRA, we can deduct the contribution from our income taxes (meaning we will only have to pay tax on $45,000 in income to the IRS). At 59 1/2, we may begin withdrawing funds but will be forced to pay taxes on all of the earnings (capital gains, interest, dividends, etc.) that are earned over the saving years. On the other hand, if we put the same $5,000 in a Roth IRA, we will not receive the income tax deduction but when we reach our retirement age (70 ½ up to the 2013 law), we would be able to withdraw all of the money 100% tax free. And just in case we need the money in the account (even though I suggest not to touch it at all), we could withdraw the principal at any time. We have to pay penalties if we withdraw any of the earnings our principal contribution has made, though.

This is the first important difference. They have their own advantages and disadvantages with this difference alone. Some people might say that our tax bracket when we are retired will be smaller since we don't generate as much income as in our productive age. But at the same time, we can also say that we better pay our tax right when we contribute so we don't have to worry about tax later when the rate might go up, especially with our government's estimation that in the year 2003 our Social Security fund will run dry if they don't make any changes (which is usually by raising our tax rate).

And the main or crucial reason that personally influences my decision when choosing between these two is that if we plan our retirement properly and early enough, usually the end result of our retirement account will be gained mostly (a much higher percentage) by compound interest over time, not by our total contributions during all that time up to our retirement. So I personally prefer being taxed out of my total contributions (which is usually much smaller) compared to being taxed out of my earnings after the compound interest over time (which is way bigger in most cases). So I personally suggest the Roth IRA as your first choice if you are eligible/ qualified. Unfortunately, not everyone qualifies for a Roth IRA. A single person filing their taxes can make up to $110,000 annual income in order to be qualified to open a Roth IRA, while married couples can make up to $173,000.

The second important difference is that in a traditional IRA, it is mandatory for us to start withdrawing our money in a certain amount. If we fail to do so, half of the mandatory amount will be confiscated automatically by the IRS! While in the Roth IRA it is much more flexible. We can choose to start withdrawing at any point of time in our retirement age and as much or as little as we want. We are also allowed to leave it there for our children, too. So we can use all of our retirement money for anything we decide at that time, either for ourselves or for our children, too!

So Roth IRAs have much more flexibility! In addition, with the Roth IRA allowing us to choose when and how much to distribute, we can maximize our retirement value, too! If we are already great in managing our finances, then at the time we retire we will still be great at managing our finances! So chances are we will have some easy-access cash so that we will be able to wait a little bit more for the market to go up again just in case the mutual fund market is down at the time we retire.

There is a common confusion that became a paranoid myth about worrying too much when the mutual fund market is down. Some people get freaked out and right away want to jump out of the boat. They will take their money out as soon as possible when they see that the market they are in is declining. They think it is wise to take their money out as soon as possible before it declines any more. And when the market they put their money in is rising, they will put more money there, hoping that they will enjoy the golden era of the rising market. That sounds pretty logical, doesn't it? No!! Again, if we do our homework, it is likely that we will find at least one mutual fund company which is not stupid and has decent performance (if we still have a badly performing company then we didn't do our homework correctly! Might as well not waste our time doing it, right? If anything is worth doing, it is worth doing right). If the market(s) of our decent mutual fund company is down right now, it actually means that their price per share will be lower! It's just like the share price is on sale! The share price "sale" here should already attract most ladies (just kidding ☺). And for guys, come on…. why not buy the same quality thing for a lower price? Remember that in mutual funds, each category is usually made of the top ten companies so our well researched mutual fund companies who perform decently, won't allocate their money to the constantly bad performing companies within the same category! And if the category still fails on us, that means that one sector/category is totally collapsing. By the time that happens, I believe we will have way higher priorities than worrying about our market. :)

Even though the ROTH is usually the better choice for most middle class and below people, there are other differences between the two that might affect us in a great way in some particular situations. So in order to get the best advice for our particular situation, talk to a financial advisor, not a broker (some people are still confused about the difference between these two professions). Why? A financial advisor works for our interest since they get paid a percentage of what we make. The more we make the more they make, so they'll work hard to benefit us so that it will benefit them, too. Meanwhile brokers are just traders who make money if they make any trade. So whether it's good or bad for us, it doesn't matter to them as long as they make money through the trade. So if we have any family or friends (or worse, a friend of a friend, etc.) who are coincidentally brokers, don't just right away take the easy shortcut and trust them to manage our retirement! Do our homework first all the time!! Remember "If you fail to make a plan, you're planning to fail!" Always do what we need to do first, then what we want to do!

We can analyze how good they are just like I explained earlier in subchapter Shop Around. If they are willing and able to explain to you all the benefits and losses of all the reasonable options, then they are good. If they do it in a humble and caring way, then they are awesome! If they only tell us about the pros without any cons, it's kind of too good to be true. If they tell us the cons only when we ask, then they just want to lure us in by hiding the cons. Right away flee from that kind of person! What if they emphasize the cons more than the pros of all the options? Then they don't really want our business. Either they are not smart or bitter toward their employer. :) They shouldn't even bother learning about anything with more cons than pros, right? Neither should we!

So, when we want to have a meeting with a financial advisor, we need to shop around properly. Don't just open the yellow pages then go to the first one we see or the one that's most attractive. Do your homework and research by first making appointment by phone. If the secretary, receptionist, or even they themselves sounds polite, caring, and well educated, then you should put them down on your list of financial advisors that you really want to talk to. Put at least 3 financial advisors that have that great characteristics on your list. Doing all that sounds like too much work, right? Wrong! If by sacrificing an extra 5-6 hours of our lives we could gain a couple hundreds of thousands or even millions extra doesn't seem right for us, then we are either already wealthy, we are lazy or we are plainly not smart enough! Actually even the wealthy won't choose to be that lazy and choose not to care about all that difference they might be able to gain! The truly wealthy people (ones who build their wealth from scratch not through luck like inheritance, lottery, gift, etc.) will always be wise and diligent! So, that will actually leave us with only these two excuses, just lazy or just plainly not smart (or both??).

And of course, stay as far away as possible from people who don't do it themselves but love to give advice to others! I call those kinds of people NATO, which is supposed to be the abbreviation of the North Atlantic Trade Organization but I use it as No Action Talk Only, NATO. Be very aware of this kind of person! They won't be good at anything, anywhere, anytime, especially when handling our retirement investment!! Basically you can talk to and ask advice from people who have done it properly and prevail themselves, that's the basic hint. Everyone is entitled to their own opinion but we are the ones who have to decide whether to believe and follow or not. So, do your homework properly and diligently, if not, we'll get mislead by the false teachers who are lost themselves ("a blind guy leading a blind guy" sound familiar?). Or maybe we still get the right teacher but they never do what they say (NATO, No Action Talk Only or in other words a hypocrite) so we will be inspired by the false example. Both of these scenarios are bad for all of us. This applies to any aspect of our life, too, of course. For example: getting a personal trainer who is out of shape (a round shape doesn't count ☺), getting advice about our marriage from a couple who each has been through countless divorces and re-marriages themselves, learning how to drive from someone who has gotten three tickets (or has had a collision) in the last 12 months, like getting some help for addiction from other addicts, and a lot more. You get the idea. Always seek counsel from someone who we look up to and has done a great job in what we want counsel about.

There is a whole lot more to learn about Roth IRAs and traditional IRAs, but if we do not want to spend a lot more time or energy than now, you'll have to figure out which one will work better for your situation, then just pick one and start saving. It is way better to just go ahead start saving with all the knowledge you have at this point then do nothing at all while you try to figure out what the perfect scenario for you is. Just like how I suggest getting a job when we are jobless, it is far better to start working anywhere than do nothing while we try to find our dream job. But again, I strongly suggest the Roth IRA first because of all the previous reasons I've explained except if we are not qualified enough (when we already make a pretty high income) or just had a great luck (got a big inheritance or won the lottery, transferring any estate tax) that is a strong enough reason not to. But again, people who experience all that are supposed to be already well off. :) So for most of the middle income earners and below (currently most of us will fall in this category, remember the 80/20 principal? Only 20% or 1/5 of us will be sharing 80% of the wealth available in our life, and 80% or four fifth of all of us will share only the 20% of the wealth available in this life), Roth is always the way to go.

All of the above are the main ways to invest for our retirement. But what do the numbers look like at the end (when we retire)?

Here is an example:

Let's say that there is a 30 year old couple with an annual household income (both their incomes combined yearly) of $50,000. Let's assume that their employer(s) offer a 401k benefit and up to 6% of their employees' income that is being contributed to their 401k account, their employer(s) offer to match $1 for every $1. If the 30 year old couple opens and contributes to their 401k, they'll contribute $3,000 per year or $250 per month ($3,000 per year divided by 12 months/year) and their company matches $250 per month which will make their contribution to their 401k $500 per month!!). Based on Dave Ramsey.com Investment Calculator, this couple will have $1,757,139.60 in their 401k account when they are 70 years old!

Then if they both fund their Roth IRA to the limit allowed ($5,000/year/person or $416/month/person as regulated in year 2013) at a 12% return rate mutual fund with a 4% inflation rate. When they are 70 years old, already absorbing the inflation, they will still have $2,923,881.72 ($1,461,940.80 each) tax free!!!

So the 30 year old couple, by saving $1,082 per month ($832 for both their Roth IRA plus $250 for both their 401ks) which is 26% of their income, at a 12% interest rate, at age 70 years old when they retire, they will have total money of $4,681,021.30! Almost 3 million dollars of it is tax free!! The rest (1.85 million dollars) are pretax so you will pay less tax on your income through all those saving years! 26% of their income is actually a little bit smaller compared to what they pay for their income tax bracket which is around 28% (depends on which state they live in, too) for their $50,000.00 annual income! So if it doesn't really bother us when we pay our taxes because we have to do it anyway and it is an automatic withdrawal (except in a few cases like we own our own business, etc.), why not do it for our own retirement? Might as well make it a discipline and an automatic process just like paying taxes but it's for our very own future, right? Right!! :)

And that's only if they never increase their income during their 40 year career journey!! (Which is very unlikely! C'mon, who wants to get paid the same for the next 40 years?? I sure don't!) And that's if they only invest through the two vehicles I mentioned in the example above (401k and Roth IRA) while as we all know there are more to ways to choose if they really want to earn more for their retirement. So it's amazing to think that any of us could have that kind of retirement money which is about $4.7 million just by resetting our way of thinking and committing a little discipline.

Remember, if we really want to change our lifestyle permanently, we have to change our habit. And habit is molded by our actions and all our actions are always based on our way of thinking. We have to change our way of thinking to be able to finally change our lifestyle! Always fix the basics first, our foundation first! Everything built on it depends strongly on the foundation! So choose and prepare our foundation properly.

Some of us might think that it's way too hard to save $1,082/month. Remember that it's for two people, so each only have to save $541/month which is about the same amount of money if we cut our super fancy "toys" which is not too fancy anymore since everyone else also has them. Remember what we used to call a cell phone is a device to make a phone call and maybe text. Now, what we mean by cell phone is really an i-Phone, Smartphone, Android, etc. Then those people who have that kind of cell phone will most likely want to have tablet, i-Pad, etc. Then at home (just like they don't have enough "toys" to play with), they most likely want to have a PS 3 or an XBOX 360 with all the cool gadgets and extra equipment. When they have all that stuff, they most likely also have cable and its upgrades such as DVR, etc.

Above all the "it's not that expensive for the features we got" toys, what's worse have to pay their monthly fee or subscription fee or online fee or whatever you want to call them. It's a routine cost that will add up quickly on top of the price they already paid for the device or equipment itself. At the same time, they will definitely buy a nicer and newer car even though they will have to make another monthly payment for it for the next few years. What's next? Ooh, let's get full coverage for our "baby" car, and the list will keep going on. Don't you see? It's not about the action itself but the habit built out of those "little" actions is what we are supposed to worry about. The bad habit of spending our hard earned money for something we want too easily. Then, we will leave ourselves not being able to use our hard earned money for what really matters, what we really need, especially in the future. If we want to spoil ourselves for only right now and right here, don't you think we are a little childish, well ….a lot childish, actually. So, always go back to the basics, always care and act for our future and others', too.

And not only our bad habit in spending carelessly, the worse thing is that people who have all those fancy "cell phones" or "needs" will most likely have habits of wanting to use all the features or apps (applications) that they already paid for. They will want to make the most out of what they already paid for!! So at work, during their family time, at movies, in meetings, or almost at everywhere they go, if they think they have time to spare (even sometimes when they're not supposed to), they will most likely try to use their fancy toys and gadgets! And that will make their time, focus and energy spread thin when they are supposed to focus on the right thing. Isn't that a bad cycle and we have to pay a lot more for it??! It's so sad to see a family in the restaurant who are each busy with their own "toy" while waiting for their food to be served. The dad is busy with his tablet, the mom is busy with her cell phone, the daughter is busy with her cell phone and the youngest son is busy with his PSP. No conversation, no family time, just a bunch of individuals going out together to eat their meals in their own ways. It's ironic (even though it's common) to see a waiting room in any sport facility which is full of parents who are busy with their "toys" and then say," You did great, buddy!" or "Good job, sweetheart!". I truly believe that they all care about their children. It's just their habit is starting to eat their life up without them realizing it. I believe that they will cheer for their children ecstatically when the "real" game (at least that's what they think) is on, but in the process, we start to lose our focus since we are too "busy". It's just like a baseball bat grip; we think it's easy to just hold a grip onto baseball bat. But if haven't practiced holding a grip properly and frequently enough, even though we hit the baseball at the right angle, the bat might slip a bit or there is not enough power in our wrist and grip so that we won't hit how we should.

The most common fun "toy" now is the cell phone. Seriously, if you think you really need that cool phone, try to answer honestly "What kind of real necessity is there in our life that we can get from the Smartphone other than luxury and fun?" I thought so, except if you're a businessman or an individual who is required to travel a lot, you might really need that kind of fancy cell phone. If we don't have to travel a lot or if we are not a businessman, I don't think it's a real need to use that fancy cell phone at churches, in the workplace, meetings, family time, sport practices, college class, etc. We actually can live by using a regular old-school cell phone! Again, I am not against the fancy or high tech cell phones, just please remember what we are here for. Do not get eaten up by what we have. Master what we have, not the other way around.

The second most common "affordable" habit is grabbing something to drink or eat at places that serve them instead of preparing them ourselves. "It's only $4 and I can start my day out great with one of the best coffees out there." "I'll grab a quick breakfast at this or that place, it's only $6." If you add all those up, that's like $5 on average, plus tax and tips (depending on where we live and where we go to get them), it'll bring them to about $7/day. With 25 working days/month on average, that habit will cost us $175/month. And usually, people who do that will most likely like to dine out, too. Some maybe once a week and others maybe more frequent.

With those two (cell phone and grabbing a quick drink/food) as starters, the way we think about spending our money in other aspects of our lives will change, too. Having laptops, tablets and their kind, game consoles and their kind, dining experiences and their kind, socializing and their kind (some people might prefer clubbing), etc. All that will cost us way more than $541/month, trust me, I guarantee!! Remember earlier we learned that most of them will try to make the most out of all their fancy "toys"? Well, they put their effort in the wrong things and times. They actually should make the most out of the income they have earned for their obligations and futures, like preparing an emergency fund, paying off their debt of any kind, paying off their vehicles, paying off their house, preparing for retirement, etc. Again, I'm not against any of that technology. They're really good and cool if we use them properly (function wise and time wise). It's like talking about which weapon is the best weapon for martial artists. It's not about the weapon; it's the martial artist who handles them that really matters. We can have all those fancy "toys" or devices, just don't forget our higher obligation. In our family's case, in those 6.5 years that we lived to our fullest by being joyful (from inside our heart, soul, and mind, toward our surroundings) and being simply content, people still respected us as who we really were and not for what we had. Our lives still went well and were balanced without having to have all those "everyone has it" devices. Then, after the 6.5 years, we could do anything we wanted since we didn't owe anybody anything, it's all truly ours, not only by the paper. :) And the most important thing is that we have learned and experienced how to be wealthy from scratch which will make our way of life appropriate not just to gain, but also to maintain our wealth consistently.

Dave Ramsey, a great Christian-based financial expert, showed this simple yet pretty accurate formula of how much we should save every month to gain a particular amount of money we desire for our retirement. The first time I found out about this from the FPU (Financial Peace University) class held in my church, I was so excited and in awe! Our tradition and knowledge background gave us a head start when we joined the FPU class on 2007. We have always had $5,000 in our bank all the time as our emergency fund, we haven't had any kind of debt, we had always been paying everything off right away, and we had almost paid off our home mortgage. We hadn't started our retirement and children's future, though. So when Dave Ramsey showed us (from the FPU class, not in person ☺) some basic ways available for us to do so plus his awesome motivating formula, we were so pumped to do some more detail research and get it started!! Woo Hoo!!

I will explain a little bit more about the options available though. Here's how it goes: First, we need to seriously consider about what we need (or really want ☺) for our retirement. There are two ways to do that, either we decide how much of a lump sum we want when we retire or how much income we would always have every year when we retire. The first way is usually more tempting than then second way since you're gonna see a much bigger number which makes everyone's eyes turn green (the money kind of green not the mutant kind of green, even though I really love the X-Men movies ☺) While the second way will make the number much smaller but actually I personally prefer and suggest the second way, that's what we do for our family. This is where Dave Ramsey's formula comes in really handy, just as Batman's brilliant preparation against Superman in "The Dark Knight Returns" graphic novel written by Frank Miller. :)

Why is Dave Ramsey's formula really good for motivating people to get started and planning their best as financial "Batman" (the most well planned super hero)? Here we go:

The lump sum option surely made me drool, too! But honestly, we, as human beings have the tendencies to use all sources available. It's just like our society right now; employees use all their paychecks as soon as they receive it, governments use all the available sources they can until sometimes we almost run out of some, MMA (cage) fighters use all they have in their arsenal (striking, takedown, submission, cage control, etc.) to win fights, students use all their resources from technology to additional courses available to achieve their best performance, I use all the resources I know and I can to write this book (man!! It's seriously hard to write a book for the first time but it's possible and rewarding! Winners think and live that, losers think and live the other way," It's possible and rewarding but it's seriously hard to do!" Winners never quit and always end–strong while losers always quit and end weak!), even little toddlers or kids know how to use all the resources they can! Remember when we were little kids and our dad got really mad at us? What did we do then? We usually run to our mom, right? And vice versa. If you forget (or pretend to forget ☺) then just look at our own little children now, as sweet and innocent as they are, they already know how to choose or use all the best resources! :) So, using the most of our resources is not always bad, sometimes it's good. It all depends on what we use them for and how we use them.

In this case, we will have the tendency to use our big lump sum of money more freely especially when we start feeling that our body is getting older, and our joints and muscles are getting worn. We will start thinking we should enjoy the most of our money before we get too old to enjoy it. As a result, we might go back to square one, exactly like the time before we changed our way of thinking and lifestyle, back to being a free spirit, living one day at a time style, go with the flow, etc. And before we know it, we will run out of our retirement fund! And it would be way too late to build that big of a nest egg up again that'll be enough to support the rest of our retirement for we don't even know how many more years! (Except if something tragic happens, but don't we all hope that nothing tragic happens?) Basically the first choice will give us less control. We might feel like driving a super slick and fast Ferrari (or at least a powerful Dodge Charger or Challenger just like in The Fast Five movie! That movie is awesome by the way!! At least for boys ☺) but without fully functioning brakes!

The second one will make the number much smaller but it is more realistic since we can break it down to our yearly income (I'm personally still amazed at how much yearly income we can make without any work required as long as we do it properly now!!). It will help us to stay true to our goal and capacity. If we can estimate how much money we can get every year, we won't be too far out of our proper budget when we enjoy our retirement. It's like the white line on the street. It's like a speedometer on our vehicle, etc. And, the best part is just about to come…….
Are you ready?

If we plan properly to retire on a yearly income basis and we also don't know how many more years we'll live, then the way to go to achieve that is by living out of our retirement (nest egg) money's interest only. That means that our interest which is averaging at 12% of all our retirement money will be enough to support our retirement needs and wants, so it doesn't matter whether we live until 80 years old or 120 years old! We'll never run out of our retirement principal money itself, we just live out of our interest only!! The principal will always be there!

When we pass away, that principal money can be passed onto our lovely spouse and children. If we are single, we can pass them onto other relatives/people by making a will or trust. For some of us who get the privilege to know when we are about to pass away (I personally prefer not to know ☺), we should be so excited and joyful since we will have a much better life, actually the best life we can ever have, way beyond our imagination and it will last forever, too!! Heaven is the most ideal place for anyone, some of us might not think of it that way but that's the ultimate truth. Heaven and hell are for real. So if we don't or haven't believed that, we better start believing before it's too late (just like in retirement, we better start saving before it's too late. ☺).

If we can't be excited and joyful when are about to pass away just because we know that we are about to leave our big lump sum of retirement money to someone else, that will be ironic. How so? That means that even after we are wealthy, we still only think about ourselves and are not sincere in leaving the big principal to the appointed loved one(s) in our will, if any. That means that in all the life we had, either we never truly loved or cared for anyone or all who we truly loved or cared have already passed away. And if we don't have anyone appointed lawfully, the state will get all our retirement treasure. All of those scenarios are kind of ironic, don't you think? So start sharing and showing your love. Start caring for others' wealth and futures, too. Even though we have no one that we truly love or care about after all those years, we will actually still help our state. So we should be proud of ourselves and be joyful and peaceful since we know we do a great favor for others until the last breath we have in this world.

If we can truly apply the right mentality, we will enjoy our retirement much more. We can enjoy the most of our retirement as we have planned it. We don't have to worry about how much we need to spend so that our retirement will exactly (or at least close to) run out when we pass away. We also don't have to worry about whether we have enough just in case we live longer than our estimation of when we are going to pass away. We don't have to worry about all that since we already have peace and contentment with our retirement and inheritance plan.

If we are still not sincere in leaving our retirement savings to someone else or to the state, that means that we are still self-centered! If we are still like that, self-centered and attached too much to our earthly treasure, we won't have as peaceful of a retirement in this world! And the worst part, when we are attached and worry too much about our earthly treasure here, usually we never really worry about the bigger guy upstairs (that's what most people call God now) then what makes us think that He (the bigger guy upstairs) will worry about us later when we come up in front of his sight? And trust me, hell is the last place we want to be in. It's the most miserable place with the most tortures, cries, screams, temptations, heat, cold, pains, stresses, angers, worries and a lot more and all of that will never end!! They will last forever! And forever is a very long time. How do I know about all that? I have never been there and I myself never want to tempt or test myself to go there just to check out whether it is real or not. I don't think anybody on their right mind would want to do that, either. If there's any, good luck! I strongly suggest that we all believe that it is real. In the worst case scenario, even if it's not real (which I strongly disagree with), believing that it is real will make us better people, anyway! It'll make us want to use our time, energy, treasures, joys, strengths, talents, etc. for our God and other human beings. If everybody believes and shows that in their lives, too, our world will be a much more beautiful world, don't you think? I believe so. So, start believing and truly loving our true God, other people and then ourselves (again, truly loving ourselves is not the same with spoiling ourselves or being selfish!)

So I honestly prefer to set my goal at the annual basis calculation.

Dave Ramsey provides us with this inspiring formula and chart. Let's say we're gonna put our retirement investment in a good growth mutual fund which is averaging a 12% annual growth and also assuming our inflation annual rate is 4% so we are looking at 8% net annual growth.

First Step :

First, we'll have to shoot for a nest egg amount so that we can live our lives out of its pure 8% interest it'll gain every year.

Annual Income (in today's rate) you wish to retire on: $_____ Divide by .08 : $_____

Second Step:

After we have estimated the huge nest egg needed, then, the next step is to find out how much we should save per month to gain that nest egg depending on how much time we have left to save until we reach our qualified and/or desired retirement age (in this case, we assume 65 years old).

$_____ x _____ = $_____
(Nest Egg   (8% factor   (Monthly Saving
Needed)   for our age)   Needed)

8% Factors Table (select the one that matches our age when we start to commit to saving. ☺)

AGE	YEARS TO COMMITED SAVING	FACTOR

25	40	.000286
30	35	.000436
35	30	.000671
40	25	.001051
45	20	.001698
50	15	.002890
55	10	.005466
60	5	.013610

We can see easily that the earlier we start the smaller we have to save to reach the same amount of money on our retirement time set. Let's use the previous example of the 30 year old couple, let's say they want to have same amount of annual income at their retirement as their productive age (25-60), which is $50,000. According to the 8% factor table above, they will need to save about $272.50/month ($625,000 nest egg at age 65). If the very same couple decide to enjoy their $272.50/month for a luxurious lifestyle (dining out more, fancier apps for their cell phones, extra features for their cable subscription, etc.) for the next 5 years and start to save for their retirement then, they will have to save $419.38 to gain the same $50,000 annual income at their retirement. That's 53.9% (one and a half times) more than what they should've been saving if they would've started 5 years earlier to gain the very same $50,000 annual income at their retirement!!

If they wait for another 5 years, it's gonna be $658.88/month (141% or two and a half times more!!), and if they want to "enjoy" their lives for another 5 years, then they have to pay $1,061.25/month (289.45% or almost four times more)!!

So, if that same couple wait until they are 45 years old then start to save for retirement, they will have to save almost 4 times harder to be able to reach the very same goal! But what if any of us just learned all these concepts when we were already 45 years old or more? Well, we better start as soon as possible then!! It's not about what we have, it's always about what we do with what we have at any point in our life!! If some people don't know these concepts until their late age and regretted it, I strongly suggest not to!! Do not regret anything! That's the worst feeling anyone can have, regretting something, wishing we could change something in the past, imagining what if we would have done differently, etc. We are who we are right now, is only because of whatever we have done and whatever happened around and to us in the past. So if some people know these concepts in their late age, at least they already "enjoyed" their lives for so many years with their extra "$272.50"/months, right? So they already had their chance. They kinda already enjoyed their "early retirement". :)

If some said that they haven't been enjoying their lives so far and are still too late to realize all these concepts, then they should know that the way they live their lives is not working, so they better change their way of thinking and be better as soon as possible. Basically, no complaining! Sharing is fine but then just move on with whatever we have right now for days to come, that's the true warrior spirit!!

All the big and great achievers have done the same, too. Most well accomplished professionals, all world class athletes; all winners do that, too!! Losers always try to find excuses about their past or present condition to avoid the extra hard work to achieve greatness they should've been able to grab! Losers always quit and that's why they never win! They never have enough willingness and commitment to taste their own victories and successes since they will quit before they succeed! Winners always try to find ways not to quit until they get what they really long for in their lives. Winners will never quit on their dreams, except if their dreams are irrational, but winners will dream with the proper set of mind, plan and preparation, though. If they dream without all that, then it'll become a fantasy, not a dream anymore! Remember NATO (No Action Talk Only)? This group is the one who usually have fantasies since they only talk or think about it without any action to follow up. :)

So no matter how our condition is now or in the past, no matter how old we are when we realize all these things, it is always better late than never. As long as we start changing our mindset properly and soon plan our work then work our plan with discipline, we'll be in a much better shape in the future compared to if we keep waiting or worse, don't do anything about it at all.

The earlier we start the better because it'll be easier. Just like anything else in life, let's say we heard that a big tornado and tsunami are coming our way and that we need to evacuate, any normal person usually will try to prepare then evacuate as soon as they can. The same concept applies to anyone who has been in a fight. Whenever something is heating up and the other guy is starting to bulge their chest and rush—toward us, we should know that by that time, we should be ready to: 1) flee (run) 2) dodge/evade or 3) put our hands up and go at it. :) Another example is when a student knows that they will have finals in two weeks but they kept thinking, "Ahh...it's still two more weeks, it's no use to study now, I'll forget it by then". When finals is like three days away and they say, "Hmm... I still have three days left for the finals, I still got time to catch up on my studies still, but first, I gotta check this brand new long awaited game to refresh me before I cramp my life and schedule with studying hard for my finals." And then with only one day left before the finals, they'll start to study hard and play catch up. Anyone who has been in this situation knows that the result will be devastatingly bad for them, in finals and if they never change, in their life, too.

Some might protest, "Andy, you keep giving us the disastrous or bad situations as examples, what about something more positive?" Alright, here are two simple and most popular scenarios. First, let's say I really admired and liked a girl in my college freshman year. I knew that she felt pretty close to me, too, but I'd like her to be my girlfriend, not just a friend. Unfortunately, I never asked that question, either I was being over confident or just plain stupid (being over confident if I don't think other guys could win her heart over me and being stupid if I am just too scared and shy to ask the question). Being as admirable as she is, there are other guys who like her, too, of course. So someday later (after a pretty long time) when I realized that I really need to pop that question, she already said "yes" to someone else who is also pretty close to her as a friend, too, at the beginning. Good for that guy who has the common sense and guts to ask the question properly at the proper time.

Well, it's too late for me by then. Except if they broke up. :) (by the way, this is just an example; it is not based on my real experience……. Or is it? ☺)

Some people might say that it is okay if we're the ones who broke them up as long as they are not married yet. I don't personally agree with that, if we let our chance pass us by, and then we want to get it back, it'll take a lot more work to get that chance back, if any. Or let's say we successfully broke them up then we get back together, what prevents others to do the same thing to our relationship then?? The key is how I and the female friend feel towards each other. If we really like each other at the level that we both will sacrifice a lot of stuff in our life, then go for it. I always support people going for their dream and when I say dream, I mean the proper dream in which we aim, plan, and prepare to reach that dream, otherwise it is called a fantasy! Not a dream! But again, if I really have planned and prepared to really be more serious with my female friend as I mentioned in the example above, then I would've asked ask the question at the proper time (sooner).

And our retirement is a plan that we can decide and do by ourselves unlike the example above where two hearts and minds are affecting each other's decisions. Our future and retirement is totally up to us. So whether we seize or pass the chance to plan and prepare for our future/retirement, that's purely our decision. I really do hope that everyone will make the best decision for themselves that they feel is the right thing to do at the time and be content to live with the consequences later.

Just a few reminders again, delaying pleasure is one sign of maturity (a great line I heard from Dave Ramsey). One more great concept that I live by is that laziness pays off only for that moment we are being lazy but not later. Meanwhile, diligence is the other way around, it'll be harder for that moment we are being diligent but it will pay off later. The beauty is that some people are able to change their point of view and love being diligent. By doing so, they enjoy the planning and preparation (the sacrifices, the process) and they'll also enjoy the later time (the great time, the result)! And I believe everyone can do that, too. How? It's actually as simple as this: if we all can shoot for our dream and really want it bad enough, then we'll enjoy the process of getting there just by focusing ourselves on the end result, the reward. If we can't enjoy, or at least be committed to the process by focusing ourselves on our ultimate reward or end result, that means we don't want our dream badly enough. It might be caused by either shooting for too high of a dream (fantasy) which is not logical or we are just plain lazy. Neither is the right way to live our lives. And the worst is when we have no dream at all, then there's no purpose in our lives or reason to want to get better at anything, we will just do whatever to survive but not to thrive! Everyone should have a dream! If we haven't had one, try to think about it and then act on it by planning and preparing our best to reach our dream (again, not fantasy!).

The second popular "non-disastrous" example is just like a young couple who is looking for their very first dream house. They do all the right things like getting a pre-qualification from the bank and mortgage company for their potential loan (again, it's best if we can pay it off right away but the chances for people to be able to do so is slim to none, so at this point, logically most people will need a loan for their first home mortgage), getting a realtor, looking around and analyzing as a couple with their realtor, checking all the checklist, etc. Then they find their used dream house. They really like it but they want to think about it more. They feel that they might find a better used dream house. Finally, they come back to their first love of that dream house they found earlier. They make an offer but they're too late by 3 hours, someone else gave their offer to the house owner and the owner took the offer.

Both the "non-disastrous" situations above are real. In fact, they are from our very own experience! The first one is about my approach to my female friend in the proper way and the proper time, that was my first girlfriend which was in 1995 (and I am still married to her since 2001. ☺). Fortunately, I am the one who asked the question at the right time (pheww... it's not easy, but it's rewarding). There was another guy at her church who was pretty close to her, too, while I knew her at our university. Well, it might have been because of the fact that I could bring her to her church and had some visits with the church people, then the other guy saw us together. I didn't even know him back then, so I really didn't mean to rub it in front of him at all. Unfortunately, since he liked her, I believed he always paid attention to her and wanted to always be around her but then he was like, "Whoa!! ...wait..wait.. who is the Teddy Bear she's with tonight?" (Actually I didn't look like a Teddy bear back then, but... actually I don't look like a Teddy Bear right now, either! It's just my silly storytelling style...you can think of me as a James Bond kind of guy if you want... :), just kidding). On the other hand, he couldn't bring her to our university and had some visits with the university people hahahahaha!!! No...no... I'm just kidding, I didn't even know that he was pretty close to her until after we were officially together (my former girlfriend who is my wife now, might have been afraid to tell me at that time, she thought that I'd confront him ☺). Later I asked her if she ever had anyone close to her that might be her potential choice for being her boyfriend at the time I approached her, then she told me about this guy from church. It was also a relief for me that I asked the question at the proper time because she actually liked both of us as her close friends and was actually waiting for whoever asked first, pheeww... that was close!

And the second one is our own experience with our first dream home. We waited a little bit to think about it which usually is wise since we are not rushing into it. But at that time, we had truly done all the research, planning, and preparations, so it was time for us to make a great decision on a great opportunity. Then we decided to get the house only about one and a half days after we looked at it. Unfortunately, the house owner already took someone else's offer about 3 hours earlier from the time we proposed our offer. We were a little disappointed since we just missed our first dream house by 180 minutes. But then we remembered that God is always good and that He always works in everything in our life for our prosperity in His way and in His time, so we believe that sooner or later, we'll find the best dream house for us (which might be better than the first one). There's a saying " It'll happen if it's meant to be," that's true but we also have to plan and work hard for everything under our control, then everything beyond our control, we just give it to God, just like in The Adjustment Bureau (Matt Damon and Emily Blunt) movie. :) And we did find the best home for us about 2 weeks later and at that second time around, we didn't think for hours or days, just a few minutes since we already did all our planning and preparations, plus we already had our first time, disappointing experience in passing up the opportunity. :)

Basically we need to decide at the proper time for anything in our life. The proper time to decide in anything is when we already truly understand what we are doing, either by properly preparing ourselves or by having learned from our experience. If we don't truly understand what we are doing when we try to make a decision, it's called rushing. If we know what we are doing when we make a decision, it's called proper timing. :)

II) Children's Close Future / College Planning

UTMA/UGMA vs. Section 529 Plans vs. Coverdell's ESA

Even though there is a lot of debate whether a bachelor degree is worth the cost or not, I strongly recommend all of you to embrace and promote school/college to your children. Earlier in this book, I already explained about the three main beneficial habits which we can gain from school: a logical and systematical way of thinking, discipline, and perseverance. I believe that we always have to prepare our best for our future and others'. So, if we have children, it will be noble and great if we have the desire and ability to help them with their college, including the tuition fee. As we all know, college tuition is not cheap nowadays. It actually increases faster (6% average annual increase according to savingforcollege.com) than our average inflation (4%)! If we really are noble and great parents, we should prepare ourselves to help our children with preparing themselves for their college specifically and prepare for their close future, overall.

There is a plan/program that is not specifically for college or education but it's for our children's future overall, which can also be used for their college/education purposes, too, of course. It is called UTMA/UGMA (Uniform Transfer/Gift to Minors Act) account. An UGMA/UTMA account is basically a custodial account which means we have to hand the control over the fund to our child when they reach a certain age, usually 18 for UGMA or 21 for UTMA (depends on the legislating state). The great thing is that before then, we have total control over it just in case they don't grow like we nourished and educated them to be (just like the Batman, right? Always be prepared for the worst! ☺). We get a little tax break for the first $2,000 of income (the first $1,000 is tax free and the next $1,000 will be taxed in the child's tax bracket which is usually smaller than the parents') we make in the fund. And we have to pay full tax for the rest of the income as our income until the child reaches the qualified age, then it will all be taxed in their tax bracket. There's no income restriction to join this plan. The annual contribution limit is $14,000 ($28,000 for us and our spouse) and we have great flexibility in our investment decision. This is what our family has prepared for our two great sons, Joshua (6) and James (2). But again, just in case in the future for any reason we think that they don't deserve the money we have saved for them, we have total control over it until they reached their qualified age. We really do pray and wish that they will grow and shine the best they can as God meant them to be, so that we could gladly give them their close future's gift. :)

So, the UGMA (Uniform Gift to Minor's Act) and UTMA (Uniform Transfer to Minor's Act) are nothing more than custodial accounts which are created at a bank, brokerage firm or mutual fund company that is managed by an adult for a minor until they reach the qualified age of 18 to 21 (depending on state legislation).

Even though these UGMA/UTMA accounts aren't education specific plans, they are still considered the root of education savings accounts since they have been around way before 529 College Savings Plan and Coverdell ESA's. And parents have been successfully using these accounts to accumulate significant amounts of money for their children's college/education, too.

The latter plans are the two popular college/education specific plans: They are the 529 College Savings Plan and the Coverdell's ESA (Education Savings Account).

In the 529 College Savings Plan, we have more benefits compared to the UTMA/UGMA account as long as we use the saving plan only for higher education/college. We always have control over the fund as far as who we want to give the money to, it will grow tax free, and it'll also be tax free upon distribution (like Roth IRA for college)! If we don't use the saving plan for higher education, we'll have to pay tax for the income we make from the fund and a 10% penalty. There's no income restriction to join this plan, the total contribution limit is between $100,000 - $350,000 (depending on the legislating state) but we are more limited in our investment decisions.

The second one is the Coverdell's ESA (Education Savings Account) which we also always have control over the fund, it grows tax free, it will also be tax free upon distribution if it is used for primary, secondary or higher education. There are some income restrictions for who can join this plan (only singles with income under $95,000/year or joint income married couples with income under $190,000), with a $2,000 per year contribution limit but we have great flexibility in our investment decisions.

Why consider this UGMA/UTMA account while we have other plans/programs which are education specific with better benefits? Well, let's see the advantages and disadvantages:

First, the advantages of UGMA/UTMA accounts are:

1. We can use them for more flexible purposes, not limited only for college or education.

So it'll be a perfect scenario if our child can get a scholarship later since that means that they are bright and disciplined enough to be able to get a scholarship. It means that they really deserve the fund we have saved for them for anything else they might need, like the living expenses, extracurricular things, business, experiments, or even their later retirement.

What if they don't get a scholarship? That's still perfect (and more common, too), since they will really need it for their college/education, that's why I said "perfect" if they can get a scholarship. But please don't get caught with a bad habit that selfish people have if their child gets a scholarship later, some might say, "Hey, they already got a scholarship anyway, so I could use some of those funds (or even worse, all of those funds!!) for myself". That's messed up! But honestly, I believe that won't happen to any of us if we have been willing to save with good discipline for our child(ren)'s future. Why? Because we already set our heart on a good deed and have good discipline on it, so if someone thinks or actually does that, chances are they haven't set their heart properly and won't be disciplined enough so the fund is usually not that much of a help anyway. :)

2. We have 100% control over the fund until they reach 18 or 21 years of age (depending on the legislating state).

   So, if the worst case scenario happens (which we all hope will never happen), the child grows up as someone we really can't trust with the fund (improper behavior, rebellious, irresponsible, etc.) then we can take over the fund 100% as long as they haven't reached the qualifying age.

3. We have unlimited options on how or where to invest the fund.

4. The first $1,000 we gain from that fund will be tax free and the next $1,000 (and above, when the child has reached the qualifying age) will be taxed on our child's tax bracket which most likely will be much lower compared to the parents' tax bracket (up to the 2013 regulation).

5. It has a very high annual contribution limit, $14,000 for singles and $28,000 for a married couple. That means we could have much more investment potential to be grown beneficially.

6. There is no income limit on opening an UTMA/UGMA account. Anyone can open this account for their child(ren).

The disadvantages of UGMA/UTMA accounts are:

1. After those $2,000 income tax benefits, we have to pay at the parents' tax bracket for the rest of the income we make from the fund if the child is under 18 years (21 for UTMA) of age upon withdrawal. If the child has reached 18 (21 for UTMA) years of age, they will have to pay at their tax bracket whether they're going to college or not since it's all their money/asset now. This won't happen with the other two popular plans which are all tax free as long as the fund is used for college (529) or education (ESA). But honestly, when our children reach their qualified age to be legally entitled for the money, their tax bracket will be minimal.

2. Since this is considered the child's asset so it will affect the child's ability to get any school aid. The bigger the fund in their UGMA/UTMA account, the heavier it will count against their student's financial aid application. In my opinion, though, if parents are really committed to preparing a special account for their child(ren)'s future, I really don't think they even think about counting on financial aid. What would we choose? Getting financial aid (free money) meaning we're not in quite good shape financially or not getting any financial aid but we're in good shape financially? I personally prefer the latter option since we're in control. We don't have to count/rely on other's help whenever we can.

The advantages of 529 College Savings Plans are:
1. They will grow tax free, so all our gain from the fund will be tax free.
2. It will be tax free upon distribution as long as we use it for higher education.
3. We always have 100% control over the fund which guarantee that it will be used fitting what we think the best for our child's college/higher education.

4. We can transfer/change the beneficiary if it isn't used by the original beneficiary.
5. There is no income limit to open 529 Plan account. Anyone can open this account for their child(ren).

The disadvantages of 529 College Savings Plan are:

1. We will have to pay tax and 10% penalty if the fund is not used for the higher/college education specific. So, it won't be too good if that happens. Either we pay tax and a 10% penalty (which won't happen if we put them in UGMA/UTMA accounts or have more options in ESA, at least) or we have to change the beneficiary to someone else who we don't really intend to in the first place. In some cases, though, we might be able to request a penalty free distribution if our child(ren) get a scholarship but we still have to pay tax which will fall in the parents' tax bracket (usually higher than the child's tax bracket).
2. Very limited investment options meaning that we cannot choose more promising / potential investment available other than what they offer. That means we might get a lower increase from our fund.
3. Just in case the worst scenario happens and our children don't have the proper way of life when they grow up, we most likely have to pay the tax (in the parents' tax bracket) and 10% penalty.

The advantages of Coverdell's ESA are:

1. They will grow tax free, so all our gain from the fund will be tax free.
2. It will be tax free upon distribution as long as we use it for education specific, primary, secondary or higher education.
3. It has more options and flexibility in the investment compared to a 529 plan.
4. We always have 100% control over the fund which guarantees that it will be used on what we think is the best for our child's education.

5. We can transfer/change the beneficiary if it isn't used by the original beneficiary.

The disadvantages of Coverdell's ESA are:

1. We will have to pay tax and a 10% penalty if the fund is not used for education specific purposes. So, it won't be too beneficial if our child(ren) get a scholarship. We could either pay the tax and 10% penalty (which won't happen if we put them in a UGMA/UTMA account) or we could change the beneficiary to someone else who we don't really intend to in the first place. In some cases, though, we might be able to request the penalty free distribution but we still have to pay tax which will fall in the parents' tax bracket (usually higher than the child's tax bracket), just like in the 529.

2. Very low annual contribution limit, $2,000/year, compared to 529 with total contribution limit between $100,000 - $350,000 and UGMA/UTMA with annual contribution limit of $14,000 for singles and $28,000 for married couple.

3. It has an income restriction for who can join this plan. This plan is only available for singles with annual income under $110,000 and married couples with annual joint income under $220,000. So the wealthy cannot join this plan, they better prepare and save wisely themselves for their child(ren) :) I believe that won't be a problem at all for the wealthy if they really earned their wealth properly (since they already know and exercise everything properly so that they can be wealthy) but it's a totally different story if the wealthy get their wealth just from some luck without properly earning it. :)

4. Just like in the 529 plan if the worst scenario happens, our child(ren) don't have the proper way of life when they grow up, we most likely have to pay the tax (in the parents' tax bracket) and 10% penalty.

Some of us might say," But Andy, what if any of us don't want to invest for our children's future even though we have children?" or "My parents never did that for us, why should we?" It's all up to you but I personally suggest doing so since it will show our: 1) pure love for our children and 2) character as human being. How so?

1. To show our true love to our children: Remember that love means joyful sacrifices? And remember that we really shouldn't just think only about ourselves but also about others? So supposedly, our children are much more than just "others", they are our children! Our fruits of love, our legacy! We are defined by what we do, not by what our positions are. For example: if I am an alcoholic (which I am not, this is just an example ☺), what will being a father turn me into? An alcoholic father!! Except if I commit to change what I do! Again, we are defined by what we do, not by who we are officially (this quote was even used by Katie Holmes to Christian Bale in the "Batman Begins" movie ☺). So if we really love our children, we really should be joyful in sacrificing our time, energy and money for something useful for them. The more time, energy and money we spend on someone or something, the more it truly shows how much we love that particular someone or something.

2. To show our character: If you have been reading the book this far in the right order, you would know by now that I don't compare what we can do to what others (including family) have done to us. We're not that shallow, just like in any of the great movies, sometimes the good guys are tempted to just kill the bad guy and then a true friend of the good guy will remind them not to do so since that will just bring the good guy to the same level as the bad guy (which is bad!). Others or people around us might have done bad things to us. But when we start comparing ourselves to them like that, we tend to wonder why we bother being a better man or woman, right? I totally understand that, but again, be the better person! Be the bigger person! Be the best we can! Why do we want to follow the footsteps of ones that we don't respect or appreciate that much anyway, right? Just like in the

X-Men movies, if we always want to do to others what others have done to us (at least that's how we feel), then all of us will be the Magneto character, hateful & revengeful! Trying to even up the score all the time! Be like Charles Xavier in the X-Men movies, not Magneto. Even though Magneto sometimes has a good point to some extent, overall, Xavier is the noble one. Even though Xavier has the power to do otherwise, he chooses not to, he always chooses the best for everyone, not only for himself or his kind (I know, I may love X-Men stories too much!! But hey, they really have a great message, though. ☺). So we always can do better for our children than what our parents did for us, if our parents never did that for us. Every hero starts from zero, not every great parent had great parents of their own. Sometimes they just have to realize not to follow what their parents did to them and decide to be better parents for their own children. What if we already have great parents? That's even better! It should make it easier for us to see and follow how to be great parents since we have experienced it themselves. :)

So yes, I strongly suggest all of us to invest for our children's close future/education (after we have invested in our retirement, of course, remember that a blind guy can't lead another blind guy. ☺) except if it's way too late (not enough time) to start our mutual fund investment to grow as needed or how we want it to be. If that's the case, still save for our children, just not in mutual funds, start saving in the lower risk account(s) such CD, money market, or even a checking account (make sure to shop around for the best rate with the least cost first, of course). And always be as loving and nourishing as possible in every aspect of our lives (time, energy and treasure) while we can.

Actually, if we plan properly for our retirement, we will be able to live out of our interest only, while the big lump sum of our principal money will still have a big chance to support, or even alter our children's life and condition. So why bother with all this stuff I mentioned above just now? That's why I call them our children's close future/education. The problem of thinking that our inheritance for our children is going to be enough is the timing. Our child(ren) will only get their inheritance when we pass away. If nothing unusual happens, we will pass away in our old age. By that time, our children will most likely be an adult already; their way of thinking and lifestyle will already be molded in their character. It's harder for them to change their way of thinking since it's already rooted in their life that far (especially if they have an improper one). If we prepare for their close future when they grow up from a child to a young adult, that timing is the best for them to learn, grow, discover, analyze and thus, it will mold their way of thinking properly for the rest of their life. Many psychological researches have proved that most (not all) adults' way of thinking will reflect how they have been inspired, taught, prepared and supported while they were growing up toward adulthood. Actually this is common sense. I believe that the research is just to confirm this common sense. The younger we are, the easier for us to learn something since we're still like a pretty clean and soft sponge. The older we are, the harder for us to learn something new (even if it's for our own good). Just like an old sponge which has been used so many times and it's getting really dirty and hard, it will be really hard for the sponge to absorb anything by that time. :)

So, do we have to sacrifice more (work harder and smarter, spend less, save more, etc., basically think less about ourselves) to prepare for our children's close future (after preparing for our own retirement, of course!) even though we might still leave a big inheritance for our children? Yes! The key word is "might" in the sentence above. If we all plan our retirement properly, we should only live (roughly) on our interest so that we don't have to worry about how long we'll live later in our retirement. But remember that when we are older, we are more vulnerable to any kind of health problem, from diabetes, cholesterol, heart problems, uric acid, kidney failure (all kinds of health problems that are mostly caused by an unhealthy diet or inactive life) to joint problems, bone problems, nerve problems (all kinds of health problems caused by aging, especially for active athletes with multiple previous injuries). I don't say that we will get all those kinds of health problem when we are older. I just say that we are more vulnerable to them. It all depends on how we live our lives (most of the time, sometimes it's just God's way to make us stronger and wiser, just like in Job's story in The Bible). So, just in case we get any of those health problems, we might use our retirement money more than we expected. We might use more than only our interest. Thus, we might not leave as big of an inheritance to our children, if any. So while we can, let's prepare our children's nourishment and education our best. Again, this only can be done after we have already prepared our own retirement. We wouldn't (or shouldn't) be able to help our children as needed if we can't help ourselves. It's like any airplane flight's emergency procedure, always put on your own oxygen mask first then help others.

I personally believe that the above plan is the best for our family. We do what we believe and we are really happy (actually joyful, but happy will rhyme better ☺), healthy, and (about to be) wealthy.

And also, we are so blessed that we realized and made that decision at our relatively young age (31). It doesn't matter when (how old) we realize or make the decision and commitment to do all that above, it's the intention and commitments themselves which matters. The action itself is the most important thing! If we know about it and make a commitment later in our life, that's great, it's better be late than never. If we know about it and make a commitment early in our life, that's even better! But even if we start realizing it late, it means that we already enjoyed our "retirement" early. ☺ It's a privilege to have the chance to be our best and our best for others, especially our loved ones. So let's get started being our best! Let us be great and noble so that we can influence others, too, at least our own children. When to start? Literally as soon as possible while we have the chance, so no regret at all later. What a beautiful life and world we will have if everybody is their best and does their best for others, yayyy!!!!

Just in case, the last, worst scenario happens. Let's say that our children were doing fine, they grow up properly under our true and proper loving way in their nourishment and education. But unfortunately, when they are adults (after using all their close future/college saving that we've prepared) they started to behave inappropriately (which is very tiny chance if we have done everything properly while they grow up, that's why it's the last, worst scenario). Well, if we have tried our best in our prayers and efforts but still can't change them to be better (I am truly sorry if this ever happens to any of us, I really hope not), then we have a lot more money for our retirement. We can do a lot more than we can dream of (for ourselves or others who we think deserve the money most) since we'll have the interest plus the much bigger principal. But again, this is really the worst scenario, though. I believe every parent in their right mind will never wish this to ever happen.

III) Business / Fun

Now that we are done understanding and investing for our retirement and also for our children's future (if we have any children), we can start thinking about our own close future's planning, either for business or fun. Most people I know usually save for a few months/years for their dream vacation, home, car, etc. A few of them save for a few years for their principal to open their own business or new line of work, but the most common reason I hear is for their dream vacation. It's good either way because that means that we are planning for our particular goal in our lives. Just make sure we do first things first. The ideal priority order as I go through with you in this book is: have an emergency fund of at least $4,000, pay off our debts, have a reasonable home (if we don't plan to move around soon), start our retirement saving, start saving for our children's close future, pay off our home mortgage, finally harvesting and sharing time. I'm not saying that we shouldn't have a vacation or fun at all before we have done all the ideal priorities above. No! We should live, too! We should make money and make memories. That's awesome!! But if we keep going on vacation every 6 months while we have $8,000 in debt that is very wrong! If we have a brand new car while we can't pay one of our family's medical bill that is totally not cool! Having a nice BMW car while we only can afford to rent an apartment in a not-too-safe area is very not smart! You know what I mean. Basically be responsible and be an adult! Be Bruce Wayne (Batman) who always prepares for everything and the worst. Be Clark Kent (Superman) who even though he has the power to do anything, uses them wisely for others' need and future, too. Be Charles Xavier who used to have a close ally and friend who had a tempting yet wrong way of using his power and ability, but still chose to be the noble mediator. Be like mother Theresa, be like Abraham Lincoln, be like Walt Disney, be like Dave Ramsey (if you don't know who they are, please Google them ☺). You know what I mean. We should have a balance between making money (our need, our obligation) and making memories (our want, our right). If it's not in balance, our heart, mind, and soul will be unbalanced, too. While we have been preparing all those ideal priorities in our life, we also have enjoyed family vacations to Disney Land (California), Disney World (Florida), Universal Studios (California and Florida), Las Vegas, The Grand Canyon, Yosemite Park, The Great Wolf Lodge and other places, too, for our family vacation. So if we can do it in the proper balance with our average income, then you all should be able to do it with your income! Be like me! :) Hahaha...!!

There are two ways to do that saving for a few years:

1. Save in a checking or savings account in which the end result of our few years of saving will be almost as great as how much we put into it during that few years since we won't have too great of a rate of return, but it's a guaranteed amount since it's usually guaranteed by

the FDIC and also has a good liquidity (we can put in or take out anytime we want)

2. Save into a mutual fund account which will be more risky since they're not guaranteed by the FDIC and have less liquidity in the withdrawal but if we are fortunate enough and are doing our research thoroughly, we might be able to ride the glory years with a way higher rate of return (that will multiply our saving's value).

Those two ways have their own positive and negative sides. How to choose them wisely is usually based on how flexible we are with the schedule of our plan. If our particular plan (either for business or fun) for the next few years could be moved around pretty easily without hurting anyone or causing any major damage, then we really should go with saving in a mutual fund account. But if our particular plan's schedule for the next few years is already set and have to be done in that particular set time to avoid hurting anyone or making any major damage, then we should go with saving in a less risky account.

For example: Let's say I want to plan a dream family vacation. Well, actually for our family, every family vacation is a dream family vacation! If it's not a dream vacation, why should we even bother spending our time, energy, and money just to do it? Remember the wise saying that I talked about earlier in the book? "If something is worth doing, it's worth doing well!" Some of us might say that a non-dream vacation is still better than no vacation at all, so might as well make that non-dream vacation become our dream vacation then or just be an adult and wait until we really can achieve our dream vacation! So let me rephrase it from "dream family vacation" to "luxurious/costly/expensive family vacation," that's why we need to save up some money in the next few years, right? :)

Okay, back to the example. Let's say our family's luxurious/expensive vacation will cost us about $17,000 and we plan to do it in the next 5 years! I know what you want to ask," Wait...wait...Andy, do you really spend that much money for a luxurious family vacation?" Nah, we only do that once in every ten years on average, so actually it'll cost us about $1,700 per year for our family of four. That's why we call it luxurious/costly/expensive, right? :) For some families (or worst, most families ☹), that's worth only a few months of their "everybody has it" and "it's not bad for what we pay." :) Seriously though, just keep all the records of our spending and then check the complete statement for all your credit cards, debit cards, checkbooks, cash usage. You'll see how much you spend per month for your primary needs (real necessities to survive or need to have), for your secondary needs (good to have) and tertiary needs (luxury or fun/comfortable to have). And since people rarely keep track of their spending, trust me, most of them will be shocked to see how much they spend for their secondary and tertiary needs. Basically they spoil themselves too much!

Anyway, even though our schedule to achieve that goal is in the next five years, if I know for sure that I wouldn't hurt anyone (my wife, my children, my other family or friends whom we might have promised to go on our luxurious/expensive vacation together, etc.) by moving it either earlier or later, then let's put our few years savings into a mutual fund account. Why? Because a mutual fund is not guaranteed by the FDIC or any other company, so our close future investment's chance to lose or gain money depends on how the market performs when we put in and take out our investment.

Basically, we want to put more money into our mutual fund account when the market is down, which means some companies' share price is going to be cheaper, just like the scenario when we buy the very same quality stuff but on sale!! The worse the market, the cheaper (bigger sale) some companies' share is going to be. On the other hand, we want to take out the money from our mutual fund account when the market is up, so some companies' share price that we already have will be sold at a higher price, aha!! :)

If we really do our homework, we will choose at least the pretty decent mutual fund company and they usually will have the good, strong or well-known company under their mutual fund portfolio choices. So when any of them are facing a pretty rough time, they will rebound back stronger and strive for the long term. When any of them really are facing a bankruptcy, other solid and strong companies (might be as well-known or not) will buy them because they can use their image or brand that might already be patented in the customer's mind and beliefs. And remember, this is for our close future investment only (which is less than ten years).

With the reasoning above, I strongly suggest always putting some money in when any decent performing mutual funds' share price is down which means they are on sale. They won't really affect our middle/long term goal since they'll either bounce back strong or end up being bought by another decent company (which is stronger at that time) later on.

Of course, on the other hand, we always want to take out our investment while the decent performing mutual funds' share price is up so we can get some extra advantages.

Chapter III : The Simply Great Strategy

This strategy is a tribute to Dave Ramsey's Baby Steps in his Financial Peace University program, combined with our own success strategy from our beliefs and original culture. Yayy!!

Why did I put all these steps here, at the end of the book?

If I put them at the beginning of the book, most people will just try to read this part about the steps and then won't even finish the motivations and explanations in the rest of the book which is much more important. Actually those are the most important part of the book!! The inspiration by our own real life experience, the understanding through the step by step private tutorial style, the clarification of our proper way of thinking, the facts around us, the analogies (examples) of our financial conditions through movies, sports, games, etc., all those will drive our emotions and logic to a higher understanding so that we are motivated and able to decide what's best for ourselves and be at peace with the consequences in our lives later.

When we have already read, understood and agree with all the points of view and principals in this book, then we are ready to take the practical steps as our summary, just like building our house on a strong foundation. If we read these steps at the beginning and do just that without following up with deeper understanding and agreeing with all the points of view and principals, most likely we will quit or fail sooner or later because our foundation is not proper/strong.

If we really want to change our lifestyle, we always have to change our hearts and ways of thinking first, then we can change the way we do things. When we keep repeating the new way of thinking and acting, it'll become a new habit. From then on, it will start rolling smoother and before we know it, we already have a new lifestyle.

Always build a strong foundation, a strong start. It's like when we push a van by ourselves, we think that it'll be really hard. In fact, we just need to believe that we can do it with all our might and effort. It'll be a little hard at the beginning, but once we keep focusing our might and effort toward it, it'll move. Once it starts moving, it'll be a lot easier to push since we already started the momentum. This is based on my real life story when a lady needed help with her van which suddenly went dead on a sloping road. I first looked around to find someone else to help me with that but since there was nobody at that time, I thought it would be almost impossible but actually it's not that bad when I focused all my might and effort into it. Honestly, I myself couldn't believe that I did it! :)

As I mentioned earlier in this book, human beings only believe what they want to believe. That principle applies to every aspect of our life, like our favorite college football team, our spouse, our working place, our political party, our religion, etc. Once someone believes in something, it's almost impossible for somebody else to change that person's belief, except if that someone opens up his heart and mind, if not, the chance will be slim to nothing. If any of you don't believe it, go ahead and try to convince someone else who already believes in something, to change his/her belief. And ......good luck!

Again, our lifestyle is highly affected by our habits, our habits are highly affected by what we do, and what we do is highly affected by how we feel and think, what we believe is good, right, effective, efficient, powerful, fun, etc., you name it. So get as much knowledge as possible and then decide which path we want to choose to commit ourselves to. If we choose the right one the first time, we will succeed faster compared to if we chose the wrong decision and try to fix it. And it'll be worse if we keep choosing the wrong decision and keep trying to fix it. So, gain all the knowledge we can and then think (and pray) seriously before we decide.

About reading this book, from all the people who read this

book, let's say only about 85% really understand what this book is all about. From all who already understand this book, maybe only 50% agree with the idea (yes, understanding doesn't necessarily mean agreeing). From all who agree with the understanding they got from this book, maybe only 25% who commit themselves to apply it in their life. From all who commit, what percentage will really finish (not quit because of whatever reason might come up later) what they commit to in the beginning? So if the reading part is not done properly, what are the chances they really achieve what they long for in their future? So please read this book in chronological order, if any of us decided to just jump to this section of the book or by accident flipped to this section, please go back to the first page and begin reading it in the chronological order I intended. Sorry, no shortcuts, guys and girls. You are only allowed to skip around this book when you have already read it from cover to cover. :) If you keep skipping around, this will be just another finance book. You won't get the maximum potential you can get from the book. Trust me!

Now last but not least, the simply great strategy is here.

The simply great strategy for preparing or fixing our financial conditions is:

1) **Build a Real Emergency Fund: $5,000 (Depends on Our Comfort Level But at Least $5,000 For Year 2013)**

    We seriously have to build this real emergency fund ASAP (as soon as possible). Work smarter/harder and/or spend less in the next few months, not years! If we can't save $4,000 in years, I personally don't think you are serious enough. Might as well quit and leave this serious matter for ones who are serious about it. :) This real emergency fund is only for real emergencies such as: things that may hurt us worse physically (not spiritually or emotionally since both of them are very relative for each person so we can't use them as our measurement) or may make us lose our life or someone's we really care about (significant other, direct family, a true best friend). Our real emergency fund is not for a "to-die-for" outfit, dress, accessories, new restaurant, show, etc. If you want to use your real emergency fund for all that stuff, you'll have to build a luxurious "need" fund or fancy fund or whatever you want to name it as long as you have fully funded your real emergency fund and paid all your debts of any kind. We always need to have some fun, but we need to do it properly and within our means. We always need to do first things first, important things first, things we need to do first then things we want to do. Always do our obligations first then we can demand our rights, work hard first so that we can earn our rewards, right? Right!!

Why do we need to build our real emergency fund?

First, so that we will be ready when any real emergency happens. We shouldn't wait and/or rely on others' help, grace, favor or pity when it comes to our emergency need(s), except on God. Others have their own real emergency need(s), too.

Second, so that we won't have to borrow (more) money from a bank, loan shark, etc. and being in (more) debt whenever a real emergency happens in our life.

$5,000 is my own personal standard for our family's emergency fund from 2002. The bigger the better but it's all up to our own honest comfort level. I said honest which means no one can say," Oh, I only need $200 for my real emergency fund, so I'm done with this step, what's next?" That's just delusional or plain lazy but yet they want to rush their way up. They will misrepresent our principals greatly! Honest means honestly think about how much we need to feel comfortable just in case anything really bad happens. It all depends on what we do for a living, our lifestyle so far, how many people are depending on us, how deep our love is for others who depend on us, how much we care about planning, etc. If we plan to build our emergency fund in the next few months (or better, weeks ☺), we will start our new habit which is working smarter/harder and/or spending less! That new habit in the next few weeks/months will make us taste our very first success/accomplishment over our very own financials by successfully building our own real emergency fund.

Some might build their real emergency fund in a few weeks. That means that they really put in their focus and effort, so that they can do it in a pretty fast time. Meanwhile, others might build their real emergency fund in a few months. They have the advantage of having more perseverance than the ones who do it in a few weeks. Both groups, the faster (only needing a few weeks) and the slower (might need a few months) have their own advantages. But again, slower here doesn't include the ones who need years to build their real emergency fund, that's just plain lazy or not serious at all. If anyone with their best focus and effort couldn't save $5,000 in a few years, they might have a special condition or limitations. And if they have one, God is so fair and kind that He usually sends other compassionate people or organizations to help these people. But if we are healthy and do not lack in anything, there no reason for us to not being able to do so I'm sorry if I'm kinda strict in this case but that's true, though, and I come with a pure good intention to make all of us better. ☺

2) Make Current Budget Positive (Eliminate All Debts Except Mortgages)

After we have our real emergency fund built in our own honest comfort level, now we need to make an honest assessment of all our savings and debts of any kind to make a proper budgeting sheet/plan.

We have to subtract all the debts we have in any kind from all our real savings we have.

Debts of any kind will include but are not limited to: any kind of credit card, any kind of loan (including school), any kind of payment except your home mortgage (automobiles, any technology or entertainment system, etc.), any kind of debt (if we ever owe to anybody else, which we really shouldn't), etc. Our real savings means any kind of savings we have, including but not limited to: Checking accounts, saving accounts, money market accounts, CDs, retirement accounts (401ks, Roth IRAs, IRAs, non-qualified/regular mutual fund accounts), stocks, bonds, etc.

When our debt total is bigger than our savings total, it will make the previous subtraction formula have a minus/negative total. That's really bad, that means we live beyond our means, are not wise in managing our money, don't have self-control, etc. It might seem harsh but it's the truth. We should be able to live within our means, only spend part of what we make and save the rest, and control ourselves to mostly get what we need not what we want.

We always have to try to pay off the debt with the smallest amount in it first, not the one with the highest interest rate. So, let's say we have three kinds of debt. On the first one, we owe $1,000 with a 15% interest rate, on the second one, we owe $5,000 with a 27% interest rate, on the third one, we owe $8,000 with a 25% interest rate. We should always try to pay off the first one first, the $1,000, even though it has a smaller interest rate (15%), then the second one, the $5,000 with a 27% interest rate and then the third one, the $8,000 with a 25% interest rate.

Some people might say that we should try to pay off our debt with the highest interest rate first since we will pay more interest. Well…. if we are that smart in math, we won't be in debt in the first place ☺ (quote from Dave Ramsey). I personally agree with Dave Ramsey, always pay the smallest amount of debt first, and don't worry about the interest rate. With the exception of having two with about the same amount of debt, then of course I really want you to pay the one with the highest interest, first. If we have more than one debt and they vary in the amount, always try to pay off the smallest amount first, and then keep going to the bigger one gradually. Why?

This credit card scenario is actually similar to many of our real life situations. It's like playing video games, we got to fight the easier opponents first before we get to fight the tougher ones. It keeps building up like that so that finally we are good enough to fight the toughest opponent. It's also like our school or college, we have to do some homework, papers, quizzes, etc., on a gradually increasing level in quality and/or quantity, and then we have to have our finals which is like the ultimate quality test. It's also like in any sport competition, we should battle/race/compete against about the same level competitor in the beginning, then if we keep building our position to rank high enough, we will get the chance to go the finals or compete for the championship and win. And I believe that there are a lot more analogies you can think of. All of them have the same rule, if we pass the smaller challenge/test/goal, then we can move on to the bigger one. If we skip to the toughest/hardest one right away, we will surely fail and get frustrated because we are not trained or prepared well enough for that! We are not ready yet, that's why we have to keep practicing, warrior! :)

So always try to pay our dues starting from the easiest level first and then gradually advance to the harder ones and at last, we will be ready to knock off our ultimate opponent. By the time we face our ultimate opponent (the biggest amount of debt to pay), we are already pretty well trained and prepared if we keep winning/successfully paying off all our smaller debts so far. In addition, we also already gained momentum and confidence if we do it this way. If we are disciplined enough to be able to knock all the previous opponents (smaller amount of debt) then we are surely ready to face the ultimate opponent (the biggest amount debt!!) and win (pay off every single debt we have, by sticking to the game plan). Yayyy!!

Whenever we focus on paying off our debts one at a time, we also still have to pay the minimum amount on the other debts we have, to avoid any more penalties, fees, or any further worse scenarios. We always have to be responsible for what we've done in the past. If we always live within our means and save, we will never be in debt. If we live beyond our means and can't control our desire to want something as soon as possible, etc., then we will usually be in debt. So we already had our fun while we lived beyond our means, right? Then there will be a time to pay the dues. I know it sounds bad, but we can do it! We can come back to our old school way of life, be a good manager of our own finances and be a champion of our own life!

What if we haven't had fun even though we are in debt (living beyond our means)? Well...... why did we even bother doing stuff we didn't really enjoy and still get ourselves in trouble then? Why did we even live beyond our means and still not have fun? Being in debt and still not having fun? That's just the most childish excuse! It's like we know it's not fun to get burned by a fire but we still try to burn ourselves (doing things we don't really enjoy) and then complaining later about how we have to deal with the burn wound and all the bills that come with it! Duh??!! Or someone who knows that falling from a high places will hurt but still tries to jump off a two story building's roof to make a YouTube video sensation without any proper preparation (like a special mattress) or exercise (learning Parkour/Free Running), then whining about how to deal with the injury, the medical bills caused by the injury and how they couldn't work and make any income...... Duuuhhh??!!

3) Have a Cushion Savings at Least 4 Months' Worth of Our Living Expenses

After we have built and maintained our real emergency fund, have paid off all debts (except for our home mortgage), now we still need to save at least 4 months' worth of our living expenses.

Why? The reason is just in case we get unemployed and have no income at all. Since our emergency fund is only for a real emergency (a once in a while thing), how do we live our lives (routine things)? Get a loan or credit card? (If this idea still crosses your mind now, I'm so sorry and I truly wish you the best in the future) No!!! C'mon, really?? No!! We should never be in debt! Especially when we have no income! It's just like trying to make a deal when we have nothing, no bargaining power at all. If we owe something to another person while we have nothing to pay, we are the slave of that particular person. Except if we are planning not to pay them (which I am really against). If we borrow something, we better treat that thing we borrowed properly and return it properly, too. If we can't do that, then don't ever borrow anything from anybody. You are not ready to borrow anything! So we always need to have savings at least worth 4 months of our living expenses just in case we ever become unemployed at any time in our life.

Now, why do I suggest at least 4 months' worth of our living expenses? Why not 1-3 months? I said at least 4 months just in case we can't find a job in the first few months after we are unemployed. The bigger the savings, the better, it means we have more money available just in case we still can't find any job for a longer period of time (which I really hope doesn't happen!). And that doesn't mean that we have to use all (almost all) of our savings before we start to work again. We can work as soon as we get a job and we can use the rest of our savings (worth 4 months of our living expenses) for the same purpose just in case we become unemployed again in the future (which I hope doesn't happen but it's always better to be safe than sorry ☺).

I understand that when we become unemployed, we usually get a little (or a lot) shocked, depressed, maybe a little hopeless, feel broken, etc. Some people might take longer than others to get out of that shocked mode. We usually also have post-power syndrome if we can't find the same level job or position. Even though we are strong enough to get over our shocked mode quickly and are ready to work in any position/company, we also might still want a little break before we start working another job. I personally don't like being idle, especially if it's too long. Being idle for too long will spoil us: corrode our minds, emotions, physique, and skills. That's why I prefer to be idle about 4 months maximum, in order to get another job and start working again. I'll get whatever the best job available is at that time even though it might not be my dream job or a profession that I went to school for, but remember, it's better be working in any company than not working at all!

Never be idle for too long!! At some point in time in our life, we might be idle but do not stay idle for too long, we got to snap back into the game, guys and girls! Just like in any sport, football, basketball, baseball, tennis, any racing sport (of course ☺), in any martial arts or contact sports, all of the sports we know and even in chess (even though we might think that there seems to be a lot of idleness, they actually keep thinking way more than we, the non-chess players, do). So being idle for too long is never good in any way in any sport!! Can we imagine a wrestler or MMA fighter being idle?? A football player being idle? Even if we can't imagine them being idle, we know what's going to happen next, they are beaten, defeated, left behind, etc. That concept applies in our life, too, actually! There are some wise sayings like: "An idle mind is the devil's workshop," "Just as iron rusts from disuse, even so does inaction spoil the intellect." In my own words, "Not every change is for the better, but to be better, we definitely need to change!"

Don't be idle for too long! We'll either get left behind or get spoiled if we do so!

We experienced that first hand! My wife and I are both are engineers (graduated from Indonesia). When we came here, we couldn't do much with our former country's degree, we could transfer only about 22% of all our graduated classes and had to go to school again (needed more money). At that time, US $1 = INA Rp.10,000! So no way we're going to spend money like that when we just arrived here. We just wanted to work as hard as possible and save some money first. We planned to never be in debt and to keep improving our lifestyle. If we're stagnant, never increase our income, can't catch up with our average inflation rate, then we have to change our plan. We might have to go to school again, take extra courses/training to keep us updated, find another job more rewarding for our abilities, or just open our own business. As long as we can keep improving our overall life quality, we are fine with it. We will always work hard and smart. So, we didn't wait until we found an engineering job. We just worked our best at any place we could. We have worked at fast food restaurants, in retail, a martial arts school, golf club, at a vending machine company, and at a middle class restaurant during our first 4 years in the US. Mostly we each had two jobs at a time. It seems like a lot of jobs in such a short period of time, but actually it wasn't that bad, since we didn't dwell in jobs/companies that didn't suit us even though we tried our best. We were always loyal to jobs/companies that appreciated and rewarded us as long as we tried our best to contribute to their success. We prefered not to keep changing jobs if we didn't have to. I know some people who keep changing jobs consistently until I think that it's their passion/hobby to change jobs, finding new things to do or be in a new environment. :) But I personally don't prefer to keep changing jobs except when we have to. I don't mind trying out other jobs as long as we keep and do our best in our current job. Why? Just in case the other job(s) that we try don't work out well with us, we still have our primary income from our current job.

Anyway, my personal preference of maximum time for being idle is 4 months. I will tell you the reason which might be harsh but it's the truth which will wake us up and actually inspire us (at least that's what I hope ☺). If we can't find any jobs in 4 months (or approximately 17.3 weeks or 122 days or 1/3 of a year!!) that means either the job market that we want is really bad or we are not as good as we think we are. That's simple, right? If we are truly honest with ourselves, those are the only two answers, which means we really shouldn't be too picky about where to work.

If the job market that we want is really that bad or we are not as good as we think we are, then just get the best job available for us at that time. Work our best at our current job while keeping our eyes peeled for opportunities in the job market we really want. By doing so, we can support our own living expenses, especially if we have a family or someone that really depends on us. We better do something rather than doing nothing at all to support our own and our family's lives!! Some people say that the right time will come for them to get their dream job while living on government welfare or unemployment support or food stamps, etc. But trust me, continuing to wait for the right job or the right moment or our destiny, etc. just won't cut it! All those are just excuses they make to cover up their pride or laziness or the fact that they live in fantasy (are delusional), or even worse, a combination of all of them! Any of those three scenarios is bad, being too proud, being too lazy or being delusional, especially when you live on someone else's account or government support.

Actually, the government support also means every citizen's support (account), too! How so? When we all have our healthy minds and bodies set to work hard with integrity and take pride in working with our very own hands, we all pay tax and some part of that tax money will distributed to help/support any citizen in need.

Unfortunately, not everyone who gets our government support really deserves to get it. Some of them are just being lazy or too proud, and some are just delusional. Some are really in need. People who don't agree with my opinion are usually the ones who are taking advantage of that silly system, too, directly or indirectly, in the past, present or near future, or the ones that really believe that our country, The United States of America, really has that many people incapable of working. I honestly don't believe that our great country has that many people who really are incapable of working with their own two hands. They might have one or two disadvantages compared to others in their capabilities but I don't believe that they really can't work at all with their God given body, mind, heart and soul. Basically, if someone doesn't really deserve the government support but is still getting it, it is actually like they are reaching their hands into our wallet and taking some small amount of it without our permission. They get their permission from the government who gives out that support without carefully reviewing them!

So people who are being too picky to work and are still saying that they can't find a job, that's just plain wrong! It's pride, laziness, or craziness (or all of them!!) There are tons of "hiring" signs everywhere, like fast food restaurants, full service restaurants, retail, gas stations, banks, grocery stores, toy stores, video stores, electronic stores, any rental company (auto, apartment, furniture, etc.) to any office job position, data entry, book keeping, etc. The jobs are greatly available, the opportunities are out there, and it's whether we really want to work or just saying that we want to work. There is no such thing as a dead end job, there are just dead end people who always complain, always overvalue themselves, always think that they deserve better, but all they do is whine and complain. People like that always think that their employer is unfair and crooked; they think that so many things are so wrong and nobody does anything about it, while they themselves don't want to act. So again, too much pride or laziness or craziness plus the attitude problem such as whining without acting (NATO ☺) are sure signs of dead end people. Please, don't fall to this group of people.

Some people even dare to say that they're waiting for God to open the door for them. Really??! Here is a funny story about this waiting-for-God excuse:

A guy was about to drown in the ocean, so he prayed to God for help. A small fisherman boat approached, but he refused the help offered by the fisherman, saying," No, thank you, I already asked God for help." Then a motorboat came by and they offered to help him, but again he refused their help saying," No, thank you, I already asked God for help." Then a big ship came by and they offered their help (you might already know his answer, yup!), but for the third time he refused their help with the same answer. Sure enough, this "strong faith" guy died soon after the last ship passed by. When he met God upstairs, this guy asked God," God, I prayed and cried out to You for help and I've been faithful waiting for Your help, not others. But why didn't You help or save me?" God answered," I've tried to help you three times but you kept refusing every one of them, foolish guy!"

The lesson is that we should not abuse our faith in God. God gave us a heart, mind (brain) and soul, hands, feet and every other part of our body for a reason, to be used for many purposes. If we only needed faith, then He wouldn't even give us all the other tools, right? We would be shaped just like Pac Man (not the former great boxing champion and Philippine's former vice president, Manny Pacquaio's nickname, "The PacMan" but the old Nintendo game's Pac Man that shaped like a ball with only eye and mouth ☺) we wouldn't need many of our body parts, just roll in faith, right? No! God equipped us with hearts, minds, souls, and bodies to be used. He created all those for a purpose. Just like any creator, they always create something for a purpose. If not then why even bother creating it at all? Especially our God,

He always has the greatest purpose in everything He creates and lets happen.

Some people even use a Bible quote that says we shouldn't worry since our Father in Heaven (God) always take care the birds in the sky, the lilies in the valley, even though they don't have to work, etc. I tell them that it is very true! We shouldn't be too worried because the more worried we are shows how little faith we have. But the Bible never mentioned that Jesus told them not to work, either! He only taught them not to worry but He never taught us not to work! We still can work our best and not worry, actually that's what He wants all of us to do! Keep working and don't worry! That's the best scenario we can have! It's a great balance between logic and faith: we show our faith by not worrying too much about things in our life that are beyond our control and we also show our logic by using all the healthy parts of our body for good use, including working.

What about continuing to work but still always worrying? That's kind of bad since it means that we only use our own logic and power, but not our faith. If we rely only (mostly) on our own logic and power, we will get burnt out sooner or later. Trust me, there are many things that are beyond our control. There is a higher power in life and I truly believe it is God. For people who don't believe in God but in the evolution theory, here is something to think about: Do they really believe that they came from apes descendants? If they really believe so, shouldn't they be more comfortable drinking an ape's milk than a cow's milk then? Okay, back to our main topic, the best plan is to always work and not to worry. To keep worrying while we work is not good since we will get burnt out sooner or later. What about not working and continuing to worry? That makes sense. :) And we better do something about it! And last, not working yet not worrying either, that's as bad as the other three, since that means we only have faith and abuse it since we don't use our logic that God also gave to us. We take our faith in Him for granted. We always need balance in our life. So the best thing is to keep working and not worry.

Basically, on top of our real emergency fund, I suggest to have savings worth at least 4 months of our living cost just in case we can't find any jobs in those 4 months if we ever become unemployed. If we want to give ourselves more cushion, that's even better because that means that we really care (because we prepare for the worst scenario) and humble (because even though we're good, we know that we are still vulnerable of being unemployed). And the more we have a cushion saving, it shows how we've gotten to the habit of being well-prepared and humble. And those are two of the greatest characteristics in human life. The great news is that usually people like that will still work as soon as possible when they get unemployed (if ever) even though they have already prepared a decent cushion saving because they already have their mind ingrained with the proper lifestyle (well-prepared and humble). :)

4) Buy a House (If We Are Still Renting and Not Planning to Move in the Next Few Years)

Some people prefer renting to buying a house. I already explained the pros and cons of renting and buying a place to live. I always suggest to people who ask me about buying a property rather than renting it, as long as we fulfill some criteria, especially about how long we plan to live in the same particular area. The longer the time span we plan to live in the same area, the stronger I suggest to buy. Why? If we plan to live in the same area only for a short period of time, it's not worth doing all the proper steps needed for buying a property to live in, such as doing some research about the area, the prospect of the market price, school area, mortgage companies or banks, realtors, property inspectors, termite inspectors and the house itself. All those can't be properly done overnight. It takes time and it depends on how much time we put into it. In our personal experience, we spent about 16 hours doing all the research and shopping around. It took us only about two months (started in December 2004 and we closed on the house in February 2005). And the 24 hours were not necessarily spread out evenly, like 12 hours a month, 3 hours a week, it's just a total of 24 hours during those two months.

Our priority order is always like this: God first (have personal time with God, serve at a Bible-believing and God-loving church), then family (spend time together for both obligation and fun), then obligation (which are mostly work and doing things around our lives, such as chores, etc.), then the last one is our hobbies (something fun we want to do). We live our lives with that priority order properly and responsibly, of course. We can't be great at the first two priorities (God and family) if we don't do our third priority: obligation in order to live our life! How can we say we love our God if we don't show respect at all by not using all the talents and gifts He has given us to make a living? How can we say that we love our family if we don't do our best to prepare the best life for them? That's called lying or delusional! We always think about God and our family so that when we are at work, we have the positive energy and mindset. That's what it really means. But it doesn't mean that we work very well and be successful and never really prepare time for God or our family, that's very materialistic! So apply our priority order properly and responsibly!

During the time we were looking for our first dream home, we always followed our priority order. Our first priority is always God. We always make time to get to know Him more everyday by reading, watching, listening, and discussing. Our second priority, family, was only the two of us since we hadn't had any children at that time, so we had a lot more time and energy on our hands. :) But honestly, we are truly glad to spend time, energy, and money with our lovely children now, it was actually our plan to have bought a house first before we had our children so when they were born, they would already have a place called home. And God is great because in 2006, our first son, Joshua, was born! Our third priority was the obligation to make a proper living, which is work in our case. We always worked hard and were responsible. Each of us almost never called in to work, maybe about twice a year on average, tops. The number of times we call in to work shows how much we love our job. The more we call in, the more we don't like our job, the less we call in, the more we love our job. If we love our job, we will have an extra push to overcome whatever reason might make us call in. And unfortunately, it's the other way around, too! We will get drained more easily when we hate our job. So if something comes up that might make us to call in, we will certainly want to call in since we think we'll kill two birds with one stone (to save our energy and time to solve the problem that comes up and to stay away from the job we hate). Remember, always love to work hard! No pain no gain, no work no play, no victory without sacrifice! And our fourth priority, our hobby, at that time was researching and shopping around for our first dream house we would hopefully call home, soon. So, we decided to focus all our might, energy, and time, on doing our mutual mission. By having the proper first dream house, we believed (and still do) that God and our family will be happy and content. It's also our responsibility to have our own place, not always borrowing someone else's place. :) And, it'll also be much more convenient and fun to have our own place. So by doing so, we fulfill all our priorities. Aha! :) We dedicated ourselves to the hunt for our soon-to-be home sweet home, just like a strong Impossible Mission Force (IMF from Mission Impossible movies), The Fast Five team ("The Fast Six" will come out in 2013, too!), "The Avengers: Earth's Mightiest Heroes", and of course, The X-Men. :)

But again, everyone has their very own scenarios and commitments in their life. Just remember one principle that stays true all the time but most people forget or don't believe anymore: "The more we put into something, the more we get something out of it," except if there is a hole. :)

So, I strongly suggest buying a property to live in when we plan to stay in one area for a decent amount of time. Why? Because we will own something! We are not just using our money for rent, because then when the contract is out after some time, we still have nothing!

5) Starting Your Retirement Investment (401K, Roth IRA, Regular Mutual Fund)

After we have built our real emergency fund up to at least $5,000 (or more, depending on our own comfort level) and have already made our current budget positive, we are ready to live our life from square one, the beginning, with a clean slate. When we have prepared for the worst scenario of unemployment by saving at least 4 months worth of our living expenses, that will add peace to our mind. And when we are ready to begin a fresh start and have a decent peace of mind, usually we are stronger when we start and face our life!! Then, we should be ready to decide on how long we plan to stay in the same area so that we can decide whether to buy or rent a property to live in.

So, after all the worst scenarios (real emergencies and unemployment) and our present lives' matters (current budget and place to live) have been solved properly, we are now ready to prepare for our future, our retirement!

We have to:

a) Fully fund our 401k account until we reach the limit set by our employer that they'll match (if we put more than that particular limit, we won't get matched at all), only when it is matched by our employer (free money). If they don't match at all, never fund our

401k account (because the mutual fund companies our employer offers usually don't have that good of a return), and might as well continue to our next step, which is …..

b) Fully fund our Roth IRA account until the limit our regulating state allows, which so far is $5,000 a year and $6,000 a year if we are 50 and older. If we contribute more than the limit allowed, we will have to pay a penalty. Our money will grow tax free and it'll be tax free, too, when we take it out. If we are not qualified to open a Roth IRA (for example: we have too much income, etc.) then....

c) Fully fund (same as the Roth IRA limit) our traditional IRA, and just in case we don't have enough time to let our IRA investment to grow to its potential (we are way too close to our retirement age, 70 1/2), then just do …..

d) Any other kind of investment. Just find the highest interest rate of return with the least amount of fees (in any kind) through any FDIC insured account, such a CD, savings account, money market or checking account.

Just a friendly reminder, 401ks, Roth IRAs, and traditional IRAs, they all are just the vehicle for our retirement that gives us benefits such as free matching money from our employer (401k), tax-free growth (both Roth and traditional IRA) and even tax-free distribution if we already reached our qualified age (Roth IRA only)! As a fun analogy, we have a Honda Civic, Toyota Corolla, Hyundai Elantra, Nissan Versa or Sentra, Mazda 3, Ford Focus, Chevy Sonic or Malibu, etc. They all are compact sedans with their own strengths and weaknesses. We have to make a decision according to our own priorities, but how we drive them is a totally different story. All those compact cars with their own strengths and weaknesses are our 401k, Roth IRA and traditional IRA, how we drive them is our research, analysis and decision about which mutual fund company we trust and how our portfolio should be for our investment. So choose your vehicle wisely, then drive it wisely, too. :)

My personal preference is just how I put them in order above. You might have your own preference based on your own priorities and analysis. I just enlightened you with the basics. Just like in martial arts, when your basics are strong, you can continue strongly even though you might have a different preference.

6) Children's Future Plan (UTMA, 529, Coverdell)

After we are done planning and committing to our own future (retirement plan), we can start planning for and committing to our children's future (school, college, any kind of education, close future). We have three major options that give us the most benefits. Here is the summary:

a) If we think our children might get a scholarship when they go to school later because they are very good and are excelling in anything that our country and schools need or are interested in, either academics, sports, music, etc., then get the UTMA (Uniform Transfer to Minor Acts)/UGMA (Uniform Gift to Minor Acts).

If we want to be safe in case our children might not want to get any higher education or might not grow how we would love them to be as an individual (which no parent ever hopes) for of any reason, then get the UTMA/UGMA.

If our main goal is to give our children a head start in their young adult life whether they go to school or not, then get the UTMA/UGMA account.

If we care about all the stuff above more than we care about getting the benefit of tax-free growth and withdrawal only when we use them for their higher education, then we best get the UTMA/UGMA as our vehicle for our children's future.

b) On the flip side, if we care more about the benefit of tax-free growth and withdrawal (when we use them for higher education) than we care whether they deserve it or not, or whether they'll get scholarships or not, then we best get the 529 College Savings Plan for our vehicle for our children's higher education

c) Just like in our second major option, the Coverdell ESA (Education Savings Account), has very similar characteristics except that the Coverdell can be used for any level of education, such as primary, secondary and higher education and it has more investment options and better flexibility compared to the 529, but the contribution limit is much smaller. So we best choose this Coverdell if we have the same goal as the 529 but for a shorter term. We will have less time to save if we want to use our investment for their elementary school (age 6-7) compared to their college (age 18), that's why they have more flexibility and options in the Coverdell so we can adjust it better.

My personal preference is just the way I put it, UTMA/UGMA, the 529 and my last option is the Coverdell.

I know that I won't be as good as people who have specifically studied and have had a lot of experience in their real life in investing. So, my most important job is to research, analyze and decide my best choice for our family's investment as the initial step, then I let the professionals take care of the investment details with our monthly committed contribution. Just like dental appointments, about every 6 months (for best upkeep and maintenance) or at least once a year, we should revisit our investment portfolio ourselves through the website or by meeting with our financial advisor. This portfolio checkup also applies to any other mutual fund investments we have, too, of course, including but not limited to 401k, Roth IRA, and non-qualified mutual funds.

7) Pay off Home Mortgage and/or Ride the Golden Years of Our Economy

After we have done all the steps above and still have extra money to be saved or invested, then we should start thinking about paying off our home mortgage (and other big mortgages if we have any) or invest more for our own close future.

I personally prefer to pay off our mortgage first as you all already know from our life story. Why? Again, back to our main principle, never borrow anything in our life if we are able to own it ourselves! The problem is that we usually can't afford to pay off our home mortgage with cash right away, that's why we need the mortgage loan, but still, we have to return/give back whatever we borrow as soon as we can. When we have paid off our home mortgage (or any other if we have any), then we will have all the power to use all the money that usually goes to our monthly mortgage for our investment and/or fun!! Can you all imagine a life without any payment except for food, utilities and fun??! No credit card payment, no car payment, no school loan payment, no entertainment system or furniture payment and finally, no mortgage payment???? Won't that be awesome and sweet?? It'll be really cool!!

The second option for us when we still have extra money after doing all those previous steps above is to ride the golden years of our economy by investing some more money toward our close future (business/fun) or retirement while we pay our mortgage regularly until it's paid off.

Some people say that they can gain more benefit by saving their extra money in their investments which gives them a better rate of return than trying to pay off their mortgage. It might be true to some extent. Let's say if we only have to pay 3.75% mortgage interest and we can gain about an average of 10% return on our mutual fund investment, only by the numbers, it seems that putting our extra money toward our investment is a much better thing to do than putting it toward our loan principal for trying to pay off our mortgage. Unfortunately, the 10% return we get from the investment is only from our extra money, maybe around $1,000 - $5,000, that's how much most people usually have as their extra money if not less!). That amount is relatively small compared to the seemingly smaller 3.75% mortgage interest, but we have to pay the interest from the huge lump sum of mortgage we owe, maybe between $70,000 - $200,000. That's how much most people's homes cost, depending on where they live. In this example, we could gain a return from $100 - $500 (10% X $1,000 - $5,000) yearly by investing our extra money but the interest we pay annually will be $2,625 - $7,500 (3.75% X $70,000 or $200,000). So the seemingly large interest percentage only works if it is applied to the same amount of money. Remember, I mentioned how important it is to always compare apples to apples? Usually, our extra money is relatively small compared to our mortgage loan, except when our mortgage is almost done. For example: when we only have three years left on our 15 year mortgage, usually the payment breakdown will shift from mostly allocated toward our interest in the beginning of the 15 year term and now mostly will be allocated toward our principle. That's the time when we might consider putting extra money toward investments rather than toward our effort to pay off our mortgage!

That's why I personally prefer (and have done) the first option which is to pay off our mortgage as soon as possible by paying extra money toward our loan principle all the time as long it doesn't hurt our family's simply great strategy: have a real emergency fund, pay off all debts, have savings worth at least 4 months of our living expenses, pay all the living expenses relatively easily and wisely, have our retirement prepared, and have our children's close future prepared. Actually, before we ever heard about all the kinds of beneficial vehicles for our retirement and our children's college/future, we already decided to pay off our mortgage as soon as possible so that later we can save and invest with a lot more power in our hands.

8) Harvesting and Sharing

Now is the time to enjoy all our hard work and discipline!! Yayyy!!! It's the time to harvest! This step is finishing of all the previous steps. But it will ultimately be completed only if we enjoy doing it and at the same time we share this great way of life to others. We can't just enjoy our new lifestyle and let other people live how we know for sure is wrong. We might think that it's not our business to tell them what to think or do. That's true, I totally agree with that. But here is a good thought:

Let's say our best friend who is so dear to our heart, got a terminal illness and most doctors don't even know how to treat it. We really love and care for this dear friend. We always help each other when needed; we share our thoughts with each other, laugh and cry together, grow together. Unfortunately, all that is about to end. Coincidentally, we have an extended family member who lives on the other side of the world, also gets the same illness (or symptoms). On that side of the world, their medical or health practitioners successfully recover our family member's health and soon enough our family member is totally healed while our dear friend here, is getting worse and worse. Even though the treatment the health practitioner used over there might not be familiar or may even seem strange or weird, don't we honestly want to at least tell our dear friend here about the health practitioner over the other side of the world who healed our family member?

I certainly do. I know most of us will answer the same, too. For ones who answer to the contrary, just remember that we are defined by what we do, not by who we are or what position/relation we have. To make it clearer and easier, basically, we are what we give to others.

We are what we give to others. If we give our community nothing, then we are nothing to our community. If we give troubles to our friends, then we are troubles to our friends. If we give genuine love to our family, then we are a genuinely loving person to our family. If we give only money to our children and not much else (time and energy), then we are a guinea pig/checkbook to our children, not real, good parents. We are what we do. We are what we give/contribute to others. It's that simple! Some people might deny this statement, but sorry, that's a fact! And usually people who deny this are the ones who don't really give/contribute to others, anyway. :)

We should share any good news/things with others, especially if we ourselves already enjoy them. For example: In 2011, my favorite action movie was "The Fast Five" (with Vin Diesel, Paul Walker, Dwayne "The Rock" Johnson, etc.), my favorite drama movie (with a sport theme) was "The Warrior" (Joel Edgerton, Tom Hardy and Nick Nolte), my favorite super hero movie was "X-Men: First Class" (you might have already guessed that ☺), my favorite action spy movie was "Mission Impossible 4: Ghost Protocol", my favorite action thriller was "Sherlock Holmes 2: The Games of Shadows" and the list can go on. So if I know anyone who loves movies but hasn't seen any of the above, I'll strongly suggest them to watch it because I've seen all of them and genuinely enjoyed every minute of them! Another example is when we tell our friends enthusiastically about one of the greatest football games/MMA fights we have ever seen, when both sides are so evenly strategic, smart, fast, strong, tough, athletic, and both sides have the strongest determination possible to win the match so that we all get the best entertainment out of it with respect for both sides.

We, as human beings, are social beings. We love to share great things and news with others, so why not embrace this finance stuff, too? Will it be too personal to talk about our families' or friends' financial condition/problems? It depends on how much we care about them, in spite of how close we are to them. But, Andy, how can we care about someone we're not that close to? Well, if we went to a public restroom and found out that the floor is covered with something unpleasant to see or smell because one of the toilets are stuck and overflowing, when we get out and see someone else about to come inside, wouldn't we want to warn them about that condition? C'mon, any decent human being should have a basic conscience to warn others about that condition. At least, tell the next person who is about to come in about that, at most, and hurry and tell the authorized person about that condition so that they can fix that problem as soon as possible.

Just like the great motto from the Spiderman stories: "With great power comes great responsibility" and if we combine that motto with another wise saying "Knowledge is power," we can summarize them into "With great knowledge comes great responsibility!" :)

So, sharing the way and process is the first and main part of the sharing. It doesn't necessarily mean that you have to offend them by looking down upon or judging them, or to show off your condition, but just let them know that there is interesting knowledge that you have learned and applied yourself and got a pretty cool result! That's it! If they are interested in more details, you can surely go as detailed as you both are comfortable with. You shouldn't feel any pressure at all about the result. You just share the great news, just like sharing/recommending great movies, great games, great diet programs, great deals, great restaurants, etc. It's not your obligation or responsibility whether they are interested or not, whether they will succeed or not, the important thing is that at least you try to share the great news and accommodate the best you can as far as you (and they) are comfortable with.

The secondary sharing part is sharing the result of your new lifestyle (your wealth) which is the harder part usually. But again, just like the original great motto from the Spiderman stories "With great power comes great responsibility". Our power now is our wealth, so we have a greater responsibility. This very same idea has actually been applied to our government's (actually, every other country's, too) tax law: the wealthier we are, the more tax we pay. It's not only because the amount is bigger since we make/have more, but also the percentage number itself is bigger compared to the percentage number of others who make/have less.

We have also heard this saying "There are two things that we can't avoid, death and taxes." We shouldn't do our part just because we have to and there's no other way around it. We should really want to do it willingly.

It's the way to go for any giving act. Why?

First, from the receiver's perspective, they will appreciate the gift/help more when they know/feel that the one who gives/helps is genuinely doing so. It means that the giver really cares about the receiver, and is not just doing their job by force or persuasion. For women, think of how joyful and proud you are when your husbands offer (and really do it, too, of course, not just offer, if they only offer but never really do it, then they are NATO ☺) to help you cook, garden, clean, or buy some groceries, or bathe the kids, etc. on their own, not by your request or command. For men, think of how joyful and proud you are when your wives offer (and do it, too ☺) to mow the yard, massage you, change your car's oil, bring the kids to wrestling or MMA practice, etc. on their own. It's awesome, isn't it? For all of us, when we were little kids, didn't we feel great when our mom and dad wanted to play, teach and have fun with us even though they were busy or tired, without being asked at all? Of course! I know that some of us who are decent and/or blessed enough have already done and/or experienced that. So it is clear that for the ones who receive the help/gift, it feels much better when they know that the ones who help/give are genuine.

Secondly, believe it or not, it works both ways. When we genuinely help/give to others and don't expect anything back, deep in our heart, we will feel warm comfort and contentment knowing that we are willing and able to help/give to others. This warm feeling will send a message to our brain and our brain will have soothing peace. When our heart and brain are at peace, they can work to their best potential, commanding all our cells, molecules, endorphins, muscles, joints, tendons, etc. to do their best, too, in a positive state of mind, just like in the movie "Limitless" (Bradley Cooper, Robert De Niro) but instead of the NZT pill from the movie, the warm feeling in our heart is the trigger for our brain to work its best. :)

So, if we give nothing to any good cause, or to our families, friends, and surroundings, that means we are nothing to our families, friends, and surroundings, too. We are defined by what we give in our life. And if we give, we might as well give with our best intentions whole-heartedly so that the gift will be benefited most by both sides, the giver and the receiver. Just like the wise sayings I mentioned earlier in this book, "If something is worth doing, it's worth doing well" (with all our heart, mind, energy, time and all that jazz ☺) and "We will excel (accomplish better) when we do something (giving) that we really love (whole-heartedly)." Those two principles will complement our main principle in this topic: "With great power (wealth) comes great responsibility (to use them wisely for good cause to our loved families, friends, and surroundings)" since "We are what we do."

If we are only concerned with what we can get/gain all the time, without thinking about contributing/giving to others, we will be financially fat, not financially fit! Only caring about the intake without any outtake. Dave Ramsey (the famous Christian financial expert) says that it is just like a pond with all the water flowing in but with no way out, the pond will surely stink! My good friend, Johan Luhulima, once mentioned that it's important to be fit, not fat, in our Christian belief. We shouldn't just be full of Bible knowledge but never really practice it. If we do so, we will be Christian fat, not Christian fit. This theory actually applies in all aspects of our lives. It's always important to be fit, not fat, in our health, in our financials, in our beliefs, in our knowledge, in our family life, in our friendships, in our hobbies, etc. Let me explain a little bit more about the difference between getting fat and getting fit. In health, if we are only busy eating all the calories, like fat, sugar, oil, protein, carbohydrates and alcohol (all kinds of income/intake/collections) and never really work out (do something good/healthy for us and others) to burn all the calories we get, we'll just be plain fat, not fit. What comes in must go out! :)

There are a couple more wise sayings: "Quality over quantity" (It's not about how many but more about how good), "Technique over power" (it's not about how strong but more about how, when and where to apply), and "Age before beauty" (It's not about the surface/external look but more about the heart/internal quality). It's also like Steve Rogers before he got injected with super soldier serum in the "Captain America" movie. :) So it's not only about what we have, what counts is what we intend to do with it. It's not about how much we make, what really counts is how we handle it.

"Andy, why do you explain so much about giving?" Simple, because most of us don't have the proper understanding about giving. Most of us don't really give a thought about why and how we give, who, when, and where to give, especially about the percentage. Most of us who give, just give out of spontaneity or how we feel. Again, we should give or share on a percentage, so it will always be proportional with what we make/have.

Chapter IV : The Relief

Pheeww.... I felt a great relief when I finished this book. After about 3.5 years of writing and revising, thousands of hours {(2 hour/day x 365 days/year x 3.5 years) – 15% break) = (2,555 – 383.25) hours = 2,171.75 hours! That's like 54.3 weeks nonstop of 40 hours/week working!} researching, learning, and thinking the best way to present my ideas in a new fresh way which is combined with motivational pep talks, inspirational personal life examples with real numbers and scenarios, easy to understand yet solid techniques, a well thought strategy, a lot of fun analogies through life, movies, sports, etc., hardship, challenges, and concerns I had to go through as a first time author, finally my first book is finished in the best way possible. While writing this book, I kept asking myself. How is my book different than any other finance books out there?

First, we have done it (all the strategy steps I put above including paying off our mortgage) ourselves. And we have done it in our first 6.5 years living in the U.S. Thanks be to God only for allowing and inspiring us to do so. There are so many people or organizations out there, who teach about something but they haven't done it themselves, they just learn the theories and get fired up to share them for whatever purpose they have.

Second, we were always happy (joyful) and healthy while doing so. All the people who know us won't feel bad when they see our lifestyle. We didn't have to live through "hell" to be able to do so. We just need to re-tune our way of thinking and feeling properly.

Third, we are average income earners (if not lower). So if we can do it in that time and fashion, you can do it, too! Especially people who have better income than us. C'mon, don't you want to be worry free and debt free, to be truly wealthy (not only rich)? We worked in retail and restaurants while we completed all those processes. I believe you can do it, too! I really do believe in you, now is your time to believe in yourself! If you don't believe you can do it, that doubt in your brain and heart will send the message to all of your body parts, all the muscles, joints, endorphins, bones, blood vessels, kidneys, etc., including your brain and heart, too. They will not perform well if you already commanded it like that. It would be like an NBA coach saying," Sorry, guys. I really care about you all and I've trained you my best, but this is it, we won't have a chance to beat this team at all. It's great to work with you, though…" Don't!! Don't ever do that to your dream! I know you can do it; it's just a matter of how much you want it and how good you discipline yourself.

Fourth, God blessed me with teaching talent. It's one of my strong gifts from God. Fortunately, I've also done/experienced what I teach. :) God has blessed me with the will, ability, and opportunities to teach martial arts (for traditional and sport purposes) for about 21 years, to lead choir in churches, schools to children and adults (in separate choirs), to tutor Math and Physics, to lead a Bible Study group, to counsel some families, friends, and colleagues in need, to work in various kinds of jobs that require me to make other people understand any particular system, products or service. All of those have built and molded me in how I use the gift that God has given me: teaching. Some people are really good at what they do but aren't that good at teaching them. We see this example a lot in athletes since they are in the spotlight more than teacher, lecturer, preacher or writer. :) But that happens a lot. I am so grateful to be blessed with this gift from Him.

Those are the main reasons why I kept going forward writing this book. There are some other indirectly correlated reasons why people want or can learn from me: I've been married for more than 12 years (18 years since we started dating) with my first love in college. I am blessed to have the best wife in whole world! She truly is the best wife...for me, though she may not be the best for anybody else. I believe that everybody will say the same about their wife, too (I hope ☺). Anyway, my wife is truly the best for me, everybody else has their own best wife. :) We raise, nourish, and educate two sweet and great sons (age 6 and 2) who truly love us (at least up 'till now, I'll tell you how it goes when they are teenagers in my book at that time ☺). I have parents who've been married for 47 years. We have lived and strived in two different continents, two countries with totally different cultures, backgrounds, weather, and beliefs. We have been elders at our church. We have been active in choir and musical drama. I have been working out and sparring with many great martial artists. I truly believe that all those experiences and people around me in my past and present, helped mold me as I am right now and I am so content and grateful for being who I am. It might not directly correlate to the reason why you should check out this book but it will surely affect who I am as the writer. :) My family has been living in Oklahoma for about 11 years by the time I publish this book. We are so blessed and proud to be Oklahomans. It's a great place to grow as a family. It is simple, humble yet great. Just look at OKC Thunder (2012 NBA Western Conference Champion), Shannon Miller (Olympic gold medalist), Pat Burris (7 time National Judo Champion), Rafael Lovato Jr. (2011 Abu Dhabi World BJJ Gold Medalist), Mat Hoffman (legendary BMX rider), Scott Sabolich Prosthetics and Research (world leader in prosthetic care and improvement), etc. :)

I am truly blessed to be known by our great God, Jesus Christ and amazingly transformed by choosing to know Him closer. Actually He knows everybody from hair to toe, it's just a matter of whether we are willing to know Him more or not. In my personal preference, I choose to know Him more, to know Him closer. It works beautifully for us and I believe it will work for any of you, too. He always protects my family from any kind of danger, hardships or temptations that are beyond our abilities. If He brings us to it, He will bring us through it. He always blesses us with His abundant love through all the people I meet and all the things happened in our lives. He always guides us in our life through all the experiences, opportunities, even the challenges, hardships and temptations, too. He always leads us in making our best decisions from thousands of different options in our lives. And the most important thing is that He always forgives me when I am bad. I don't always listen to Him. Even when I listen to him, sometimes I still don't obey His lead and wisdom. I even betray Him, too, sometimes. I might do all those either with or without my consciousness. The great thing is that He always forgives me for all my transgressions since He knows that I am a weak human being who was born in flesh. That's why I always appreciate and give thanks to Him in everything (not for everything)! Forgiving me doesn't mean just being tolerant of me, He also disciplines me and even chastises me, if necessary, to make me a better person as He meant me to be, in His best way and time. Sure, I had some rough paths in my life (conflicts, heartache, depression, got burglarized, got scammed, calamity, bullied, etc.) but they all are just parts of His plan used to build my faith, character, diligence, and intelligence even more. Some people say that I'm the happiest man on earth with a smooth and jolly life, really? No!! It has its ups and downs. It's like you have to experience both the ups and downs on any roller coaster. The key is that you have to enjoy both the ups and downs to gain the maximum benefit of a roller coaster's purpose. It's the same thing with our lives, the key is that we have to enjoy both the ups and downs to gain the maximum benefit of life's purpose! :)

I am also grateful to my parents who raised and taught me stuff in a very unique (in a good and not too good) way. Without them and their way of raising and teaching me, there wouldn't be the Andy who I am right now. I can't stop thanking my sweet and wonderful wife for always loving, supporting, teaching, inspiring and forgiving me. She's one tough lady! Also, I am so blessed to have our two super sweet and great sons. I truly love them and they really do make me proud. Here are a few examples of how sweet they are: Both of them, at their very first Birthday celebration (the little one's was in January 2012), even though were provided with Birthday smash cakes and motivated to have at it, they just looked at it and didn't want to go crazy with it since they knew that usually their parents teach them not to be messy. ☺ Or when we asked our first son when he was 5 years old what he wanted for 2011's Christmas, he answered," Eemm…. It's up to you, Mommy and Daddy, I will love whatever you give me because I love you both so much!!" Awwww…. That reminds me of Isaac (a very sweet and obedient son), Abraham's only son in the Bible story, who was about to be sacrificed to God by his very own loving father who always put God first in his life. You know the rest of the story (if not, sorry, you can Google it or check it in the Bible, Genesis chapter 22, verse 1-19). Of course, our case wasn't as extreme as Abraham and Isaac's case..☺ Lucky us, I honestly don't think I could do what Abraham did. I would try to bargain my best with God to see if there's anything else I can do instead, the most noble thing I would do is to bargain with God by offering myself instead of my son. But Abraham did exactly as he was told without any bargaining. He believes in God ultimately and he knows that everything is created by God so that God has the right to take it back or change His creation. Abraham ultimately obeyed God and that's why he is the father of faith.

I personally believe (and apply it, too, of course ☺) that we have to always do our best in everything as long it's under our control and give everything beyond our control to God. A simple way to say it is "Always do your best and He'll take care the rest." If someone doesn't do their best and keeps saying that they have faith that God will take care of it, I call it "abusive faith" or faith without action. That's taking God for granted. He is not our genie or Aladdin's magic lamp or a super powered bodyguard! He is our creator who uniquely respects us, His creation, that He treats like His own children. As we all know, a good father will teach us right from wrong. A good father will always show example by action, not merely by words. On the other hand, dictators are examples only by words but not actions, they'll say," Do it because I said so!" or "Do as we say, not as we do." Seriously? Who will follow that??! The ones who follow them either have a hidden agenda or know something that we don't. ☺ So, we also have to do our best to go along with our faith! Just like the motto "Ora et Labora" which means "praying and working."

I am also inspired by the late Randy Pausch and his book: The Last Lecture. The reason why he is writing is not only to teach people about achieving their childhood dream and leading their life properly, but also it's a book for his children so they can know him beyond pictures, videos, and words from families, friends, and colleagues. With his book, he can show how he thinks and feels as a husband, a father and a great person. I saw a billboard about him, saying, "Randy Pausch, inspiring us about living while he is dying." That truly inspired me to write this book since I could pass away anytime, anywhere, for any reason, too. My life is in God's hands. I don't really worry about it but at least I have prepared my best so my own family, all families, friends, and colleagues (even the ones who might not like me, too ☺) can know how I feel, think, act and live. I hope this book can be one of my legacies just in case I pass away suddenly while I still want or need to share my blessings and way of life with others who I care about. I really care about my family, friends, and colleagues. I also care about our great state, Oklahoma, and our country, the beloved United States of America. I cared about my former country, Indonesia. Actually, I wish that all the people in the world would at least try their best to be good and responsible. I believe our life will be much more beautiful and the world will be in much better shape if we do so. I hope this book can really inspire all of us and help us to get better in life, at least in this tough economy season.

Most of my families and friends say "Everybody loves Andy!" or "He's always happy!" I am so honored that most people feel and think that way. I am so thankful for every one of them who express that to me, too. Unfortunately, I am sure that there are some people who don't like me, somehow, somewhere, sometimes. I hope the amount is the minimum but there will be some. Realistically, we can't please everyone, every time, everywhere. Think of Jesus, the noblest character we'll ever know who is 100% God and 100% human, who did nothing but good and the people still crucified Him. He is truly noble since He was willing to sacrifice like that even though He could easily turn the tables if He wanted to. He is the real X-Men's Charles Xavier, the true Superman's Clark Kent. He has died for us so that we can live for Him. We should really try our best to follow His example since He does what He preaches. How about me always being happy? Why am I always happy? Simple, I always try to find any reason to be happy in any situation, even the bad ones, too. Why? Because I won't make the bad situation better anyway by staying mad, angry, worry, sad, depressed, etc. Actually we will make matter worse by dwelling on all those negative emotional conditions since it will affect how we feel, think and act toward other things and people in our life. We won't be able to perform our best if we dwell on those negative emotions. People will see our negative emotion through our face and body language and I don't think that will make anything better anyway. So why do so? Might as well be happy and get excited for our journey ahead. The bad situation still happened to us but we can choose to be joyful and do better or choose to dwell in it? I choose to be joyful and do better in my next journey!

So my book is about understanding (hopefully agreeing with) and applying the simple yet proper way of thinking with real commitment so that all of you can enjoy the most of this beautiful life, especially through finance.

We are a 36 year old married couple with two young boys. We've already built our emergency fund, have no debts at all of any kind, have built savings worth of at least 4 months of our living cost, have paid off our home mortgage, have already built our own retirement savings, have already built savings for our children's close future and even their later inheritance, and lastly, we have also already built a medium term investment just in case we need or want to use it for any purpose in the next few years. And the most important thing is that we do all that with our income from working in restaurants, retail, and as teachers.

So if we can do it with our middle class income, everybody else should be able to do it, too, since we are the average income earner. Remember that only 20% of the society falls into the high class income earner (the 80/20 law), 80% which is most of us, including me and my family, will share the rest of the potential left. :) It's okay, we shouldn't be jealous at all. As I said earlier, the top 20% already paid their dues mostly (at least their biggest due ☺). The good thing is that we don't have to be in that top 20% to be able to enjoy our lives to the fullest. It's not what we have/get that matters, it's what we do with what we have/get that really matters. Plain and simple. Just like what Randy Paucsh said, "We cannot change the cards we are dealt, just how we play the hand" or the "Kung Fu Panda 2" movie's line when the Soothsayer gave Po (the Kung Fu Panda) great advice, "Your story may not have such a happy beginning, but that doesn't make you who you are. It is the rest of your story, who you choose to be that makes you who you are. So, who are you, Panda?" And also when Po (the Kung Fu Panda) tried to pass on the message to Shen (the villain), "You got to let go of the stuff from the past - because it just doesn't matter! The only thing that matters is what you choose to be now." We can learn a lot from movies sometimes. Well, actually it depends on what kind of movies we watch and how we interpret it, too. :) The Shawshank Redemption movie has a lot of great lessons we can learn about life. Especially the part when Red (Morgan Freeman's character) explained to his friends in prison: "It's a funny thing about the (prison) wall, here. First, you hate it. Then, after time passes, you get used to it. Enough time passes, we will depend on it." The prison wall in this great movie represents any bad lifestyle in our real life, in this case is living in debt. So, please be careful.

And lastly, with this book, with all my effort and time writing it: my thoughts and feelings about life and our surroundings, my family's experience and real numbers, all the examples and tips, I really wish that all who read them will have a warmer heart and cooler head, more things to smile about, more peace in heart and mind, yet can also gain fueled adrenalin, bigger commitments, better planning (and executions ☺) and most of all, a better life, in as many aspects as possible, especially the financial aspect, of course.

1) The Reminder (Anti-Relief ☺)

Below are reminders for us to not easily get caught in the trends and lose grip on ourselves in achieving our true goal in life. Here are some of the scary (anti relief) facts of our society (I also put which part of this book tells how to prevent or fix these scary conditions ☺):

- Mybudget360.com says that one in three Americans don't have any savings to their name, so that they will surely be unable to make their mortgage or rent payment for beyond one month if they lost their job, and 61% are unable to make payments beyond five months!

- The Reuters.com said that more than two-thirds of Americans are now living paycheck to paycheck, according to a survey released on September 19th, 2012 by the American Payroll Association.
The survey of 30,600 people found that 68 percent said it would be somewhat difficult or very difficult if their paychecks were delayed for a week.

{**Chapter III : The Simply Great Strategy,** point 3) Have savings at least 4 months' worth of our living expenses, always save for the worst case scenario and don't be idle for too long!}

- According to CNBC.com on Sep 16th, 2009, 30% of workers with salaries of $100,000 or more said that they are living paycheck to paycheck, according to the survey of 4,400 workers nationwide, that's 9% more than 2008!! Overall, 61% said they always or usually live paycheck to paycheck, and went up from 49% in 2008 and 43% in 2007.

{**Chapter II ; The LoVE-ly way to prepare or fix our financial path:** 1) preparing or fixing our way of thinking, point e) how to manage, not only how to get money and things, the bottom line is that our income relates proportionally to our lifestyles but good budgeting (managing) relates proportionally to our real net value (wealth) so it's not only about what we have, what counts is what we do with it. It's not about how much we make, what really counts is how we handle them}

- A new report from a government (FDIC) survey on Americans' access to basic banking services last Nov 29, 2011 says that in at least 25.6 percent of U.S. households, close to 30 million American households (60 million Americans) are either unbanked (don't have any bank accounts) or under banked (using non-traditional banking services like pawn shops and payday lenders). At least 17 million Americans have no bank accounts!
{**Chapter II ; The LoVE-ly way to prepare or fix our financial path:** 2) Preparing or Fixing Our Way of Doing (And Committing To Make It As Our Habit), subchapter II: Saving, always shop around for the bank or financial institution with the highest rate of return (interest) you can get and the lowest total cost/fees if you want to save your money there}

- The Federal Reserve is another good source of credit card and other debt statistics. Current statistics on debt gathered by this US government agency include:

a) The size of the total consumer debt grew nearly five times in size since 1980 ($355 billion) to 2001 ($1.7 trillion). In 2010, it stood at $2.4 trillion, then grew one and a half times. The worst is that in the third quarter of 2011, our total consumer debt fell to $11.66 trillion, that's five times in only a year!!

b) The average household in 2010 carried nearly $6,500 in credit card debt.

- According to Lundquist Consulting, a research company based in California, there were 115,000 bankruptcy filings in November 2010.

- According to the Bankruptcy Statistic of US Court Website, during the calendar year 2010, more than 1.5 million bankruptcy petitions were filed by individuals with predominantly non business debt, an increase of 9 percent over the number of filings in the calendar year 2009. Approximately 71 percent of these cases, the same percentage as in 2009, were filed under chapter 7, in which a debtor's assets are liquidated and the nonexempt proceeds are distributed to creditors.
{**Chapter II ; The LoVE-ly way to prepare or fix our financial path:** 1) preparing or fixing our way of thinking, point a) have a different attitude, don't get caught by the trends and point e) how to manage, not only how to get money and things}

2) The Closing

Remember the 80/20 rule? We might not be in the top 20% of this world (or even of this country ☺) but the good news is that very same 80/20 rule also applies to everything in every other aspect in our lives. We could be the 20% of all the middle class Americans who are not living paycheck to paycheck or even better, we might be the 20% of middle class Americans who are debt free and living joyfully with our ever improving contentment! With the inspiration, examples and knowledge in this book, I really hope that all the readers will be in that 20% group of middle class Americans who are joyfully debt free.

I am really sorry if I happened to offend anyone, any institution, company or any system. I never meant any harm to anyone; I just want to present the facts, data, principals, understandings and experiences as honestly as possible to open a clearer horizon for your vision and mission, financially. The rest is totally up to you. I sincerely wish you all, the readers, the best in life! It might be bumpy in times, but life is beautiful overall. We gotta enjoy it just like a roller coaster, we need both the ups and the downs to enjoy the whole great sensation of it. And when hard times hit us, just think of these two points of view:

1) It could have been worse (so be grateful)
2) If it really is the worst, well…. it's gonna be nothing but up from here (so be excited!)

So either way, we will find something to smile about. :)

Mission accomplished! Well, at least for me. :) And how about you? Go for it and get it done!! I believe you can do it, too!!